Additional praises for
The IT Value Network:
From IT Investment to Stakeholder Value

"This book is required reading for any CIO who wants to demonstrate and drive the investment possibilities of technology. A seat at the table with business awaits the reader."

—Steve Gestner
CIO & EVP, Resolve Corporation

"The IT value network is a comprehensive and excellent consolidation of the current thinking on IT value-based management—especially relevant in today's current economic climate. The concepts of triangulating value and the six degrees of IT value hit the mark, providing great management insights. IT and business managers wanting more from their IT investment dollar and the ability to effectively communicate the value proposition to the CXOs should read this book."

—Drew McNaughton
Chief Technology Officer, Axia NetMedia Corporation

"IT vendors and professional services companies wishing to improve their value proposition and partnership with their CXO clients will find the IT value network invaluable. The concept of expanding a firm's IT value footprint beyond an internal perspective is enlightening. Driving stakeholder economic value across the firm's value system and value network is visionary and, as Tony states, will create network advantage—great read by Read."

—Dale Neilly
VP Sales & Marketing, Radiant Communications

The IT Value Network

From IT Investment to Stakeholder Value

Tony J. Read, Ph.D.

WILEY

John Wiley & Sons, Inc.

Library of Congress Cataloging-in-Publication Data:

Read, Tony, 1958–
    The IT value network : from IT investment to stakeholder value / Tony Read.
       p. cm.
    Includes bibliographical references and index.
    ISBN 978-0-470-42279-3 (cloth)
    1. Information technology—Cost effectiveness—Evaluation.   2. Capital
investments—Evaluation.   I. Title.
    HD30.2.R425 2009
    004.068'1—dc22   2009015526

    ISBN-13 978-0-470-42279-3

Printed in the United States of America

10 9 8 7 6 5 4 3 2 1

To the Read family:

Rhonda Lee
Martine
Charlie
Pauline
John
Gary
Nicky
Lisa
Naomi
Jonathan

Family Stakeholder Value

Contents

Foreword

E xecutives around the world are trying to get a clear answer to one fundamental question when faced with significant IT investment proposals: Where's the value? *The IT Value Network* provides a framework to answer that question. It systematically outlines effective techniques and tools for the measurement and management of IT investments to deliver a comprehensive and enlightening answer.

My career started in finance and I have held a number of CFO roles around the world, in different industries, within dynamic companies. The industries may have been different, but they all had the common challenge of ever-increasing IT investment demands, which required unquestionable justification.

If I take my 10 years at FedEx as an example, customers often talked about the great service, the knowledgeable couriers, or the vast fleet of aircraft covering the globe overnight—but it's the IT investment that enables the "experience" behind the product or service. Consider the FedEx capability for you to track the movement of your precious package around the world from the comfort of your own home. Justifying IT investment requires a strong business case, which should include quantifiable drivers like customer experience. *The IT value network* aptly refers to the necessity of triangulating the value through a value index, determining stakeholder economic value.

Justifying IT investments goes beyond cost savings; it's fundamental to your differentiation as a company—your strategic advantage. Consider the FedEx IT capability to provide your business with the opportunity to reconfigure your supply chain to minimize inventory, or the offering of a customized product from a single location, with service across the world. The decisions you make on your IT investments, sitting at the heart of your business, are one of the most important decisions you will ever have to make as an executive—so they better be informed! *The IT value network* framework enables you to make informed decisions: capturing, enabling, optimizing, and realizing business value.

My past eight years have been with Vodafone, in the telecommunications industry. As the CEO of Asia, Pacific, and Middle East region, I get the opportunity to see markets/countries in various stages of development—from mature to emerging. I see the profound impact that mobile telephony can have on a country's rate of development, as a key part of the country's infrastructure. There is obviously a lot of interest about the mobile technology evolution path, from 2G to 3G to LTE; taking us from pure voice services to high-speed exchange of data on the move. Consider the growth of the smartphone like the iPhone, or mobile broadband connectivity to your corporate IT applications via your laptop. However, these technology investments are just enablers.

The way telecommunication operators, and indeed most companies, will differentiate themselves is through their IT choices and how those choices will provide unique and compelling products and services. In the case of the operator, choices that allow customers to make the most of their time, whether in the office, at home, or on the move. IT agility and value options are a necessity within today's business, driving current and future returns and intellectual capital, which drives shareholder wealth. Bad choices make for bad economics. Thus, the need to appropriately migrate away from traditional "industrial age" measures to more effective "informational age" techniques to manage and govern IT investments, as effectively covered within *the IT value network*.

At Vodafone, we want to ensure that our customers stay connected to the people and the information that are central to their lives—via voice, text, instant messaging, e-mail, music, communities, news, and applications both social and work related—whenever, wherever. *The IT value network* helps you explore your company's value system and value network, building network advantage, a concept for sustained competitive advantage.

Being on various company boards, many of which have other shareholders represented, I reiterate the book's mantra: that maximizing shareholder economic value should be a primary consideration. *The IT Value Network* not only provides guidance on how to assess the trade-offs, it also outlines methods of triangulation, when a single perspective is too narrow a line of sight. The book also provides an IT investment governance model that goes beyond the pure "industrial age" regulatory compliance, internal controls or audit requirements, to more effective "informational age" considerations, required to run a company in today's fast paced global economy.

The IT Value Network is a thought-provoking book that is rich in content and one that will continue to be referenced beyond the first read. I passionately believe in IT as a key differentiator, where mistakes set you back years and can be fatal to your business and your competitiveness. Tony has brought his extensive IT management and consulting experience to focus on addressing a real need—making an informed decision on how to value IT and ultimately make the right call for the future of your business. I am fortunate that I get his advice for free. You just need to pay the price of this book—an investment with a great ROI. Enjoy the read.

Nick Read
Regional CEO Asia, Pacific, and Middle East, Vodafone Plc
Board member of China Mobile and several Vodafone subsidiaries

Preface

The modern computing era started more than 60 years ago with the advent of early digital technology, but debate remains about whether organizations have seen the expected value from their information technology (IT) investments. In the current economic climate, the tendency is to focus IT investments on short-term profitability. Yet successful firms cannot ignore future business opportunities for long-term growth and competitive advantage and for building strategic options for agility under uncertainty. Establishing confidence in future IT value provides the impetus to invest now, despite a recession. The emerging reality is that attitudes toward IT value are changing to accommodate new paradigms such as value networks and value systems, which are driving intellectual capital and company valuations. The goal of this book is to provide insights into IT value-based management and to maximize stakeholder economic value—beyond shareholder value. The IT value network framework presented here provides current and new, multidimensional measurement and management approaches to gain sustained competitive advantage or network advantage from IT investment and spending.

As managing partner of Read & Associates, I have traveled the world working with various companies to capture, enable, optimize, and realize IT value. As I journeyed through sunny days and cloudy days, periods of boom and doom, there was always an opportunity to realign IT investment and connect the dots for a higher IT value proposition. It's amazing what new constellations you can configure from stargazing—but this book is not "pie in the sky"; it's grounded on proven techniques, as depicted in various client cases. The IT value network approach has been deployed in many companies within the high-tech, telecommunications, computing, banking, financial, retail, and professional services industries. The book covers a multitude of various financial- and organization-based tools, methods, and techniques for practical application in the real world, including an IT value network maturity model for current practice assessment.

The IT value network presents a business focus on IT value, bridging the value gap between the CIO and CXO. Thus, the book's intended audience is for business and IT leaders and managers wanting to get more out of the IT dollar—and why not, given a \$3 trillion annual global IT investment and a 2009 economic recession with a credit crunch. The IT value network builds a comprehensive IT value proposition, extending beyond company boundaries and leaving nothing on the table. Academics and students engaged in the fields of IT management and the economics of IT will also find this book valuable. It discusses multidisciplinary fields, including finance and accounting, decision support, organizational management, information economics, portfolio and project management, business strategy and planning, and value-based IT management. The book challenges conventional approaches to IT value measurement and management, identifying lost value. The IT value network provides a comprehensive toolkit for IT value-based management, organized as follows.

Part I: Status Quo—Where's the Value?

Part I considers the following topics: reflecting on six decades of IT investment and discussing future IT investment direction. Classifying IT investment spending—the four "S" category model. Conventional asset valuation is contested, challenging traditional norms of IT investment evaluation. Lost value is identified—no bang for the buck—providing IT value observations within the banking industry.

Part II: Triangulating the Value—Somewhere Here

Part II considers the following topics: how traditional and emerging financial-based and organization-based IT value measures are defined, creating a strong value-creation business case. Financial and accounting measures alone are just not good enough; value needs to be triangulated through strategic, operational, stakeholder, and agility value lenses, culminating in an IT value index scorecard. The IT value portfolio is discussed, citing stars and black holes.

Part III: Six Degrees of IT Value—There IT Is

Part III considers the following topics: IT value management, which covers capturing, enabling, optimizing, and realizing stakeholder economic value. Six degrees of separation from IT investment to stakeholder economic value exist; proactively managing the six degrees of IT value will unlock and realize stakeholder economic value. Each degree of IT value improves IT value management, providing an iterative cycle for enhanced network advantage or sustained competitive advantage.

Part IV: IT Value Network Clients—Did IT, Got IT

Part IV considers the following topics: Four client cases are discussed, within the banking, financial, retail, and high-tech/telecommunications industries. Each case describes the company challenges, the IT value network solution, and the subsequent stakeholder economic value impact. Realized IT value is discussed.

Part V: Emerging Reality—Do IT, Value IT

Part V considers the following topics: applying thought leadership, with respect to new paradigms and emerging concepts, including social networking, value networks, network portfolios, value network analysis, exchange value, value systems, value options, risk management, collaboration, and value loyalty. An IT value network maturity model and implementation checklist enables stakeholder economic value maximization for your company.

IT investments are becoming more than just business enablers or assets on the books; they provide capability that can drive the business. Thought leadership should migrate toward information investment with the aim of getting a bigger bang for the buck from the "I" in IT and from the "I" in CIO, accounting for intellectual capital and 80 percent of market capitalizations. The IT value network will make a difference in the way your company manages and measures IT investments for network advantage or sustained competitive advantage. I hope you enjoy the book and resonate with the IT value insights that are highlighted.

Acknowledgments

Throughout my international career as a corporate executive, consultant, and university professor, I have been fortunate to meet many wonderful people. This book relects a journey of discovery, which could not have happened without the contributions of many knowledgeable and insightful colleagues. I am blessed with my own value network.

In writing this book, I particularly want to acknowledge three groups of terrific individuals who have provided support and encouragement, specifically:

- My clients, for collaboration in the best practice cases: Heather Reisman (CEO), Michael Serbinis (CIO), Dan Leibu (VP Strategy & Planning), and the PMO team, from Indigo Books & Music. Gwyneth Edwards (CIO office) and Steven J. Bandrowczak (CIO), from Nortel Networks. NA Bank and NA Credit Union wish to remain anonymous; therefore, contributors cannot be mentioned, but thanks to many (you know who you are) for your insights and support.

- My Ph.D. dissertation steering committee, assisting with the research foundation: Dr. Sumitra Mukherjee, Dr. Steven Zink, and Dr. Easwar Nyshadham, from the Graduate School of Computer and Information Sciences, Nova Southeastern University, Florida. Thanks for direction, guidance, and the many hours of editing.

- My book enablers, making the idea a reality: Joel Silver (Chief Merchant) and Bahram Olfati (Director Trade), from Indigo Books & Music. Stacey Rivera, Timothy Burgard, Chris Gage, and Helen Cho, from John Wiley & Sons, Inc. publishers. It's just great to have the opportunity of being coached and supported by leaders in the book business.

Finally, it would be remiss of me not to mention the continual support from my wife, Rhonda Lee. Thanks for being at my side and accepting the countless working weekends; now it's time to play.

PART I

Status Quo—Where's the Value?

I T costs typically constitute 2 percent of a company's revenue, but it can easily exceed 12 percent, culminating in 2008 to a \$2.6–\$3.0 trillion global IT investment. But the value derived from IT is questionable at best. Part I of this book attempts to provide a better understanding of the nature of IT investments and conventional valuation. Despite continued IT investment growth, realizable shareholder value is often absent or suboptimal. Yet firms maintain the status quo by applying traditional approaches to measuring and managing IT investments or spending.

In the current economic climate, the tendency is to focus IT investments on short-term profitability, starving growth because of deflationary concerns. However, successful firms do not ignore valuable future business opportunities or long-term growth. Projecting confidence in future IT value increases the likelihood of investing now. Chapter 1 examines IT investment growth and trends during the past six decades, from early computing to cloud networks. IT investments are also classified according to a four "S" category model, defining characteristics for effective evaluation. Future IT investment considerations are subsequently explored, providing a backdrop or context for more effective valuation approaches, as discussed further on in the book.

Greater management focus is being placed on evaluating and realizing shareholder value from IT investments, especially with worsening market conditions. Chapter 2 discusses why IT investments have not fully realized their value. Conventional IT asset valuation methods are flawed, unable to effectively identify and capture value. The cost of poor IT investment decisions is high, whether in failed projects, lost revenues, security or privacy exposure, or operating inefficiencies and ineffectiveness. Conventional organizational-based and traditional financial-based approaches to IT investment valuation are reviewed, identifying concerns and subsequently challenging norms. The chapter concludes by examining lost IT investment value.

The global financial services industry is under siege and has not been in such dire straits since World War II. Yet, IT investments continue to grow within the banking industry. Chapter 3 provides specific insight to the IT value dilemma within the banking industry. An overview of the North American banking industry will explain the competitive landscape and bank challenges. Subsequently, IT investment patterns will be explored, questioning whether these investments have added value to the bottom line. Various IT value observations are identified throughout the chapter; these arguably apply to the global banking industry, not just to North America. A North American bank case is also covered, exploring IT investment observations.

CHAPTER 1

IT Investment

Sticker Shock

Walking through the virtual IT "car lot," it is not hard to see why a CXO would challenge the Chief Information Officer (CIO) with respect to IT costs. Too often an IT Ferrari would be proposed when an IT Volvo could meet the required needs. The daunting task of justifying technology direction and spending variances, let alone the need for investment in the first place, is a challenge unto itself.

IT investments are becoming more than just business enablers or assets on the books; they are indeed a capability that can drive the business. IT thought leadership should transition from a traditional technology investment model to an information investment approach, getting a bigger bang for the buck from the "I" in IT and from the "I" in CIO. In today's world, the business impact of effective IT investments is potentially exponential and needs to be governed accordingly, not just as cost savings enablers.

IT costs typically constitute 2 percent of a company's revenue, but they can be as large as 12 percent, perhaps the single most manageable cost after labor. According to Gartner, this culminates in a global 2008 IT investment of some $2.6 to $3.0 trillion, with half spent on telecommunications and the rest on IT hardware, software, and services.[1] Such annual spending is comparable to the gross national product (GNP) of the United Kingdom or France, or nearly thrice that of India. In other words, globally we spend on IT nearly three times what India's 1,135 million people (20 percent of the world's population) spend on consumption, gross investment, government expenditure, and exports less imports. But the value of information is invariably unknown.

> Globally, IT spending is nearly three times the gross national product of India, where, unlike the case of India, the value is undetermined.

This chapter focuses on IT investment growth and trends. Six decades of IT investment are considered, from early computing to the World Wide Web. IT investments are classified according to a four "S" category model, which will be useful for IT evaluation further on in the book. Finally, future IT investment considerations are explored, which sets the context for IT value network measurement and management.

Six Decades of IT Investment

IT investment has consistently grown from the modern computing era in the early 1940s to the present information age. Spending on IT has expanded from fundamental computing and telecommunications infrastructure to enterprise application systems and to information and service management. Within just 60 years, IT investment went from a select few to the masses, from large organizational spending to individual spending.

Sixty Years of Growth

The modern computing era started more than 60 years ago with the advent of early digital technology. There is no one inventor who can lay claim to the first modern computer, as many contributed to today's foundation of basic computing. In 1941, the German technologist Konrad Zuse developed the Z3, which become the first functional program-controlled, all-purpose, digital computer. Subsequently, the British Colossus was created in 1943; considered the first electronic computing device, it was used in decrypting German World War II messages. A series of computing advancements then occurred in America, with the advent of the ABC, Harvard Mark I, and ENIAC I computers. The latter, designed by John Presper Eckert and John W. Mauchly, became the first all-purpose electronic computer in 1945. The design was based on John Von Neumann's report on unified storage of data and programs.

> "It would appear that we have reached the limits of what it is possible to achieve with computer technology, although one should be careful with such statements, as they tend to sound pretty silly in 5 years."
>
> John Von Neumann (ca. 1949)[2]

Arguably the first modern computer, evolved from the collective, was Federic Williams's and Tom Kilburn's Baby computer, built in Manchester, England. In 1948, 60 years ago, the components or characteristics of the basic computer were complete, memory had been added, and programs could be stored. With a random access memory of 32 words (128 bytes) and a computer speed of just over one millisecond per instruction, it may not have been fast, but it could perform many applications. It was a far cry from today's fastest supercomputer, IBM's BlueGene/L, which can process 360 trillion transactions per second[3] or a 1GB DRAM chip, which can store 8 billion bits.

> "Where a calculator on the ENIAC is equipped with 18,000 vacuum tubes and weighs 30 tons, computers in the future may have only 1,000 vacuum tubes and perhaps weigh 1.5 tons."
>
> *Popular Mechanics*, 1949[4]

The Baby or Manchester Mark I eventually became the first commercial general-purpose computer, named the Ferranti Mark I.[5] In 1951, the UNIVAC (Universal Automatic Computer), a derivative of the ENIAC 1, became the first mass-produced computer, providing a memory of 1,000 words for a sizable $1 million investment. IBM entered the arena in 1953 with the 701 Electronic Data Processing Machine (EDPM)—the first mainframe. Then IBM developed Fortran, the first high-level computer programming language. The first generation of computing started to gain momentum. IT investment started to grow, moving from university and government institutions to commerce. But at $10,000 per megabyte for an IBM magnetic disk system (currently, one-fiftieth of a cent per megabyte), it was an expensive proposition. Many thought computing was for the limited few.

> "I think there is a world wide market for maybe five computers."
>
> Thomas Watson, Chairman IBM, 1943[6]

The second generation, triggered by transistors, started a wider commercial interest in more affordable computing. The vacuum tube was dead. Between 1960 and 1964, the IBM 1401 captured one-third of the world market, selling over 100,000 computers. The third generation, driven by integrated circuits or the "chip," further transformed computing application. Jack Kilby and Robert Noyce independently created the microchip, in 1958. Into the mid- to late 1960s, IBM introduced the System/360 mainframe, and Data General started selling one of the first 16-bit minicomputers, the Nova, for $8,000.

"Moore's Law states that the number of transistors on a chip will double about every two years."

Intel co-founder Gordon Moore, 1965

Intel has kept that pace for nearly 40 years.

The fourth generation exploded onto the market with the advent of the microprocessor, invented in 1971 by Ted Hoff, Federico Faggin, and Stanley Mazor at Intel. From the late 1960s, competition grew, with mainframe and minicomputer offerings from IBM, Data General, Hewlett-Packard, Sperry Univac, Olivetti, Burroughs Machines, and ICL. In the background, the ARPAnet and the original Internet were born in 1969. These were quickly followed by Robert Metcalfe's and Xerox's Ethernet computer networking in 1973. Packet switching and internetworking, using standard communication protocols, provided computing power across boundaries.

"There is no reason why anyone would want a computer in their home."

Ken Olsen, president of Digital Equipment, 1977

The personal computer revolution followed, from the early Scelbi and Mark-8 Altair, in 1974–1975, to the Apple I and II, TRS-80, and Commodore Pet in 1976–1977, followed by the IBM PC in 1981. Add Microsoft's MS-DOS operating system and Windows, and from the early 1980s computing became a commodity for the masses. The more recent exponential computing and telecommunication utility is, of course, associated with the growth of the World Wide Web. The introduction of the Mosaic Web browser in 1993 by a University of Illinois team, led by Marc Andreessen, sparked the networking revolution. Today, voice and date have been successfully merged over the network. New all-in-one handset devices are enabling mobile commerce and social networking (e.g., Facebook). Commercial applications are going virtual, through software as a service (SaaS) and managed services. The next generation is around the corner.

"We've all heard that a million monkeys banging on a million typewriters will eventually reproduce the entire works of Shakespeare. Now, thanks to the Internet, we know this is not true."

Robert Wilensky[7]

IT investment grew exponentially from the late 1950s as technology significantly advanced from the first computing generation. Global IT

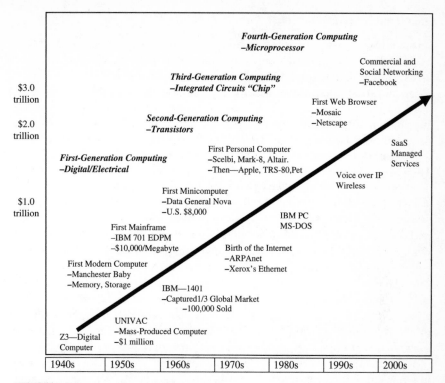

EXHIBIT 1.1 Six Decades of IT Investment

investment grew from tens of millions in 1950 to $2.6 to $3.0 trillion in 2008, as depicted in Exhibit 1.1 (nonlinear). Between the 1950s and the 1990s, annual global spending growth was averaging in the double digits. This changed with the Internet crash in 2001; subsequent growth in the 2000s has been modest, stabilizing around 2.5 to 5 percent, but with an increasing pace in developing countries. However, this still means that in absolute dollar terms, global IT investment grew from just under $2 trillion at the end of the 1990s to $2.6 to $3 trillion in 2008. According to Gartner, nearly one-third of all global IT spending is now outside North America, Western Europe, and Japan.[8] This continued growth will provide new capability and innovation within developing markets, and more competition to developed markets.

> Global IT investment has grown from tens of millions in the 1950s to $2.6–$3 trillion in 2008.

Importance of IT Investment

IT spending consists of existing and new technology investments. Costs associated with technology hardware and software (e.g., support and services) should be included within IT investment management. Certainly from a capitalization perspective, labor costs that add value to the implementation of a technology asset can be booked and depreciated. Although ongoing operational support and services are not normally seen as an investment, our argument is that human (intellectual) capital is more important than the physical asset and should accordingly be treated as an IT investment. Therefore, in this book, all IT spending is considered as an investment in an organization, differentiating between existing and new.

IT investments increase both the tangible and the intangible asset value of a company. Traditionally, IT investment has been based on tangible costs and benefits. However, it is intangible assets that now create some 85 to 90 percent of shareholder value from IT investments, focusing on knowledge-based strategies, including business intelligence and database applications.[9] This claim is supported by empirical evidence that up to nine-tenths of the costs and benefits of computer capital are embedded in unseen intangible assets.[10] Intangible assets, generated by IT, can provide an explanation for excess returns, producing higher market valuation. But the tools for managing and measuring strategies have not kept up with the vision to create value.

Intuitively, we understand the importance of information, but investing in information is another matter. Where does a knowledge management system stack up against operational systems? The challenge is that data is underutilized with latent potential, often not transformed into information or knowledge creation. The past 60 years should therefore be called the data age and not the information age, as data remains unlocked in terms of realizable value.[11] Data can be aligned to business processes through informational maps and can then be optimized or rationalized through relational database integration, but who's the owner and sponsor of the investment? Better information behaviors will lead to improved business performance, creating visible intellectual capital and valued intangible assets.

IT investments are required both for short-term profitability, supporting the current business operations, and for long-term shareholder value, enabling new business opportunities.[12] The tendency is to focus IT investments on short-term profitability, with a focus on cost containment and tight investment controls on strategic initiatives.[13] Yet successful firms cannot afford to underinvest in valued future business opportunities or long-term growth. The challenge is to reduce IT costs from operational infrastructure and move spending to strategic investments for business growth. For instance, how can networking and computing infrastructure costs be reduced, reinvesting in customer relationship management (CRM) or knowledge management systems? Competitive advantage grows out of company improvement, innovation, and change, where IT is a critical enabler. There is a need to invest in technology regularly, including associated human capital, building net worth through future capability of value, growth options, and competitiveness for shareholder value.[14]

> IT investments will become increasingly important in driving visible intellectual capital and valued intangible assets, enabling growth options that will build future enterprise net worth.

IT Investment Trends

During the next 5 to 10 years, the following IT investment trends will continue to gather momentum and become a priority for the enterprise.

Open and Service-Oriented Architecture

The value of open systems architecture is well understood, providing companies with cheaper and flexible nonproprietary protocols, languages, and operating systems. As governing standard bodies such as the World Wide Web Consortium (W3C) and the Organization for the Advancement of Structured Information Standard (OASIS) drive open access, more companies will be able to exploit standard electronic exchange for information and transactions. Strategic IT investments should include open infrastructure enhancements, alongside business-driven imperatives, considering middleware, standardized Windows, UNIX or Linux platforms, open networks, open database connectivity, Web services, and distributed computing. The importance of integrating open systems, as opposed to stringing together proprietary platforms, is key for business speed to market and agility.[15]

Service-oriented architecture (SOA) and Web 2.0 are still in their infancy, but they are growing in acceptance and commercial application. From the late 1980s to mid-1990s, SOA was focused on application programming interface (API), with J2EE type standards. Since the late 1990s, SOA has become more business focused, applying Web Service messaging (context rich) and registry (UDDI) for business applications. Exhibit 1.2 provides an architectural overview.

In designing an SOA architecture there is considerable debate as to whether to drive an enterprise-wide initiative, based on standard business processes and data schematics, or a bottom-up approach, focused on specific system integration challenges. Perhaps the compromise is to meet in

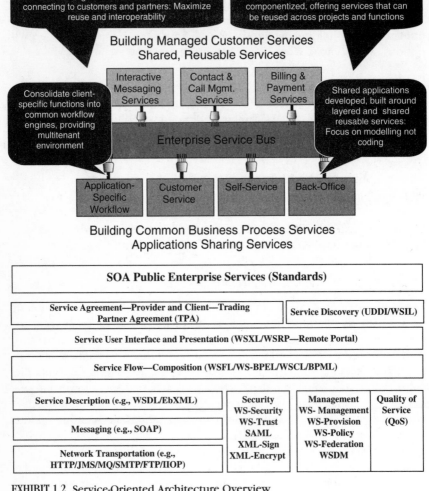

EXHIBIT 1.2 Service-Oriented Architecture Overview

the middle, focusing on an enterprise service bus (ESB), with attention to service definitions, integration, quality of service, service level agreements, security, message processing, modeling, communication, ESB management, and infrastructure intelligence.

The challenge to Web Services is separating the core legacy functionality across multiple tenants or systems to create a service interface that can be reused across multiple platforms. Thus, intermediary or aggregate services become important interfaces to basic business logic or data Web

Services. Basic services can then be wrapped together with legacy functionality. Thus, more popular Web Service applications are simple and consumer focused, including blogs, wikis, social networks, and peer-to-peer networking.

The benefits of moving to an open and interoperability service-based model include:

- **Improved returns.** Reduction of capex and opex investments
- **Personalized customer service.** Maximized lifetime value, cross-selling, up-selling
- **Real-time intelligence across business.** Liberating information for improved decision making
- **Data reliability and integrity.** Best-in-class service levels
- **Lower operational and technology integration costs.** Pay-as-you-grow utility pricing models and optimized total cost of ownership (TCO)
- **Time to market and profit.** Speed of system development and deployment, meeting business requirements
- **Business agility and flexibility.** Affordable, scalable, reliability, and global just-in-time solutions
- **System assurance and security.** Lower risk/reward trade-offs
- **Regulatory compliance.** Legislation, audit, and customer protection
- **Technology leadership.** First to market for competitive advantage, with integrated advanced technologies off the shelf

> Service-oriented architecture and open systems will become mainstream to support just-in-time service provisioning and enterprise agility.

Virtualizing Everything

From the IT organization to the infrastructure, everything will be virtualized. The IT organization will be globally distributed, connecting competencies and capabilities through the network. Today, outsourcing significant portions of IT infrastructure, including telecommunications, is becoming a norm. As IT becomes more of a commodity or utility, outsourcing becomes a cost-effective option, moving assets off the balance sheet and becoming a predictable operational cost. Total cost of ownership becomes a moot point, as evergreen services replace legacy infrastructure.

System and process outsourcing continues to grow, deploying transaction processing onshore and offshore. While core IT competencies are internally retained, especially in support of company competitive advantage, IT departments are becoming virtual in partnership with outsourced companies such as IBM, HP, and growing offshore outsourcers from India, China, and Romania. External IT spending consumes over 50 percent of total IT within the global financial industry and that is increasing as legacy systems are replaced.[16]

Even during the 1970s, virtualizing aspects of the computing infrastructure or raw computer processing was a serious option, due to the relative high cost of computers. Timesharing was an affordable business expense for large transaction processing. Today, server virtualization and storage area networks (SANs) continue to grow, optimizing infrastructure platforms and providing flexibility in support of applications and IT services. Enterprise management systems provide virtual control in the data centers. Principal players such as Microsoft and VMware are now advancing into the new frontiers of client or desktop virtualization. According to Gartner, an estimated 660 million PC desktops will be virtualized in 2011, from 5 million in 2006.[17] Thin-client computing and terminal services could be back, as in the days of timesharing and the dumb terminal, but hopefully without the green-screen look and feel.

> A company can virtualize most of IT, whereby the virtual IT resource can now work at a virtual office, on a virtual desktop image connected to a virtual application on a virtual server.

Managed Services over the Cloud

Large software vendors such as Oracle, SAP, and IBM continue to acquire software vendors and to consolidate the software market, providing a one-stop shop and preserving licence and maintenance revenues. However, the traditional software model is seriously challenged and could well die with the advent of Software as a Service (SaaS) proposition. Why pay large one-time software investment costs and significant annual maintenance (18 to 22 percent of initial investment) plus ongoing support costs, when you can pay as you use? Managed service providers (MSPs) or application service providers (ASPs) offer a company business capability at a transactional cost, with minimal or no up-front investment. Not a bad alternative, if a company can accommodate a standard service.

Thus, vendors are creating clouds of capability through network connectivity. Consider consumer clouds such as Facebook, Google, or YouTube, which provide collaboration services such as instant messaging, whiteboarding, and content management. Consumers can move within vendor clouds and from cloud to cloud, depending on the required service or social network alliances. Taking even broader steps, Web retailers like

Amazon.com are now providing corporate managed services that leverage their vast computing power and data centers. Based on pay-as-you-use, for 20 cents per hour you can have the computing power to run your Web site. Amazon.com's cloud computing now has over 300,000 customers.[18] Google runs world-class data centers; it's not surprising that it has opened its infrastructure to software developers for managed services over its cloud.

Corporate-managed services extend from network and computing management to service desk to SaaS. Traditional telecommunication companies, (e.g., Telus, Bell Canada, Sprint, and AT&T) have all been successful in managing corporate networks, and in collaboration with the likes of IBM or HP, the managed service would extend to the data center on the network. However, until recently, corporations have been more cautious of the SaaS market, reluctant to give up ownership of core applications. This is about to change, as companies like Salesforce.com and NetSuite are starting to revolutionize the market under the watchful eyes of traditional application vendors such as Oracle and IBM. Salesforce.com has provided a managed CRM service for some time, but its cloud vision extends further, given the recent partnership with Google. Businesses of all sizes will have affordable on-demand business applications, from CRM to collaborative and office productivity tools. At Salesforce.com, one million subscribers now have "free" access to Google applications, now under the watchful eyes of Microsoft.[19]

> Cloudy days ahead—the cloud will continue to absorb applications, content, and processing capability and to rain down new and highly valued on-demand services.

Integrated Customer Experience

Customer sales and service relationships are the top priorities for most companies. The expectation is that when high levels of customer satisfaction are sustained, customers will maintain company loyalty. Providing the customer with a consistent and valued experience could lead to a lifetime relationship and increased wallet share. To manage the customer relationship, over one-third of North American financial services firms purchased CRM applications in 2003, primarily from the then industry leader Siebel Systems (now part of Oracle), but also from Peoplesoft, SAP, Oracle, and E.Piphany.[20] Across all industries, CRM has been evolving, though in many cases it has not been fully successful to date. While call centers and marketing have derived value, sales processes have lagged. As an example, Bank of America implemented a CRM-based direct mail marketing program that increased response rate by

97 percent and the commitment rate by 21 percent. Further, Royal Bank of Canada (RBC) claims a 6 percent improvement in the marketing cycle, and a direct response that exceeds 40 percent, through product customization from its CRM implementation.[21] However, there is little evidence of similar benefits resulting from automating the sales processes.

Proliferation of delivery channels and the need for multichannel product offerings is driving strategic IT investments. New IT investments in channel integration include Web Services, speech recognition, integrated voice recognition (IVR), call center technologies, self-service, and live agent integration tools like computer telephony integration (CTI). Personal area networks have emerged, converging voice and data through multiple devices or appliances. For example, Internet and PC banking have evolved to include multichannel integration supported by Web Services technologies.[22] RightNow, a consumer-focused CRM application suite, has integrated Web 2.0 social networking capability with cross-channel integration (Web, voice/chat, e-mail). Ultimately, the customer will choose which channel to engage and yet expect a consistent and engaging experience. IT will need to provide a seamless integrated solution.[23]

Integration of customer information for a single view of the customer throughout the service delivery should be an IT focus. The objective is to achieve better customer service levels and improved business analytics for cross-selling (selling broader services) and up-selling (selling premium services) opportunities. Strategic IT investments include CRM, data mining and integration, collaborative computing, workflow technologies, Web Services, and business analytics. Retailers have applied kiosk technology to provide customers with profile-specific information for an improved store experience. Customized or personalized decision-making information and analysis is a critical strategic driver for many companies.[24]

> It's the experience that's remembered, not the product or service.

Information on Demand and Real-Time Business Intelligence

Information on demand is becoming the expected norm, shortening the life of fact-based printed materials like newspapers. Customers and consumers have information at their fingertips, whether through Google or vendor Web sites. Digital media is cheaper and faster to manage and disseminate. Document imaging and scanning continues to be a key back-office technology, evolving to integrated document and content management systems. Add business analytics to the mix and knowledge management systems are developing in support of digital scorecards and collaborative decision making.

Watch out for the growth in business modeling, where analytical models will be constructed to optimize business outcomes through the power of unleashing data.

While batched data processing continues to be the mainstay of most enterprises, Internet speed to market warrants real-time information. Monolithic data warehousing is still a driving force for data consolidation, but it has recently been challenged by alternative cost-effective approaches, such as data marts and enterprise information integration (EII).[25] Instead of managing enterprise data in one warehouse, an option is to manage by domain or context (e.g., sales or marketing), reducing complexity through the application of data marts and online analytical processing (OLAP) tools. But standardizing data continues to be a challenge within most companies; disparate legacy systems and commerce system constraints remain in place across companies due to a lack of implemented industry-standard protocols.

> Real-time business intelligence builds from domain-specific analytics to integrated enterprise digital dashboards.

Mobile Networking and Social Computing

Whether you are an Apple iPhone or BlackBerry fan, mobile handsets will increasingly look to laptop/notebook capabilities for new functionality, in addition to new integrated voice and data applications. Mobile internet devices (MIDs) powered by Intel's Atom chips will provide low-cost, energy-efficient capability, enabling fast Web page downloads and video streaming.[26] Corporate applications will continue to grow with short-range radio frequency (i.e., RFID) hand-held devices. Rapid adoption of next-generation mobile handsets and phones will drive new financial services and payment methods, preparing the way for mobile commerce (m-commerce).[27] Smart cards will evolve to include secure transaction processing and identity protection, while potentially offering transaction tracking.[28] Growth in mobile networking will keep the telecommunications companies strong, driving wireless and wired broadband services. However, the first challenge is to improve voice-over IP (VOIP). Quality of Service (QoS) over the network will enable improved voice services. No time for dropped calls.

Social computing will provide advancements in online technology, including search engines, blogs, and community networks. Together with collaborative applications, new information-sharing channels will come to market. Consider Twitter's success in using Web 2.0 technology in support of Barack Obama's hugely successful U.S. presidential campaign, providing micromessaging to millions of the electorate. Further, the business LinkedIn social network is about to expand, with recent additional funding for new capability.

> Integrating social computing and mobile networking could enable the next computer generation.

IT Investment Classification: The Four "S" Category Model

Understanding IT investments requires an appreciation of specific types of spending and their differentiating or unique attributes. Aligned to business drivers, such investments can be uniquely better managed and so valued. Exhibit 1.3 classifies IT investment into the four "S" categories, which include:

Shared—Infrastructure
Systems—Operations
Services—Stakeholder
Strategic—Informational

Shared—Infrastructure

Network and computing infrastructure continues to be a large portion of overall IT spending across industries, typically 50 to 60 percent.[29] The investment category includes all computers, servers, data centers, operating systems, and help desk support, in addition to data, video, and voice network facilities. To drive business operational efficiency, IT computing and network consolidation, integration, and standardization through a common shared infrastructure platform has proven to be a successful strategy for many large enterprises. Infrastructure outsourcing has been a growth industry as technology becomes commoditized and priced competitively. Growth in full-time IT staff lags overall IT budget growth, emphasizing contractual labor and outsourcing.[30]

The key is to leverage existing investments, minimizing "lights-on" operational costs and maximizing company productivity. However, shared infrastructure is impacted by company expansion and transaction or information volume. Together with technology refresh and upgrades, this warrants significant new investment. An overall investment strategy should focus on reducing cost of ownership and operating costs, while mitigating operational risk.

EXHIBIT 1.3 Classification of IT Investments—Four "S" Category Model

IT Investment—Four "S" Classification	Differentiating or Unique Attributes	Primary Business Drivers

Shared—Infrastructure
■ Telecommunications and network
■ Wireline and wireless
■ Computing servers, storage, and data center
■ S/W operating languages
■ Desktop/laptop
■ Productivity tools (MS)
■ Help desk
■ H/W maintenance and support
■ Adds, moves, and changes
■ Network operational center (NOC)
	■ Base communications, computing and productivity tools
	■ Shared across the enterprise
	■ Volume sensitive
	■ Standardized and consolidated
	■ Infrastructure outsourced
	■ Upgrades and refresh
	■ Patch management
	■ Vendor procurement
		Existing Investment
		■ Operating cost
		  – Lights on
		  – Cost of doing business
		■ Productivity
		■ Cost
		
		New Investment
		■ Cost justification
		■ Cost of ownership
		■ Cost reduction
		■ Risk mitigation

Systems—Operational
■ Application design and development
■ Vendor applications and contracts
■ Supply chain management (SCM)
■ Enterprise resource management (ERM)
■ Customer relationship management (CRM)
■ System support
■ Enterprise application integration
■ Quality assurance
■ Software as a service (SaaS)
	■ Base systems capability
	■ Transaction based
	■ Business process and workflow aligned
	■ Feature sensitive
	■ Nonstandard
	■ Integration challenged
	■ Application rationalization
	■ Process/application outsourced
	■ Feature enhancements
	■ Version control
	■ Vendor licensing
		Existing Investment
		■ Operating Cost
		  – Business sustainment
		  – Cost of doing business
		■ Productivity
		■ Net margin
		
		New Investment
		■ Cost/benefit justification
		■ Cost reduction
		■ Revenue increase
		■ Margin improvement
		■ Business process improvement
		■ Customer/supplier/ employee experience
		■ Risk mitigation

Services—Stakeholder ■ Managed services ■ Social and community networking	■ Services based ■ Business added value ■ Stakeholder requested	**Existing Investment** ■ Operating cost – Added value ■ Productivity

(Continued)

EXHIBIT 1.3 (Continued)

IT Investment—Four "S" Classification	Differentiating or Unique Attributes	Primary Business Drivers
▪ Service-orientated architecture (SOA) ▪ Web services ▪ Service desk ▪ Call center ▪ Project/program management office (PMO) ▪ Vendor management ▪ Asset management ▪ Procurement management ▪ Alerts and monitoring ▪ Reports and reporting ▪ Digital dashboard or scorecard ▪ Collaborative computing ▪ Document imaging ▪ Content management ▪ Information security	▪ Time and accuracy sensitive ▪ Collaboration and content driven ▪ Information security and privacy ▪ Opportunistic	▪ Service level agreements (SLA) or expectation **New Investment** ▪ New service levels or expectations ▪ Cost optimization ▪ Margin improvement ▪ Customer/supplier/ employee experience ▪ Stakeholder satisfaction ▪ Risk mitigation

Strategic—Informational
▪ Business strategic initiatives
Any of the above can be strategic if enables business strategic goals, plus:
▪ IT Strategy, architecture, investment management
▪ Business intelligence and analytics
▪ Online analytical processing (OLAP)
▪ Decision support
▪ Predictive databases
▪ Data mining
▪ Knowledge management
▪ Enterprise information integration (EII)
▪ Integrated middleware
▪ Distributed computing
▪ Data warehousing
▪ New or emerging technology (R&D)
	▪ Strategic business based
	▪ Informational based
	▪ Technology added value (Architecture)
	▪ Competitive advantage
	▪ Long-term returns (3 to 5 years)
	▪ High risk on returns
	▪ Higher probability of failure
	▪ Outcome (market) uncertainty
	▪ Disruptive breakthroughs
	▪ Options value
		Existing Investment
		▪ Capital cost
		  – Investment allocated
		  – Internal rate of return
		▪ Investment management
		
		New Investment
		▪ Margin improvement
		▪ New customer value proposition
		▪ New channels to market
		▪ New products or services
		▪ New revenue
		▪ New market
		▪ Lower cost model
		▪ Business agility
		▪ Intellectual capital

Systems—Operational

IT systems are transactional in nature, supporting the business operational processes, providing software applications, quality assurance, and on-going support. In support of business processes, the continuous challenge is one of system integration, seamlessly connecting legacy, custom, and "off the shelf" applications. Version control and vendor licensing can create compatibility issues and constraints, especially in light of ongoing feature enhancements as demanded by the business. Rationalizing applications is a way of simplifying the base system capability.

Integration and scalability of multiple platforms increases complexity, especially with global mergers and acquisitions. A big issue for larger transaction-based companies, such as banks, is that their incumbent legacy operational applications are becoming obsolete and cannot keep pace with change and the speed of adoption of new technology implemented by new virtual entrants. Citizen Bank typifies the use of technology to reduce operational costs and to provide remote banking through telephones, PCs, and the Internet without incurring costly retail branches.[31]

Existing system investments sustain business operations, a cost of doing business. However, the "Internet" speed of market change dictates company agility and prompts provisioning of feature enhancements or enrichment. New investment is often justified by sound business returns in year, driven by increased revenue or cost reduction, from process improvements or enhanced customer experience. A key strategy should consider process and system simplification, driving best practice and lowering transactional costs.

Services—Stakeholder

Service-based IT investments are emerging, as IT organizations evolve to become service oriented. IT is moving from a support and enabler role to a service and business driver role, moving from the back seat to the front seat. Technology is embedded in all aspects of the business, so it is becoming the business, providing higher levels of stakeholder added value. Whether through new forms of customer engagement (e.g., social networking) or through internal facilitation of real-time scorecards, IT services are growing in stature. Service desk, alerts, and reporting provide the visible value of underlying systems or infrastructure. They also extend value by providing enterprise insights, through digital dashboards, content management, or information security.

Existing investments provide operational added value, driving productivity improvement, and in support of service level agreements (SLAs). With new internal and external demands for IT services, additional investments

will increasingly drive margin improvement. Stakeholder expectations and
satisfaction are the principal drivers for new investment.

Strategic—Informational

The business strategy will define strategic IT investments, which can be
extensions to investments in infrastructure, systems, or services. There are
also strategic IT initiatives unto themselves, which formulate long-term
IT direction, including architectural road maps, investment management,
and integrated middleware. See Exhibit 1.4 for strategic IT investment

EXHIBIT 1.4 Strategic IT Investment Characteristics

Strategic IT Investment Examples	Attributes	Transformation Objective	Shareholder Value
Customer relationship management (CRM)	Customer service focus Cross-sell Up-sell Customer analytics	New customer service process New sales process	Increased revenue Increased market share
Supply chain management (SCM)	Supplier focus Procurement efficiency Less suppliers	New supply process New order process	Lower operating costs Economic profit
Enterprise resource planning (ERP)	Human capital focus Employee satisfaction Financial controls	New human resource process Improved financial process and controls	Improved net income Improved economic profit
E-commerce	Online transaction focus Transactional efficiency Global presence	New e-business model	Incremental revenue Increased market share Lower operating costs
Business analytics	Business knowledge focus Innovation	New marketing process New markets and products	Incremental revenue Innovation—New products and markets

Application rationalization	Application standards focused Middleware—connects Re-use and object coding	New application support processes Process and application streamlining	Lower operating costs
Infrastructure optimization	IT operational focus One common standard Cost of ownership Interoperability	New IT operational support processes Computing and networking streamlining	Lower operating costs
Information security	Customer and company protection focus Risk mitigation Regulatory compliance	New information security and privacy processes New operating risk processes	Capital reduction Risk reduction
IT investment management	IT investment focus Balancing investments across enterprise	New IT investment and portfolio management processes	Economic profit
Vendor management	IT Vendor focus Procurement efficiency Less IT suppliers	IT procurement	Lower operating costs Economic profit
Outsourcing	IT Partnership focus Reduce in-house sourcing Focus on core competencies	New IT provisioning and support model	Lower operating and net costs

characteristics. Strategic IT investments have specific characteristics that clearly identify them from other IT investments, and that necessitates a different approach to evaluation. They must contribute to a company's future earnings and to future shareholder value. Typically, these investments are spent over two to three years and would not be expected to start realizing value until months later, fully benefiting in subsequent years. In times of technology, market, industry, and regulatory uncertainty, the longer the period to realize value, the higher the risk of investment. Strategic investments have a 50 percent chance of failure. Therefore, existing or allocated investments need to be closely managed, ensuring that they are still valid or justified over the period of implementation.

Strategic IT investments can also be information driven, supporting management decision support, business intelligence, and knowledge management. Business analytics is growing in conjunction with infrastructure data storage and mining, exploiting the latent potential of captured data. Predictive databases and analytical software have provided companies with sophisticated marketing and service strategies to aid in increasing customer wallet share (increasing customer spending through one company).

Strategic IT investments are instrumental in modifying competition, providing diversified services, and defining new market channels.[32] Examples are many. Telephone banking has grown from 1 percent of retail transactions in 1995 to 10 percent in 1998.[33] E*Trade is one of the largest and most profitable Internet-only banks, with a competitively low $12 billion in assets. The U.K.'s First Direct is that country's leading nonbranch financial institution and has been in business for only 10 years, achieving a 2 percent market share.[34]

Increasingly, these strategic IT investments are more likely to be in the hands of the business unit, where closer control and agility enables new customer propositions, product introductions, and market opportunities for future profits. Strategic IT investment in the hands of business units places closer control on key growth options for future business success, but such investments are prone to failure and may not bear fruit for several years.[35] However, certain strategic IT investments are likely to stay exclusively within the CIO's realm, as they are specific to the IT organization, such as outsourcing, information security, application rationalization or integration, and infrastructure consolidation or centralization.

Future IT Investment

Aligning new IT investment for future gain requires a focus on the business strategic direction. Essentially IT needs to be integrated into the business, not just aligned. But the future is unpredictable, with estimated or projected returns and outcome uncertain. Therefore, future IT investments must be flexible and adaptive to change. Agile platforms must be built to accommodate the unknown. This requires a keen investment review of risk and scenario planning, determining alternative value options. Such considerations require in-depth understanding of current-state operations and architecture, with a clear vision of future states and transitional planning. Invariably, this does not happen in reality; lack of understanding results in suboptimal investments based on short-term justifications, incremental project-based approaches, and singular or isolated views.

Strategic Direction

Successful companies align IT investment to strategic business objectives. The ultimate goal is for IT to be strategically integrated into the business and to be effectively deployed to realize quantifiable returns. Yet Cutter Consortium found that 39 percent of firms do not have a formal IT strategy.[36] Further, even if an IT strategy exists, there is no guarantee that the strategy will successfully deliver the intended results. Organizational dynamics and complexities must be effectively managed for successful execution. Culture, politics, experience, and power-behavioral influence affect organizational decisions. Subsequently, strategies can mysteriously emerge and evolve rather than being well-planned and formulated. In one study, firms instigated development on only 24 percent of the strategically planned applications, based on a detailed postplanning analysis.[37]

Ernst and Young claim that impediments to strategic IT investments include:

- Lack of business leadership and commitment to revenue streams in driving the business case for IT investment
- Short-term focus on IT returns, affecting net margin and shareholder value metrics
- Scale of operations not large enough to justify the redistribution of funds for value creation opportunities
- Effectiveness of the business and IT partnership
- Availability of quality resources
- The pace of technology change and true open architecture
- The extent of data interchange standards
- Regulation restrictions, e-commerce activity, and information sharing[38]

Strategic IT investment for new channels, new services, and new customer value proposition has proved to be challenging. For instance, the banking industry struggles to make a profit out of its Internet channels; here, the banks have been unable to measure ROI. Identifying and isolating channel costs and revenue streams creates a huge problem for companies. However, there are examples of improvement; Wells Fargo, a leader in online banking (30 percent of its customer base use online banking), has been able to make a moderate profit, measuring activity-based costing.[39] Bank of America Corp. has succeeded in driving a channel profitability mentality by linking with customer costs and revenue. Customers have highly rated Bank of America's online program, which offers customers added value services such as account aggregation, bill payment, and online check images.[40]

Today, IT investment must be fully integrated into the business strategy, not just aligned, to achieve a company's strategic objectives.

Agility Considerations

As the business adapts and changes to new market or industry challenges, the company transforms. The business model may be revisited, business processes may be reengineered, new markets entered, subsidiaries sold—the business strategy evolves. As the pace of change quickens, IT executives often get chastised by their business partners as being autonomous and segregated from the business, unable to change with the business. CIOs must be more proactive in anticipating the business direction across the network footprint.

Firms with a business strategy that is based on agility and flexibility typically spend 10 to 25 percent more on IT than the industry average. Consider Dell Inc.'s strategy and significant IT investment in e-commerce and supply chain management (SCM). While firms with a business strategy based on business operations and cost reduction would spend 10 to 20 percent less on IT than the industry average.[41]

New IT investments should provide platform flexibility, based on best-practice business processes. Whether investing in infrastructure or systems, companies should pursue open architecture and standards. "Vanilla" (off the shelf) applications, with minimum customization, reduce the system cost of ownership and provide for less complex future upgrades. This is, however, dependent on standardizing business processes, which is a huge assumption to make. The CIO needs to be the best-practice ombudsman and should seek industry standard processes, unless company competitive advantage can justify unique practice.

IT investment must accommodate agility and flexibility for speed to market, especially under uncertainty.

Risk Management

Managing risk is a broad subject, but as applied to IT investments, it requires an awareness of controllable and uncontrollable risk, for existing and new investments.

Controllable risk includes cost risk (inputs, cost variables), benefit risk (outputs, return variables), operational risk (availability), organizational risk (human resource change), project risk (on-time, on-budget), and technology risk (reliability and performance). Existing investments require risk assessments on operational and technology vulnerability or failure. Whether an inadequately supported legacy system fails or information security is exposed, current IT investments or assets need to be audited and assessed for company risk. The amount of risk the company wants to absorb will dictate the amount of allocated investment to remedy. Often, this kind of new investment is nonnegotiable and a priority. Typical new IT investments are fundamentally about risk and reward, over time. This involves applying cost/benefit analysis, with discounted values or probabilities to accommodate various risk profiles, and then, on approval, applying project and change management to manage or mitigate risk.

Uncontrollable risk includes financial risk (interest rates, cost of capital), legislative risk (sanctions, constraints), market risk (price and demand), industry risk (transformation), and competitive risk (new entrants, differentiation). When identifying strategic IT investments, early understanding of the uncontrollable variables is a necessity. This requires executive IT leaders to understand the relevant legislation and competitive positioning and to be engaged with corporate development regarding possible mergers and acquisitions.

The failure rate of strategic IT investments is high, as the business environment is constantly changing, especially when uncontrollable variables are prevalent. Moderating variables (e.g., an industry sector) and the intervening variables (e.g., government and competition) are key factors in strategic IT investment risk management. For example, specific banking regulations have significant impact on IT investments. Consider the Basel Accord, which requires that capital be allocated to hedge against risk. Banks need to apportion capital to offset operational risk, which reduces available investment funds. Further, during the past few years, the United States has toughened its privacy laws as they relate to financial services.

Intervening variables are more generic to industries; they include broad legislation with respect to corporations and strategic IT investments. New laws (e.g., the 1996 HIPPA, the 1998 COPPA, and the 1999 Gramm-Leach-Bliley Act) require comprehensive safeguards to protect the security and confidentiality of nonfinancial data, individual medical records, and the privacy of children on the Internet. Evolving legislation will inevitably have an increasing impact on (1) electronic cash; (2) PC/Internet banking; (3) writing requirements; (4) digital signature and the security of electronic financial transactions; and (5) document imaging and storage.[42]

> IT investment should be treated as a value option, quantifying the risk and reward proposition.

Transitional Planning

Planning the future-state IT strategy and architecture requires proactively aligning to strategic business initiatives or imperatives. However, execution of new investments requires acute awareness of the current IT state. Existing shared infrastructure, systems, services, and project investments need to be mapped to a present-state IT architecture, determining business dependencies and drivers. An inventory of assets, processes, systems, and projects should include total cost of ownership (TCO), life expectancy, technology standards, and constraints. Knowing the current state of the IT portfolio provides the starting point for transformation to a new IT state. Trade-offs are required to meet short-term and long-term goals. The IT portfolio should be tailored to the firm's unique strategic objectives; it is a mark of the firm's future currency of unlocked hidden value as the company adapts to the future.[43]

Transitioning between the current and future state could take years, requiring intricate planning from short- to long-term considerations. The ideal end state considers the desired new technology architecture, which invariably will be compromised by shorter-term business requirements and capital constraints. Investments should keep in line with depreciated assets, ensuring that base infrastructure or operating systems do not become under-invested to sustain company operations. Thus outsourcing or managed services provides for a convenient, off-the-books, evergreen capability, paid as required through operating costs. As technology life cycles shorten, the focus should be on open architecture and interoperability, providing flexibility in design and options. Monitoring transition plans quarterly or biannually provides for a sanity check, evoking options or directional tuning as required.

> IT investments should be considered as a portfolio, balancing through transitional changes.

Operational Management

Existing enterprise investments in technology, people, and processes determine the current levels of operational and strategic capability. Future or new IT investments depend heavily on current-state operational capability. The design, development, and implementation success of a new IT investment or project are highly reliant on current IT processes, IT resources, and technology tools. Often, operational IT inadequacies constrain or prevent new investment progress. Yet many companies manage new IT investments completely independently from IT operations. IT operational management needs to be fully aligned and signed up to new IT investments.

> Complete IT investment value depends on the underlying IT operational capability, not just the management of the incremental, project, or strategic investment.

Chapter 1 has explored the history and nature of IT investments. The four "S" category model will be applied later in the book, in aligning IT investment characteristics with appropriate measures of valuation. Future IT investment considerations will also provide a backdrop or context for appropriate IT value network management. Chapter 2 turns our attention to why IT investments have not fully realized their value. Despite six decades of continued growth in IT investment, the value remains questionable.

CHAPTER 2

Conventional IT Valuation

Bottom Line

Spending on IT has continued to increase over the past eight years, since the early 2000s downturn up to the current recession, but debate remains as to whether organizations have seen the expected value from these IT investments. Greater management focus is being placed on evaluating and realizing shareholder value from IT investments, especially given worsening market conditions. In the current economic climate, the tendency is to focus IT investments on short-term profitability, starving growth under deflationary concerns. Yet successful firms do not ignore valuable future business opportunities or long-term growth and shareholder economic value. Projecting confidence in future IT value increases the probability of investing now. Whether planning for the upside or downside, companies need to develop and implement improved techniques for planning, investing, value realization, and governing IT investments. The cost of poor IT investment decisions is high, whether in failed projects, lost revenues, security or privacy exposure, or operating inefficiencies and ineffectiveness.

IT project failures cost corporations millions. The 2004 Standish Group CHAOS report claimed that from a total U.S. project spending of $255 billion, project waste amounts to $55 billion, consisting of $38 billion in lost dollar value and $17 billion in cost overruns. Project success rates, while improving over the years, remain low at only one-third of all projects.[1] However, this represents more than a 100 percent improvement since the first CHAOS report in 1994. While project management has matured over the years, business case justification, valuation tracking, and value realization have lagged.

> Spending on IT has continued to increase over the past eight years, since the early 2000s downturn up to the current recession, but the expected value from these IT investments is questionable.

29

The questionable value and challenged productivity improvement connected with IT is due to the deficiencies in IT investment measurement and associated applied techniques.[2] Based on an annual *CIO Magazine* survey, chief information officers (CIOs) are not using the right measures for evaluating IT value and success, according to their corresponding chief executive officers (CEOs). CIOs are measuring customer satisfaction, budget versus actual expenses, and IT employee productivity, instead of focusing on business capabilities and the economic value of IT investments.[3] Another study suggests that only 32 percent of IT professionals measure the impact of IT investment on business performance.[4] IT investment decision making is further questioned when there is a perceived view by IT managers that there has been a deterioration in senior management IT competency, as Carr found to be the case across all industries in Canada.[5] In addition, insufficient attention to information value or intellectual capital, as opposed to traditional asset-based IT infrastructure and systems, has further left value "on the table."

This chapter explores why IT investments have not realized their full value. Conventional IT asset valuation methods are flawed, unable to accurately measure and deliver shareholder value. Conventional organization-based and traditional financial-based approaches to IT investment valuation are reviewed, identifying concerns and subsequently challenging norms. The chapter concludes with a discussion on lost IT investment value.

Maximizing Shareholder Value

The conventional proposition is that the principal goal of a company is to maximize shareholder wealth through improving the stock price or paying dividends. Shareholder value is defined as the cumulative net present value of future cash flows, plus residual value, less debt. Shareholder value and stock price can therefore be defined as the total estimated economic value of investments, which is the sum of cash flows discounted by the cost of capital, plus the residual value of the investments. For shareholder value and stock price to increase, new corporate investment should provide a higher rate of return to the cost of capital investors could make on equally risky alternatives. Maximum shareholder returns will occur when long-term shareholder value is maximized and interim results support sustainable competitive advantage.[6] Subsequently, the demonstrable proof of IT performance is the contribution IT investments make to a firm's net profit and/or stock price. The challenge is to directly or indirectly correlate IT investment to increases in net profit and/or stock performance.

> "We see computers everywhere but not in the productivity statistics."
> Nobel Prize economist Robert Solow[7]

Research conducted on available government data in the 1980s by Robert Solow and Gary Loveman showed no correlation between IT investment and productivity, referring to the "computer paradox." Analyzing more accurate private sector data, Strassmann goes further, stating that there is no correlation between spending on IT and profitability, refuting Grosch's Law that computing power increases with the square of its costs, thus arguably producing economies of scale.[8] In 1994, Strassmann assessed 468 corporate reports of financial results and computer spending, finding no correlation with profitability, return on assets (ROA), return on net investment (ROI), or technology intensity (i.e., IT spending per revenue dollar). Nevertheless, there is recognition that computers can contribute to efficiency, competitive viability, and value creation.

McKinsey and Co. suggests that any productivity gains between 1995 and 1999 were due to managerial and technological innovations that improved the basic operations—not IT investments.[9] The study suggests the increased pace of IT investment (in many industry sectors) produced slower or nonexistent productivity growth, resulting in an inconclusive correlation between the growth of IT investment and productivity improvement. In 1996, the Gartner Group claimed that between 1985 and 1995 the net average return on IT investment was just 1 percent.[10]

The banking industry accounts for over one-third of the U.S. corporate processing capacity, providing an excellent example of the computer paradox. Banking experienced double-digit increases in IT spending from the mid- to the late 1990s.[11] This is at a time when the overall world IT market was growing at 10 percent annually, nearly double the rate of the world gross domestic product.[12] Within the U.S. retail banking industry, IT investments increased from 11.4 percent between 1987 and 1995 to 16.8 percent between 1995 and 1999, while staff productivity growth rates declined from 5.5 percent to 4.1 percent, respectively, for the periods.[13]

There are counterarguments, primarily from Eric Brynjolfsson and Lorin Hitt, who claim that since 1991, IT investments have increased productivity. Based on a study of 759 banks, IT decreased overall costs, suggesting that a 10 percent increase in IT capital was associated with a 1.9 percent decrease in overall bank costs.[14] The maximum value for IT is, however, realized when it is coupled with other enabling investments, such as new strategies, new business processes, and new organizations.[15] Their research of 367 corporations determined that the average gross marginal product (MP) on

IT investments from 1987 and 1991 was 81 percent.[16] However, Strassmann claims that applying the Cobb-Douglas production function equations and assumptions to their survey makes the findings questionable.[17] For instance, information and knowledge do not fit the framework as a cost of goods and services. Subsequent recalculations by Brynjolfsson and Hitt revised the average gross return on IT investments down to 56 to 68 percent, suggesting that one-half of the excess returns could be attributed to firm-specific effects and one-half from industry-specific effects. Brynjolfsson and Hitt, however, did state that their study produced a high standard error, suggesting that additional explanations should be sought for excess returns.[18]

Recent literature review, based on over 50 empirical studies made between 1985 and 2002, concludes that the productivity paradox has been effectively rejected, at both the firm level and the country level. Further, the U.S. Council of Economic Advisors (CEA) found that between 1995 and 1999, the increase in productivity was four times greater (4.18 percent versus 1.05 percent) in industries with intense IT investment.[19] The CEA study showed a wide range of IT performance within firms, illustrating that complementary investments in organizational capital made a difference to productivity. These investments would include decentralized decision-making systems, self-directed teams, job training, and business process improvement.[20] Technology is often described as an enabler to company performance, requiring a business-driven change to realize shareholder value. In other words, a firm needs to determine strategic objectives and initiatives, which culminate in business process change, organizational change, activity or volume change, or a new way of doing business.

There appears to be a growing convergence in research in support of the argument that IT investments do increase productivity, but such instances are contingent on complementary investments in organizational capital, such as decentralization of decision making, organizational change, job training, and business process improvement. Studies suggest that the following issues could explain the computer productivity paradox: poor measurements, lags due to learning, time from investment to value capture, redistribution of savings, and IT mismanagement. The productivity paradox in earlier studies appears to have been based on small samples and limited data; whereas recent studies have used better databases and larger samples and have included time-series data. A firm's increased productivity over its competitors should generate higher profitability. However, no direct correlation with firm profitability was found, as productivity benefits could be passed to the customer through lower prices. Better data collection and measurement methods need to be developed to show a correlation between IT investment and a firm's profitability.[21]

Many economists and business researchers have successfully used stock market value as an effective measure of business performance, yet there is little research that investigates the relationship between IT and stock price. Brynjolfsson and Yang conducted a study, assessing eight years of data from over 1,000 firms in the United States. They found that for every $1 in computer capital implemented there was an associated $10 increase in the stock price valuation of a firm. Empirical evidence suggests that up to nine-tenths of the costs and benefits of IT are embedded in the intangible assets.[22] Their model suggests that intangible assets, generated by IT, training, and organization or business transformation can explain excess returns that produce higher market valuation. Similar surveys corroborate these findings, where computer assets had a disproportionately higher value in firms with certain organizational characteristics such as greater use of teams, broader decision-making authority, and training. However, the correlation of IT spending to profitability is still inconclusive, with no evidence that IT directly affects shareholder value.

Trying to isolate cause and effect of IT investments over time has been challenging, providing contrasting evidence on IT productivity gains. Often, heuristics are used for IT investment decisions, due to the difficulties in measuring the benefits using strict accounting cost/benefit analysis.[23] Recent research interest has turned to asking, how does one measure the intangible contribution of IT investments and thereby realize the full shareholder value? IT investments alone will not maximize shareholder value, as they depend on business strategy, process, and organizational change. Conditional prerequisites for IT investment are essentially complementary firm investments that need to happen to unlock and realize the full shareholder value.

> IT investment can improve productivity, but there is little research evidence that correlates IT investment to profitability and shareholder value.

Conventional Asset Valuation

There appears to be no generally accepted method of IT investment evaluation or assessment.[24] However, there are hundreds of different measures that have been applied to valuing IT. These measures and methods can be categorized into two core approaches—financial-based and organization-based. Within each category there are conventional and emerging techniques and tools. Conventional approaches value IT investments purely as an asset, while emerging approaches broaden the value treatment. This chapter focuses on conventional organization-based strategic planning and traditional financial-based valuation approaches. Subsequent chapters focus on emerging approaches.

Conventional approaches to IT investment evaluation are asset based and typically used in industry, with extensive supportive research in the fields of strategic planning, traditional accounting, and financial IT investment measures. In a recent study on the usage and application of IT investment criteria, the top 10 measures applied in industry were evenly spread between the financial and organizational categories.[25] Specifically, financial measures include net present value (NPV), internal rate of return (IRR), average rate of return (ARR), payback, and budget. The organizational measures included strategic planning, business objectives, competitive positioning, decision support, and project planning. These measures are defined in greater detail in Chapter 4.

> Conventional approaches to IT investment evaluation are asset based and historical, lacking consideration for future uncertainty and intellectual capital.

Conventional Organization-Based Approach

Conventional strategic planning aligns new IT investments to the strategic goals of the firm. Subsequently, project planning and management delivers the expected business benefits. The argument suggests that if the investment is aligned and effectively executed, the probability of realizing the investment value significantly increases. Companies should benefit from strategic alignment between business and IT, gain appropriate management support and visibility, establish accountability of expected benefits, and consistently apply a formalized procurement process based on benefits justification.[26] IT programs should be accountable back to the business plan, IT capability should be appropriately sized to deliver the business goals, and IT projects should realize the expected value. The objective is to optimize the IT investment value by identifying the right projects, bringing them in on time, on budget, and to business and quality specifications, as well as mitigating customer, operational, financial, technological, and regulatory risk.

Strategic planning evolved from budget planning in the mid-1960s. However, it is noted that over two centuries ago there was a reference in Sun Tzu's *The Art of War* to a director of strategic planning. Situational appraisal is the main theme from *The Art of War*.[27] Mintzberg cites 10 schools of thought regarding the subject of strategic planning.[28] The design school was the first strategic planning thought process, which is still practiced today, commonly known as SWOT: strengths, weaknesses, opportunities, and threats. Supporters of the design school look to strategically couple internal resource capability and external opportunity. However, this formal-rational approach fails to consider the diversity and complexity of organizational dynamics.[29]

Subsequent schools of thought led to more structured and mechanistic approaches, like the Ansoff model of cascading decision flows. Porter defined the five-market-forces model for strategic focus—new entrants, buyers, suppliers, substitutes, and competitors. Strategic planning hit its high in the mid-1970s, subsequently falling in popularity over the next decade. Today, strategic planning is viewed in a more balanced way, where it provides a disciplined process in context to a firm's environment. Much attention is spent on planning pitfalls, which are principally based on obsession with control.[30]

Project management methodology and program management or governance office are typically used for action planning. Project management methods are used to deliver the benefits from the business case and should incorporate a rigorous process for reviewing business case change. Performance measurement would be conducted throughout the project life cycle. At project milestone reviews, decisions should be made to cancel, change, hold, or continue with a project, based on performance and business case validity. The review should also take into account the overall performance of the project's progress, as, indeed, changes in delivery schedule, deployment costs, and outcomes will have a material impact on the business case as well as the overall business plan. Tracking value realization would normally be conducted after project completion or when benefits start to flow. Various computer-aided software engineering (CASE) tools are available for project management, including the use of Gant and PERT/CPM techniques. Such tools assist in the optimization of project activities and resources.[31]

Traditional Financial-Based Approach

Financial-based techniques are typically used for assessing capital asset investments, based on standard formula for deriving returns on capital outlay. Cost benefit analysis is the traditional approach, applying structured models, breakeven analysis, cost displacement, timesaving, and/or work value techniques.[32] Cost benefit analysis ultimately strives to produce a return on investment (ROI) or discounted cash flow (DCF) for investment evaluation. Measures are commonly understood and translatable, at least among the finance professionals.

The comfort of using traditional capital asset performance measures is based on accounting principles and proven financial management models. Profits are essentially generated from sound capital investments; thus, ROI is a typical measure for IT investment performance. In addition, DCF (risk adjusted) gives comfort to financial managers in the knowledge that current value cash will be generated from an investment. DCF, however, is not always applied. One study suggests that as little as 50 percent of firms use DCF techniques, such as net present value (NPV) and internal rate of return (IRR), for project evaluation.[33]

Today, budgeting and capital plans are the principal methods for managing IT investments. Capital plans typically work within investment envelopes, as dictated by financial constraints or performance indicators. Techniques used for operating budgets include collaborative forecasting, rolling forecasting, and performance-based budgeting. Effective coordination of budgets and evaluating choices or scenarios can create a solid corporate plan. Usually, the IT operational run rate is based on some finance-determined percentage of sales or cost of sales and/or administration, with some tasking in for cost reduction. If business circumstances change in a year, management will try to hold to earlier budget plans, which are now invalid. Therefore, as budgeting is institutional, it is important to implement a rolling and collaborative budgeting process, one that reflects changing business circumstances. Charge-back mechanisms from IT to business departments and cost centers will help to increase the visibility and business engagement on IT projects and costs, but this is insufficient to manage overall budgets.[34]

Business cases and investment review boards are typically used as a method for defining and justifying the value of IT investments. Typically, ROI and/or DCF are used for project justification and selection, using IRR or single cost of money rates to an assumed risk (cost of capital). The biggest challenge within the business case is defining the benefits, especially the intangible value. Business cases are normally aligned with a business plan, which has clear top-line and bottom-line expectations and targets. A constant process for validation of both the business plan and the business case should be in place to ensure currency of underlying assumptions and monitoring of any changes in environmental conditions. Project plans are normally established to ensure execution of the business case. An investment review board for large investments or executive management for smaller projects would normally complete prioritization and selection of investments. Depending on the business plan, goals, and expected returns, business cases would be approved, rejected, or amended.

Challenging Conventional Norms

Firms invest in IT programs, in terms of capital and one-time expense. In today's information world, IT investment is much broader and varied in definition, beyond the traditional capital investments such as computer hardware and software assets. There are various forms of software, which can be purchased, rented, leased, or provided on a transactional service basis.

Further, the increasing practice of outsourcing or managed services would be expensed, shifting major spending off the balance sheet. Consulting, contractor, and specific internal labor costs associated with design, build, and testing can be absorbed as capital, providing added value to the end product or asset. However, the majority of staff costs are operating expenses, which do not get capitalized.

Typically, the largest part of IT spending is on the staff; in the banking industry, nearly one in five of total employees are IT professionals, the largest percentage of all industries.[35] Project management costs can be absorbed into base IT infrastructure or separated as a marginal line item. On the benefit realization side, IT investments are generating increased intangible asset value, from the likes of customer service improvement, application interoperability, human knowledge, supply chain improvements, business process efficiencies, and business cycles.[36] Therefore, IT investments are far more complicated in today's environment and go beyond capital evaluation models.

> Today, IT investment decisions are more complex, given that expenses outweigh capital expenditures, challenging capital evaluation models.

Financial and Accounting Valuation

Traditional measures and methods of managing and evaluating IT investments do not appear to be effective. Strassmann questions the appropriateness of traditional capital efficiency/productivity measures for IT.[37] The problem with applying ROI to new investments is that it can lead to misallocation of resources. Unlike economic value, ROI takes into account the past undepreciated investments and does not include the residual value for new investments post forecast period. Residual value can typically account for more than 50 percent of a firm's market value. ROI is essentially an accrual accounting return, which is inappropriately compared against an economic return on cost of capital.[38] DCF is more appropriate for operational or transactional IT investments, but not for strategic investments.[39] Strategic IT investments have numerous possible outcomes to factor in, each with a varied probability of occurring.[40] More complex evaluation models are being introduced, but one survey suggests only 8 percent go beyond the ROI calculation.[41]

Current accounting rules provide no standards for reporting on IT costs and investments, so IT firm spending cannot be publicly observed. This results in an inability to consistently measure the effect of IT investment on productivity or firm shareholder value.[42] Variances exist in the definition, categorizing, and accounting of IT investments and expenditure levels from firm to firm. Therefore, there are limited means of comparing or benchmarking IT within and across industry sectors. Capital depreciation rates are varied, depending on a firm's view of investment life. Singular discounted cash flow rate is applied across all costs and returns, indifferent to varying risk profiles. IT accounting practice is not consistently applied from one company to another.

Organizations need a new kind of management system built to measure the value creation of a firm. Examining only financial or accounting measures of value reflects a short-term focus and suffers from a time lag.[43] Traditional capital performance measures and methods are typically applied to IT investments, evaluating the past. These measures are based on capital evaluation models, as historically applied to a range of investments, from manufacturing plant to real estate to machinery. The key to IT cost management is to evaluate the future, not the present.[44]

> Traditional capital performance measures and methods are typically applied to IT investments, inconsistently evaluating the past and not considering the future residual value, which is a significant contribution to a firm's market value.

Budget Planning

Budgeting is the principal method for managing IT investments, consisting of operational budgets and capital budgets. The problem with budgeting is that the planning process is typically based on the previous year's run rate. Invariably, the IT run rate is based on some percentage of sales or cost of sales and/or administration.[45] Costs typically lag any sales shortfall, depleting profits. This leads to camouflaging of costs and bad accounting behavior in moving costs around the ledger to fit current commitments that may no longer be justified. Subsequently, IT management is prone to misallocate and overconsume IT resources.[46]

Too often, budget requests are set artificially high to withstand any tasking or budget cuts. Alternatively, budgets are set and spent in year against the plan irrespective of variable company performance and are often mismanaged, based on ineffective performance measures. The result is that budgets manage the business instead of the business managing the budgets. If business circumstances change during the year, management will try to hold to earlier budget plans, which are now invalid. Further, departmental budgets are not comparable in terms of return to the shareholder, measures are inconsistently applied, and lack the ability to identify where spending can maximize shareholder value. One CIO spending survey suggests that it is time to change old budgeting habits and speed up the investment approval process.[47]

Strassmann suggests that the IT budget should be equal to the base cost of the infrastructure, plus a coefficient of sales, general, and administration (SG&A), plus a coefficient of profit after tax, plus a coefficient of desktops, plus a coefficient of knowledge workers, less a coefficient of officials. Based on Strassmann's research, these factors and corresponding coefficients or weightings are determinants of IT spending. In addition, Strassmann maintains that the IT budget and planned new investments should consider the valuation of the IT assets (i.e., hardware, software, development, and training), including total life cycle costs and residual value (beyond expected life).[48] Alternatively, consider zero-sum budgeting, which includes only costs and investments that deliver the in-quarter sales projections and focuses purely on customer added value. Clearly operational costs or baseline costs need to be sustained, based on transaction volume and activity. However, poor business process management can lead to operational inefficiencies that inflate supporting IT costs, which in turn increase the cost of sales or sales support. Maintaining the status quo in budget plans is unacceptable and leads to poor cost management.

> Maintaining the status quo in budget plans is unacceptable and leads to poor cost management, especially when costs typically lag any revenue shortfall, depleting profits.

IT Strategic Planning

Conventional theory would suggest that corporate goals define strategies, which define objectives, supported by budgets, and create programs, in a cascading flow down an organization. In practice, however, the actual behaviors of management may be very different, based on motivation and incentives. It is not uncommon to find budgets indifferent to strategic objectives, which in themselves could be in competition with each other. Further, programs can be politically rather than strategically aligned, creating projects that are not part of the formal planning process. In the absence of a planning and sound governance process, firms can allow projects and budgets to determine strategy. Kaplan and Norton stress the importance of aligning and linking the budget and strategy, driving stretch targets, and applying rolling forecasts.[49] Ultimately, hierarchies of objectives and budgets are related to performance controls, and hierarchies of strategies and programs are related to action planning.[50]

In a 1999 *Fortune* cover story, CEO failure was related to bad strategic execution about 70 percent of the time—not bad vision. The tools for measuring strategies have not kept pace with the vision to create value. Firms need to develop a strategic business plan, which integrates IT, generating realizable shareholder value. However, traditionally, IT is seen as a support organization or at best an enabler to business goals. Therefore, business strategies are typically formulated well in advance of IT planning, requiring catch-up strategies to support the business direction. Successful companies ensure that the CIO is engaged earlier and often in defining business strategies, whereby IT is integrated and not just an afterthought of alignment. Consider a firm desiring to change its business model around the supply chain. Instead of defining the business processes and then considering a suitable system solution, a more effective approach would be to pursue an integrated process and system "best fit" strategy. Time to market and profit would be increased if an industry best practice mentality were introduced, building off a "vanilla" industry solution, customizing only where competitive advantage could be argued.

> Typically, business strategies are formulated well in advance of IT planning, requiring catch-up strategies to support the business direction.

Risk and Uncertainty

Due to the quick pace of technology, changing economic conditions, and volatility of market environments, IT investments and projects are inherently risk sensitive. Risks of an IT project are based on unique factors and thus are unsystematic or diversifiable. Many researchers question the use of traditional capital investment and financial measures, as these methods do not consider uncertainty, flexibility, and the opportunity of delay.[51] Traditional financial measures, such as DCF and ROI, do not capture the value of managerial flexibility within IT projects that have outcome uncertainty.[52] The higher the uncertainty in the investment outcome, the higher the value of managerial flexibility and thus the higher the value of the IT embedded option. Flexibility has a higher potential of enabling the upside while containing the downside.[53] More effective risk management tools are required to measure the value of IT investments.

There appears to be strong support for emerging techniques like the real options approach, especially when IT investments are deemed more strategic in nature, having a high-upside potential, high uncertainty, and indirect returns.[54] A "real option" is the investment in physical and human assets that provides the ability to enable future opportunities, thereby providing a higher future value to a firm. Essentially, real option analysis provides a theoretical platform for building alternatives through heuristics under uncertainty. The real options approach has been suggested as a capital budgeting and strategic decision-making technique because it accounts for the value of future flexibility in times of environmental uncertainty.[55]

New value-based multidimensional approaches to IT strategic investments and evaluation are required, beyond the traditional accounting and financial methods and measures. Firms need to hedge against adverse conditions in the future and retain an ability to capture the upside benefits by using IT to create strategic options. Decision support systems can be used in conjunction with traditional financial measures to de-risk decisions, especially in assessing options and risk under uncertainty.[56] Emerging financial management tools, like "real options," are required to measure the value of IT investments. The real options approach has been suggested as a capital budgeting and strategic decision-making technique because they account for the value of future flexibility in times of environmental uncertainty. A further discussion of real and value options appears in Chapter 19.

> Traditional capital investment and financial measures do not capture agility and flexibility within IT investments that have outcome uncertainty and potential options.

Lost Value

Managing IT investments is not just about meeting budgets and delivering projects on time; it should improve a firm's stock price or market valuation. IT justification and evaluation should include stock price impact and defined processes that derive an appropriate risk-adjusted economic value addition. This goes beyond the traditional DCF, ROI, cost savings, or low cost of ownership business justifications.[57] Further, conventional methods are not appropriate to capture the full benefits of the intangible value. Poor investment decisions are often made, invariably misplacing or leaving value "on the table." Total firm stakeholder economic value capture is required. It is clear that traditional accounting measures and methods of IT investment management and evaluation need to evolve and encompass more of a stakeholder economic "value" model, relying less on financials alone.

Benefit Realization

Identifying direct or even indirect benefits from IT investment is often a challenge, especially for shared infrastructure. Trying to isolate the cause and effect of IT investments over time is even a bigger challenge, especially when other activities or investments are attached to the benefit. Which capability derived the benefit, the technology, the process, or the people? Invariably all three, but when competing for investment, one could be argued over the other, in terms of greater value. Technology is often described as an enabler, requiring a business-driven change to realize value, such as business process change, organizational change, activity or volume change, or a new way of doing business. Therefore, heuristics are often used for IT investment decisions, due to the difficulties in measuring the benefits. Subsequently, IT investment decisions are made without capturing the full business value; or indeed they may overestimate the value.

There are various approaches to determine IT benefits. The most simplistic is to derive benefits from an integrated solution, inclusive of the required people and process investments. Other forms include fishbone or cause-and-effect analysis or NPV/probability trees. A benefits realization approach is proposed by Thorp and DMR[58] whereby the indirect relationship can be linked through a transformation process. Design and development of an IT investment initially becomes an IT asset. Subsequently, through application, the asset influences organizational performance. Through a series of contributions and suboutcomes the asset is transformed, and it provides a line of sight to a stock price driver. For example, an IT customer relationship management (CRM) investment transforms to increase revenue.

Remenyi and Sherword-Smith propose an active benefit realization (ABR) model, which defines "outcome space," describing wider business benefits from IT investments. IT investments are defined as automate (efficiency improvement), informate (information improvement for better decisions and so improved effectiveness), and transformate (change the way to do business, driving better process, products or markets). Different approaches to cost/benefit analysis could be applied to various types of IT investments. Deterministic (single-point estimates) or stochastic (range-of-estimates) measures can be used for evaluation. Stochastic or risk analysis measures would be used where uncertainty is greater.[59]

The closer the benefit outcome can be coupled to a stock price driver, the higher the perceived and, indeed, the actual value of the IT investment. IT measures of stock price will drive shareholder value. Exhibit 2.1 provides an example of an approach to define the stock price traits of an IT investment, triangulating the value using financial measures and benchmarking to industry standards. Assuming more consistent accounting of IT spending,

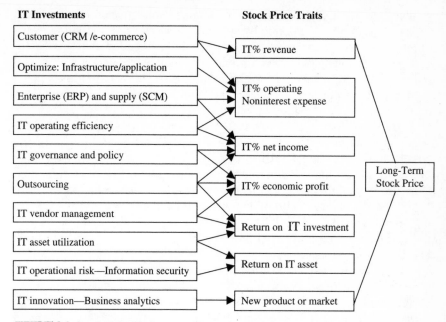

IT Investments

- Customer (CRM /e-commerce)
- Optimize: Infrastructure/application
- Enterprise (ERP) and supply (SCM)
- IT operating efficiency
- IT governance and policy
- Outsourcing
- IT vendor management
- IT asset utilization
- IT operational risk—Information security
- IT innovation—Business analytics

Stock Price Traits

- IT% revenue
- IT% operating Noninterest expense
- IT% net income
- IT% economic profit
- Return on IT investment
- Return on IT asset
- New product or market

Long-Term Stock Price

EXHIBIT 2.1 Stock Price Traits

then benchmarking the ratio of IT spending to sales, general, and administration (SG&A) costs or to information workers could be a good measure of IT value and performance. Stock price traits as an IT valuation approach better reflects the contribution to a firm's longer term stock price or market value.

> Heuristics are used for IT investment decisions, due to the difficulties in measuring the benefits, exaggerating value, or leaving value on the table.

Intellectual Capital

The tools for managing and measuring informational strategies have not kept up with the vision to create intellectual capital. Traditionally, IT value has been based on the tangible costs and benefits. However, studies suggest that it is the intangible assets that now create some 85 to 90 percent of shareholder value, focusing on knowledge-based strategies, including information and content management, business intelligence, and collaboration.[60]

IT investment significantly impacts the intangible asset value or intellectual capital. This claim is supported by empirical evidence that up to nine-tenths of the costs and benefits of computer capital are embedded in unseen intangible assets.[61] Intangible assets, generated by IT, training, and organizational transformation, can provide an explanation for excess returns, producing higher market valuation. Yet intangible value is invariably not incorporated into IT investment measures.

Consider the value capture of a CRM investment, which goes beyond the business value of cross-selling or up-selling, beyond wallet share, encompassing the social value of presence or the network value of the relationship. Let's start advocating customer network management (CNM). Further, consider the limited thinking with respect to IT infrastructure investment, like VOIP, often justified as a cost of ownership reduction or operational cost saving. Integration of voice and data goes beyond operational value, as seen by the mobile network and social integration of virtual communities through Facebook and MySpace.

As IT investment continues to drive intellectual capital, information management will increase in importance. In addition, information security and privacy exposure is well known, contributing millions of dollars of lost value for large corporations. Loss of data, loss of time or productivity, and loss of revenue through business unavailability and negative reputation are all too common. Traditional network security solutions (e.g., firewalls and antivirus programs) have been successful against malicious code penetration, but new sophisticated and automated intrusions or attacks are targeting networked (Web) applications, amounting to as much as 75 percent of all attacks.[62]

Corporate loss is difficult to size, as many companies do not report vulnerabilities due to concern over the company's reputation. However, the annual cybercrime report from U.S. CSI/FBI suggests that today approximately half of the financial loss comes from access to unauthorized information and theft of proprietary information, with the average cost of a breach being $203,000. The MS Blaster worm, for example, cost companies, on average, $475,000 to remediate and over $4 million for large companies.[63] Small and medium-sized companies can become complacent. One study suggests that of those surveyed, a third had been attacked at least four times over the past three years.[64] New IT evaluation techniques are required to justify information management and information security/privacy investments.

Management needs to focus more on measuring the intangible value of IT, deriving the full shareholder economic value. New forms for measuring IT value are required in the information age, where intellectual capital is dominant, beyond traditional productivity, which relates more to the industrial age. More research is needed to determine the indirect relationship between IT investment and a firm's stock price, measuring the intangible benefits derived from IT investments.

The majority of costs and benefits of IT capital are embedded in unseen intangible assets and intellectual capital, which need to be quantified in the information age, beyond traditional productivity measures, which reflects the industrial age.

Total Cost of Ownership

The total cost of ownership (TCO) concept was introduced by the Gartner Group in the 1980s to determine the total cost of a personal computer. At $10,000 per year, companies took a very different view in deploying computers across the organization.[65] TCO is invariably overlooked due to the complexity of the cost analysis, which is exasperated by the absence of a standard calculation formula. Reducing the TCO is, therefore, at best, an afterthought within the IT organization. Capital and one-time project-related costs determine new investment, and ongoing support and maintenance costs determine the operating costs. However, there are also associated costs that typically do not get included, such as technical and user training, cost of outage, diminished performance events, security breaches, disaster recovery, and energy consumption. Understanding the complete costs associated with a technology decision should be required not only for new investment business cases but also to determine baseline operating costs. Total IT costs invariably are not captured.

Current shared infrastructure and systems evolve over time, where new investment is integrated, complementary, or standalone to an overarching architecture blueprint (if one exists). Legacy systems are typically the mainstream of business operations, which, though possibly fully depreciated, can incur significant support costs in maintenance or change requests. Off-the-shelf applications similarly can be costly to run when high customization has occurred and release management lags current versions. Add an underinvested computing or networking infrastructure, which introduces additional support costs and productivity impact, and the baseline IT operational costs can become significantly higher to industry benchmarks and so uncompetitive. Subsequently, the value of the IT footprint erodes over time, with increasing operational costs.

The current IT architecture should be evaluated against industry benchmarks, taking inventory of underlying assets and projecting life cycle cost of ownership. The future architecture road map provides the end-state blueprint aligned to the business direction. Transitioning takes various swim lanes, with interdependencies called out and replacement sequencing scheduled over time. Determining an open architecture provides interoperability and seamless connectivity, reducing the overall cost of ownership across the IT footprint. This assumes that IT processes and policies are effectively designed and deployed, staff competencies and capabilities are in place, and IT strategy is aligned to business goals; otherwise, independent of the technology decision, total cost of ownership will increase.

> TCO is invariably overlooked due to the complexity of the cost analysis, which is exasperated by the absence of a standard calculation formula; thus, total costs are not captured when justifying IT investments.

Business Case

Business cases are typically used as a method for defining and justifying the value of new IT investments. What would seem logical and prudent in building and reviewing the business case tends to be fraught with problems. The issues start with the lack of due diligence in considering the complete portfolio of projects required for the successful execution of the business plan. Often, business cases are selected in isolation and independently, with little reflection on the interdependence between projects for the success of the plan. Business cases are often identified in a vacuum or depend on the convictions and passions of executive champions. Intuition tends to be the principal driver, with power plays driving the agendas. Subsequently, selective and inconsistent data and measures are used for justification. The business case alone will not be able to determine the necessary trade-offs and optimal value for a balanced IT investment portfolio, which addresses both short-term profitability and long-term growth or organization-wide capabilities.[66] Portfolio management is further discussed in Chapter 7.

The challenge within the business case is defining the benefits, especially the intangible value.[67] Often, benefits are not factored or discounted for uncertainty. In addition, costs are invariably absent. Consider that Forester Research estimates that non-IT costs connected with the implementation of enterprise systems could be as much as four times greater than IT costs.[68] The data collected for costs, revenue, and capital can be selective, inaccurate, and inconsistently applied to the various formulas, projecting misleading statements that create poor decisions. Traditional ROI and DCF calculations are often inconsistent, applying assumptions that would not "hold up in court." The argument is typically based on a rationale and analysis, but not necessarily on numerical or financial rigor.[69]

The financial departments validate the calculations, but based on the information provided where they may not fully understand the business conditions. Ultimately, the business leader is responsible for the decision and his or her ability to argue and justify the case. With strong leaders arguing their case in an environment of finite resources, how does one prioritize the business cases when measures are either wrong or inconsistently applied? Where do you spend the incremental dollar for maximum shareholder return? Subsequently, business case selection optimizes divisional returns or local optimization and not firm-wide returns or shareholder value. There is a need for consistent and independent governance on IT investment.

IT business cases need to include stock price impact and defined processes to ensure that the investment brings an appropriate risk-adjusted return. This goes beyond the traditional DCF, ROI, cost savings, or low cost of ownership business justifications. A new value-creation or wealth-creating business case is required, one that focuses on shareholder value and delivery of stakeholder benefits. The business case should emphasize the key value drivers, comparative benchmarking, risk adjustments, benefit realization processes; with good data collection and monitoring to capture the value. The economic value added (EVA) approach could be considered.[70] New value-based multidimensional approaches to IT investments and evaluation are required that go beyond traditional accounting and financial methods and measures.[71]

> Business cases are identified in a vacuum or depend on the convictions and passions of executive champions, whereby costs and benefits are inaccurate, inconsistent, and not risk adjusted, projecting misleading statements that create poor decisions.

Project Management

As mentioned previously, millions of dollars are wasted in projects. There are a number of reasons why projects fail, but often it is an inept business case, inadequate requirements definition, or just poor project planning and management. Failure to scope out the business case properly and define the right measures of success is common.[72] Failure to secure ongoing executive sponsorship and a good project manager are typical. Failure to incorporate an open feedback system for project review and validity against the business case is not unusual.[73] Change and risk management is typically underinvested. When those involved measure the performance of project success, the result can be self-serving and not true to the project charter or business case. Subsequently, where IT projects exhibit poor performance, only 50 percent of firms conduct a postimplementation review.[74] Ultimately, value realization is not tracked and not delivered, resulting in, at best, unknown, and at worst, negative shareholder value.

Project metrics typically fail because of the challenges of identifying the right measures and subsequently collecting and objectively analyzing the right data. Significant resources and time are required for evaluation. Business, technical, and process measures are needed to evaluate a project.[75] An additional complexity is that IT projects tend to be more irreversible than non-IT projects, as they affect customer relationships, internal relationships, and management knowledge.[76] Companies that follow a rigorous process of reviewing project slippage against the business case and finding that the goals are not being met typically cancel early, as much as 40 percent of total projects.[77] Therefore, IT management needs to review current project evaluation measures and methods. The introduction of a project or program management office (PMO) can provide strong independent investment and project governance. More on project management appears in Chapter 12.

> Project metrics typically fail because of the challenges of identifying the right measures and subsequently collecting and objectively analyzing the right data.

Change Management

As we have discovered previously, complementary investments to IT in organizational capital make a difference to performance outcomes. These investments include decentralized decision-making systems, self-directed teams, job training, organizational design (OD), business process improvement, and internal communication.[78] When considering the broader perspective of IT contribution to company performance, it is critical to consider change management investments. Studies have suggested that the success rate of IT on change initiatives is only between 20 to 50 percent, emphasizing the importance of the inclusion of change management considerations.[79] For instance, training and education are essential for technology application and utility. Otherwise value is suboptimal—or worse, not realized. Computer assets have a disproportionately higher value in firms with organizational characteristics such as greater use of teams, broader decision-making authority, and training.

> Complementary investments to IT in organizational capital make a difference to performance and value outcomes.

Stakeholder Economic Value

Stakeholder economic value drives sustained competitive advantage or network advantage. Traditional financial measures alone, in pursuit of shareholder value, are misleading and do not capture the range of perceived and realizable values from key stakeholders, across the business value system and value network.

Determining stakeholder economic value is a science and an art. Multidimensional disciplines are required to triangulate the IT valve. Decisions are made on intuition or best guess, not financials alone, requiring higher levels of information exchange and communication. Extracting the financials remains important, in addition to capturing the views and opinions through focus groups, surveys, reviews, and debriefing. Business goals and strategies provide direction but don't necessarily consider individual executive preferences and priorities at various points in time. Ultimately, key stakeholders desire services and capabilities from the underlying technology, meeting short-term and long-term needs. IT client engagement and value management processes are required to provide a complete portfolio view to defined key stakeholders, whether functional, regional, or business unit specific.

Let's also not forget the general employee base, necessitating the need to extract user satisfaction ratings and value statements. Energy is also required in understanding the extended business network values, in dialogue with partners, alliances, suppliers, and customers. Overall, significant IT value can be lost, without capturing and delivering against stakeholder needs and expectations; ensuring effective alignment and communication of the IT value proposition. Chapter 19 discusses maximizing stakeholder economic value.

> Traditional financial measures alone, in pursuit of shareholder value, do not capture the range of perceived and realizable values from key stakeholders across the business value system and network, which is imperative for sustained competitive advantage or network advantage.

This chapter has argued that conventional IT asset valuation methods have failed to fully identify and capture IT investment value. Chapter 3 provides further insight into this dilemma within the banking industry. IT valuation observations are examined to further understand lessons learned. The conclusion remains the same: new measures and management approaches are required to realize shareholder economic value. The IT value network approach is intended to provide effective valuation methods, which are explored in Part II.

Banking Value

Financial Services Industry Global IT Investment

To compete, banks are becoming larger, with multiline and multichannel offerings. To meet national and global expansion and enable new channels and products to come to market, the financial services—and specifically the banking industry—have experienced double-digit increases in IT spending from the mid- to late 1990s.[1] Between 1997 and 1999, global IT spending in the financial services industry grew from 11 to 25 percent, particularly in personnel and hardware costs.[2] This occurred at a time when the overall world IT market was growing at 10 percent annually, nearly double the rate of the world gross domestic product.[3] During the Internet crash, between 2001 and 2003, financial services IT spending slowed year over year to 4 to 6 percent, but still the spending level is the highest of all industries at 7.3 percent of revenue.[4] From 2003 to 2007, growth in global financial services IT spending has stabilized between 5.9 percent and 8.7 percent, reaching $342.1 billion.[5] Arguably the current most important variables impacting global IT spending is the state of the institutional or wholesale banking industry and the U.S. economy, both of which from 2007 show signs of collapse and recession.[6]

This chapter discusses IT investments within the North American banking industry. An overview of the North American banking industry will explain the competitive landscape and bank challenges. Subsequently, IT investment patterns will be explored, questioning whether these investments have added value to the bottom line. A more in-depth assessment is conducted on a large North American (NA) bank, referred to as NA Bank for anonymity, highlighting IT investment observations. Various IT value observations are identified throughout the chapter, which are arguably germane to the global banking industry and not just North America.

> The current state of the institutional or wholesale banking industry and the U.S. economy, which from 2007 show signs of collapse and recession, will materially impact IT investment, reducing its growth in the banking sector to low single digits during the next few years.

North American Banking Industry

After considerable debate in Congress and at the state level, the U.S. retail banking industry was deregulated to a nationwide industry in the mid- to late 1990s, as was the case in other countries, including Canada. The Riegle-Neal Interstate Banking and Branching Efficiency Act of 1994 marked an intense period of mergers and acquisitions within the U.S. banking industry, which emphasized bank expansion across state lines. This was the beginning of a large regional and national retail bank presence, although today no one bank can claim complete national coverage.

The U.S. Federal Reserve rulings also eliminated the separation of commercial and investment banking. The Financial Modernization Act of 1999 and the Gramm-Leach-Bliley Act of 1999 provided for banks to offer complete financial services under a one-stop-shopping brand. Banks now turned their merger and acquisition attention toward brokerage and investment banks, building a wealth management business for individual investors. Between 1991 and 2001, the number of U.S. banking institutions declined 33 percent. Market growth and service diversification grew rapidly. Within just four years, between 1997 and 2000, noninterest income in the U.S. grew 50 percent to $169 billion, through fee-based services and asset securitization.[7]

The United States is the largest global financial player, and Canada is one of the smallest in the developed markets. The United States represents 42.1 percent of the 1996 world's equity capitalization market, compared to Canada with 2.4 percent. However, Canada has a higher concentration of bank interests: Canadian Imperial Bank of Commerce (CIBC), Toronto Dominion Bank (TD), Royal Bank (RBC), Bank of Montreal (BMO), Bank of Nova Scotia (ScotiaBank), and the National Bank of Canada control 86 percent of the CAN$776 billion domestic banking assets. The remaining 46 schedule II banks are predominately foreign owned, where no one bank owns more than 3.1 percent. This compares with only 19 percent of the domestic banking assets controlled by the top U.S. banks, which include Citibank (Citigroup), BankAmerica, Wells Fargo, and Chase.[8] Today, under the Financial Modernization Act of 1999, any company in the United States passing a "fit and proper" test can own a retail banking franchise license. Thus, within the United States there were over 8,000 retail banks in 2004, supporting just under 70,000 branches, with an accumulated asset base of just over $7 trillion. Foreign banks account for 24 percent of all U.S. banking assets.[9]

Recent events have challenged the global banking industry, with the late 2007 U.S. subprime lending debacle and the subsequent destabilized global financial market. Fannie Mae and Freddie Mac own or guarantee about 40 percent of the $11 trillion residential mortgage market.[10] These companies are critical for institutional lending, through the secondary-mortgage market. As the credit crunch hit hard, these companies struggled for liquidity and had to be bailed out by the U.S. federal government, placing both companies into conservatorship in September 2008. Investment banking is currently in dire straits with the collapse of Lehman Brothers in September 2008 and Bear Stearns in March 2008 (acquired by J.P. Morgan), thus decreasing available institutional credit and constraining lending. Businesses and home owners now struggle to find funds to survive, as equity values diminish.

While the global financial collapse severely impacted investment banks, the retail banking industry was not immune. The U.S. Federal Reserve bank had to intervene to provide liquidity and unfreeze the credit market, buying back $700 million of bad loans from the domestic banks. This was not enough; the U.S. government had to subsequently buy bank shares to recapitalize these institutions, investing some $250 billion from the U.S. Treasury—or the taxpayers. More may well be required, which will lead to a form of nationalization, similar to that seen in the United Kingdom, with the treatment of Royal Bank of Scotland and Lloyds TSB.

Meanwhile, larger U.S. banks have been able to benefit through "basement" acquisitions of troubled banks, such as Washington Mutual and Wachovia. Canadian banks have been able to weather the storm more effectively than their overall U.S. counterparts, due to less volatile credit holdings, requiring no federal support and benefiting for discounted U.S. bank asset acquisitions. As the credit crunch eases and investor confidence grows, attention will continue to focus on the state of the economy. To stimulate business and consumer growth, in attempts to prevent a deepening worldwide recession, interest rates have been significantly reduced globally.

IT spending by North American financial services represents over one-third of the global financial services IT expenditure, and although in 2007 growth was lower than the rest of the world, at 4.8 percent compared to 5.9 percent globally, the amount spent was a formidable $116.8 billion.[11] Despite the recent financial crisis, IT investment remains high. As complexity increases, the amount spent on IT continues to grow, to manage the vast information and transactional streams. For example, the U.S. banking industry accounts for over one-third of the U.S. corporate processing capacity.

Size matters; banks like Citigroup, Chase, and Bank of America can control their own and the market's destiny. Citigroup is the largest global bank with $902 billion assets in 2002, spending over $2 billion on IT.[12] In fact, in 1996 the top three banks in the United States spent $5 billion on IT, in contrast to $3 billion spent on IT by the entire Canadian banking sector. IT investments are necessary to keep up with competition; the bigger the bank, the larger the IT spending. This subsequently creates significant performance pressure on smaller banks. At the turn of the twenty-first century, the largest banks are spending between 15 to 21 percent on their noninterest expenses (NIX) on IT, regional banks between 9 to 17 percent, and smaller community banks between 4 to 10 percent.[13] Typically, the larger the bank the higher the IT capability for competitive differentiation.

> IT investments are necessary to keep up with competition; the bigger the bank, the larger the IT spending, which creates significant IT performance pressure within most banks.

North American Banking Market Challenges

In today's global banking industry, the key challenges continue to include regulatory reform, global competition, sophisticated customers, IT innovation, and shareholder expectations. In addition, recent bank collapses have decreased available capital and destabilized institutional or wholesale interbank lending. Market share and margin continue to be eroded within the traditional retail banks, placing strategic focus on bank performance and customer service.[14] The principal retail banking challenges for the larger U.S. banks continue to be consolidation toward a nationwide full-service provider and global expansion, but economic weakness has slowed merger growth. The exception is noted where larger banks with stronger capital bases have acquired troubled banks in financial crisis. Exhibit 3.1 illustrates the current North American banking environment, challenges, and strategies.

The Canadian banking industry differs from the overall U.S. banking sector in that the Canadian big six banks already have a nationwide presence and well-diversified portfolios, including extensive wealth management (personal brokerage) services. However, the Canadian banks are challenged with short-term asset quality deterioration and the long-term strategic disadvantage of limited national and global expansion, due to national government controls and limited capital size.[15] Specifically,

EXHIBIT 3.1 North American Bank Environment

Bank Environment	Bank Challenge	Bank Strategy
Regulatory Reform ■ The Financial Modernization Act ■ Riegle-Neal Interstate Banking & Branching Efficiency Act ■ Gramm-Leach-Bliley Act ■ Sarbanes-Oxley Act ■ Basel II Accord ■ Credit rating ■ Trading ■ Privacy	■ Competition from commercial and investment banking and nonfinancial firms ■ Operating across state lines ■ Operating across financial services ■ Compliance ■ Capital allocation ■ Capital ratios ■ Equity tracking ■ Information protection	■ Diversification of services and channels and acquisition of brokerage and investment firms ■ Regional acquisitions ■ One-stop shopping for all financial services—acquisition of brokerage and investment firms ■ Governance: internal controls ■ Operating-risk reduction ■ Reduction of debt exposure ■ Stock/fund controls ■ Information policy
Global Competition ■ Regional and national banks ■ International banks	■ Traditional regional, national, and international banks ■ Community banks ■ Online brokerage firms acquiring ATMs and branches ■ Nonbank institutions (e.g., insurance companies) ■ Nonfinancial institutions (e.g., Microsoft, Intuit)	■ Mergers and acquisitions ■ Customer service ■ Personal service ■ Full-service offering and local branch service
Mergers and Acquisitions ■ National ■ International ■ Other financial services (e.g., insurance)	■ Asset size and market or geographic presence ■ Product and service diversification	■ Targeted acquisitions in regional and national banking, nonbank institutions (insurance), and wealth management

(Continued)

EXHIBIT 3.1 (Continued)

Bank Environment	Bank Challenge	Bank Strategy
Customer Loyalty • Acquisition • Retention • Wallet share	• Buying patterns and profiles • Customer experience • Market segmentation	• Cross-selling and up-selling • Customer service • Customer relationship management (CRM) • Business analytics • Social networking
New Services and Channels • Internet banking • PC banking • Telephone banking • Credit cards • Mortgages • Mobile transactions	• New entrants to traditional banking market • New channels to market that compete on cost and 24-hour availability	• Revenue diversification and full-service offerings—noninterest income • E-commerce, Internet channels, m-commerce • Branch renewal • Integrated channels • Brand identity
Corporate Citizen • Community • Charity	• Consumer competitive options • Supporting local community	• Brand identity • Government liaison and lobbying • Charities and sponsorships
Employee Loyalty • Acquisition • Retention • Development	• Staff retention • Employee productivity	• Stock options and large bonuses • Performance measurement and management
Technology Innovation • SOA and Web 2.0 • Virtualization • Mobile networking • Social networking • Business analytics • Managed services and outsourcing	• New channels and services • Large investments • ROI • Cost and performance	• New Internet and wireless platforms—e/m-commerce • Strategic IT investments • Infrastructure consolidation and optimization • Performance measurement

Security

■ Information security, protection and privacy	■ Fraud, theft, unauthorized access	■ Information security policy, credit clearance

Shareholder Expectations

■ Share price growth	■ 12% to 15% margin growth	■ Dynamic growth
■ Dividend growth	■ Dividend growth	■ Revenue diversification—non-interest income
■ Capital performance	■ Capital returns	
■ Operating performance	■ Cost (NIX) reduction	■ Risk reduction—asset securitization
		■ Operational excellence—straight-through processing
		■ Outsourcing

according to Lum and Hilderbrand,[16] the Canadian seven major challenges include:

1. Industry is becoming more competitive, characterized by fierce competition between the largest banks; foreign competition is allowed to set up branches, and nonbank financial institutions (life insurance, credit unions, and mutual fund companies) have entered the banking market with lower capitalization levels.
2. Banks have a limited ability to expand, due to national government regulation and equity size.
3. Global competitors have advantages of size, presence, and diversification.
4. Banks struggle to balance strategic spending against cost management, with the challenge of allocating resources for growth while driving operational efficiencies.
5. Banks capability and constraints to cross-sell, determined by the ability to leverage IT and the sales forces.
6. High risk of leveraging capital market revenues for retail banking expansion, which have been extremely volatile and costly (e.g., Enron exposures).
7. Deteriorating credit quality must be dealt with, resulting from syndicated lending.

In today's banking industry, the key challenges continue to include deregulation, global competition, sophisticated customers, IT innovation, and shareholder expectations. However, with the recent financial crisis, more attention will be paid to capital and operating performance.

Regulatory Reform

Fast and wide-ranging regulatory reform is changing the competitive landscape. Since the Great Depression—and particularly from the 1950s to the 1980s—banks were heavily regulated, which protected large national incumbent retail banks from external competition.[17] Since the mid-1990s, U.S. banking legislation has liberalized the financial services industry, with the advent of the Financial Modernization Act of 1999, the Riegle-Neal Interstate Banking and Branching Efficiency Act of 1994, and the Gramm-Leach-Bliley Act of 1999. In the United States (like the United Kingdom), until recently, bank regulation was competition neutral, allowing the markets to decide on individual bank survival. Recent events in the United States (and the United Kingdom) have been somewhat unprecedented, with substantial government intervention and support for the banking industry in crisis. It will be interesting to see how government legislation or governance will change to restore confidence to the financial markets.

In Canada, no real change has occurred; the balancing act continues between open competition and regulation or government support of domestic banks. In recent times, such a hybrid model has received international acclaim. The Canadian banking industry remains under stricter controls specific to domestic merger limitations, but it has been liberalized in full-service provisioning. Subsequently, between 1994 and 2001, strong and improved bank performance has resulted in the growth of the S&P Banking Index, at a compound annual rate of 12.7 percent.[18] To remain competitive, Canadian banks will need changes to the current regulation, specifically enabling the large institutions to merge in the domestic market and to gain economies from both transaction volume and capital leverage. The merger of Lloyds and TSB in the United Kingdom created, at one point, the most valuable bank in the world.[19]

Global Competition

Globalization of financial institutions has redefined the competitive and regulatory environment and expanded customer choice, generating fierce competition from global U.S.-based players such as Citigroup, the world's largest bank, with $2.2 trillion assets in 2007. The bank has approximately 358,000 employees worldwide and holds 200 million customer accounts in 100 countries. Mergers and acquisitions, although recently slowed in growth, are still a threatening force, as is evident in the merger between JP Morgan Chase and Bank One, or the recent merger between Bank of America, Fleet Boston, and MBNA. These huge mergers had created, at the time, the third and second largest banks in the United States, in terms of market capitalization, after Citibank. For example, the merger of JP Morgan Chase and

Bank One created a combined market capitalization of $130 billion, with an asset size of $1.1 trillion and an opportunity of deriving $2.2 billion in cost savings from economies of scale and from a staff reduction of 10,000.[20] NationsBank, now known as Bank of America, used its high share multiple of five times its book value to acquire other lower-valued banks such as Boatmen's Bancshares, essentially gaining a higher ownership share.[21]

As in the United States, the large Canadian banks have pursued mergers and acquisitions, particularly across the United States, in expanding selective regional personal banking and in wealth management. For instance, the merger of TD and Waterhouse in 1996 combined one of the largest Canadian retail banks with a U.S. individual wealth management company. A similar merger took place between CIBC and the Merrill Lynch Canadian brokerage firm. Essentially, the Canadian banks are expanding their personal and commercial banking into the United States, where the opportunity presents itself, or in acquiring wealth management or brokerage capability for personal investors. However, since the decision in 1998 by the Canadian government not to allow mergers between the large national banks, the ability of the Canadian banks to grow domestically has been constrained.[22]

Customer Sophistication

The banks are challenged to align to more fragmented markets, where customers want multiline and multichannel options. Customers are becoming more sophisticated and are demanding more tailored services, rejecting the one-size-fits-all bank mentality.[23] Increasing sophistication and demanding customers call for new preferences, which are creating new service hurdles and shorter product life cycles.[24] As a result, many banks are focusing on building customer loyalty through deploying fulfillment strategies tied to customers' buying profiles. More affluent customers are moving bank savings to security investments. The younger generation is Internet ready and is comfortable using online applications for their financial services, wanting the freedom of 24-hour transaction processing. The older generation looks for ease of access to retail branches and ATMs. Regional and country preferences persist. Customer mobility is yet another issue that the banks need to address by providing fund and service access internationally.

Multiline services and products are critical to offer customer choice, leverage market presence, and produce economies of scale. The Canadian big six are already multilined nationally, dominating traditional branch and ATM services and controlling together over 50 percent of transactions in all personal financing sectors, including mortgages, consumer loans, credit cards, and deposits. In addition, the big six own over 70 percent of the Canadian investment banking and brokerage business.[25] Targeted services and product combinations offered to differentiated market segments provide retail banks with the opportunity to appeal to local or virtual market preference. MBNA, now part of Bank of America, had chosen to focus on U.S.-based credit card services, successfully achieving a sevenfold growth in market capitalization in only five years, reaching $20 billion in 1997.[26]

Exploiting third-party product offerings such as AirMile programs and the TP-Wal-Mart credit card is another key strategy for building customer loyalty and retention.[27] An example of broadening services is the growth in paying bills online. Canada is more advanced than the United States in building electronic bill-payment services to online banking consumers, driving revenue opportunities while saving on transaction costs. Online billing is more mainstream in Canada, where only 16 percent of online consumers still prefer to pay by paper checks. This is in contrast to the United States, where 70 percent still pay by check. Moreover, in Canada more than half of online consumers pay bills online at a bank's site, in contrast to the United States, where only 10 percent of online consumers pay through a bank site, preferring to use biller sites instead. Banks can aggregate bill payments and provide a one-stop payment offering to consumers, building a captive market. U.S. banks are missing a strategic opportunity, losing to biller sites and letting valuable customers get away. With an annual customer savings of $29 per billpayer and a relationship-deepening benefit of $68, banks can expect to get a bottom-line economic benefit of $97 per bill payer.[28]

Retail banks are challenged by new channels to market and by new service packaging. Charles Schwab mutual funds and E*Trade discount brokerage are becoming distribution specialists, while other banks specialize on services such as underwriting mortgages. Further challenges are coming from new electronic marketplaces with integrated services from nonfinancial firms such as Intuit, Microsoft, and I-money. The challenge in supporting multiple channels to market has increased. Rather than replacing branch visits with lower-cost channels, customers have increased their overall frequency of interaction with the banks. A recent study shows that 50 percent of customers still prefer to use the physical branch bank over other channels, and some 92 percent of customers have used a branch within the past month.[29] Customers are not channel-centric. Therefore, banks are reviewing their strategies, upgrading branches, and reducing Internet banking investment.[30] Disaggregation and reaggregation of financial assets remains a challenge.

Customer relationships have suffered as a result of fee increases and reduced service levels. Tailored customer service is exactly why the U.S. community banks have been successful, creating a localized footprint to prosper. Community banks in California have been successful at exploiting larger bank service shortfalls, focusing on supporting small to medium-sized businesses. Customer service and branding are key strategies, building customer and brand loyalty. First Union, in the United States, has improved shareholder value and customer service from interstate acquisitions.[31]

IT Innovation

IT is one of the most important factors in changing the banking industry, especially as banks look inward at organic growth.[32] Rapid advances in technology and computer power are providing new delivery mechanisms and new competition. While legislation helped stimulate dynamic growth, additional sector growth came from new entrants and new channels to market. With the advent of the Internet, broader markets could be accessed through technology. The banks plowed investment into personal computer banking, Internet banking, call centers, and now wireless banking, in addition to traditional nonbranch ATM outlets. In just six years from 1996 to 2002, Internet banking in the United States had exceeded 25 percent of the retail customer base.[33] Online banking exceeded $24 million ($50 million worldwide) in 2004, doubling since the end of 2000.[34]

The biggest IT innovation challenge for many large banks, especially through accumulated acquisitions, is the convergence or replacement of their legacy systems. While significant bank IT advancements have been made within the shared infrastructure, consolidating and optimizing networks and data centers, the operational systems have seen minimum change. Rationalizing transaction-critical applications and moving to an open integrated architecture is not high on a CIO's priorities; the perceived risk to operations and career is just too high. The lack of interoperability between business unit systems has created a huge challenge in supporting multiline and multichannel offerings. Strategically, IT investment has been aggressive in application areas such as customer relationship management (CRM), business analytics, branch renewal, and e-commerce. However, investment remains low in replacing operational transaction-based systems.

Shareholder Expectations

Despite the current economic environment, shareholders expect competitive returns, placing pressure on capital and operational performance. Increasing costs and decreasing profit margins in traditional services (e.g., corporate loans, credit cards, mortgages, securities trading) have increased operational performance challenges. Size and presence are current constraints, especially for Canadian banks competing against larger U.S. banks, which have wide market presence, cost economies, full-service offerings, and vast capital (including recent Federal injection) at their disposal. The U.S. banking industry has room for growth, especially in leveraging globally from size and presence, leaving Canada behind in pace and market value. Bank efficiency is critical with tight margins. U.S. banks have been more successful in driving their net interest expenses (NIX) ratios down to sub-60 percent, whereas the Canadian banks lag averaging mid- to late 60s. Salaries and occupancy costs continue to outpace revenue growth, causing further operating margin pressure.[35] Canadian banks face further pressure to remain competitive in the face of more highly productive U.S. banks, challenging their domestic market dominance. However, Canadian banks enjoy a strong national banking system, earnings diversification, reasonable credit quality, and strong levels of capital.[36]

Disintermediation and securitization of financial assets will continue to be a challenge, in that banks have been converting loans into securities and leveraging off-balance sheet assets for greater portfolio flexibility. However, as noninterest income fees stabilize, this option is less attractive. As capital rebuilds from interest and noninterest income, shareholders will be looking at how effective banks are at managing and utilizing capital and evaluating how excess capital is deployed. Managing capital performance will also be assessed against risk profiles and controls. Today, the banks face the challenge of the decline in mergers and acquisitions and asset securitization. Dynamic growth may have to take a back seat to organic growth through sound customer-focused strategies aimed at building back consumer and business confidence.

Banking Industry IT Value Observations

In view of the past two decades of IT investment, it is clear that the banking industry is overspending and not getting the expected "bang for the buck." IT spending has been typically focused on the top line, not the bottom line, on targeting new customers and increasing customer "wallet share." It has been less focused on operational performance. IT value has not been fully realized and a new evaluation and performance management approach is required.

No Bang for the Buck

Bank prosperity was generally improving following the economic challenges of the early 2000s. That changed in 2007 with the onset of the subprime mortgage debacle and the subsequent credit crunch. The primary impact has been on capital availability and interbank institutional lending—in other words, the wholesale business. Despite defaulting mortgages and credit squeeze, the North American retail banking industry is relatively stable, but revenues remain flat, placing pressure on operating costs. Yet, as in the past 20 years, current spending on IT continues to increase, leading to the question of whether banks have realized the expected value from these IT investments.

Within the North American retail banking industry, IT investment had double-digit growth in the 1990s and medium to high single-digit growth in the 2000s, whereas staff productivity growth rates declined within the medium single-digit range.[37] This would seem to indicate a weak, at best, or nonexistent relationship between IT investment and productivity in the banking industry. However, output measurement is extremely difficult.[38] IT investments in the banking industry are not identified and selected in a consistent and disciplined framework, providing suboptimal shareholder value.[39] The banking industry does not seem to get much "bang for the buck" from its IT investment.

Retail banks typically over invested in IT. Consider that between 1996 and 1999 retail banks spent $5,000 annually, per employee, on IT, compared to the rest of the private sector, which spent less than $440 annually per employee. By 2001, financial services IT spending had jumped to just under $27,000 per employee, declining to just over $17,000 in 2002, the highest of all industry sectors, with the exception of the insurance and telecommunications industries.[40] In commercial banking, IT costs can be 25 percent of the noninterest expense. IT costs subsequently accumulated in the 1990s to a total U.S. commercial bank expenditure of more than $200 billion, which is greater than the sum of their total present equity capital.[41] Explanation is required as to why consumer banking, which is an IT-intensive industry, has not seen improvements in labor productivity, despite long-term and substantial investments in IT.[42] Nearly one-half of internal business clients within financial services firms are dissatisfied with their IT organization value.[43]

> Retail banks have typically over invested in IT yet do not see the bang for the buck.

Top Line, Not Bottom Line

Many post-1995 IT investment in the retail banking industry were initiated not to reduce costs but to increase revenue. Investments were made in sales and customer service systems, areas where investment value is harder to measure and realize.[44] One consumer banking sector study attempted to measure indirectly the impact of IT-based services on bank performance—specifically by measuring the indirect impact if IT on customer satisfaction and service quality. The effects of IT investments on perceived service dimensions of reliability, responsiveness, and assurance were measured. However, other causal effects interplayed, such as process reengineering, which made it hard to isolate IT impact.[45] Overall, the conclusion was that through IT investment, better customer service and customer loyalty had proved to show better returns in time.

IT has changed growth opportunities in retail banking, providing service diversification options and modified competition.[46] For example, innovative telephone banking was introduced in the 1980s by Midland Bank (now a subsidiary of HSBC), culminating in more than 1 million new customers within 10 years.[47] Today, over 3,000 traditional brick-and-mortar U.S. banks now offer interactive Internet banking channels. Online banking is still relatively small, but in 2004 the number of U.S. households using this service doubled from 2000.[48] Further, relatively new entrants, like Charles Schwab, are dominating the Web-based brokerage business, claiming 40 percent of the U.S. discount brokerage market and more than 3 million customers in just three years from incorporation.[49]

Today the challenge remains to make a profit from nonbranch channels, where the banks have not proved to be effective in measuring ROI on alternative channels.[50] Essentially, online banking is customer driven and not focused on cost reduction. Services such as consolidated bill payments and account aggregation continue to add value to customers, but they are not expected to generate enough revenue to offset current bank costs. The upside to online banking is the opportunity for banks to target customer profiles and buying behavior through information management and business analytics, driving profitable up-sell (premium) and cross-sell (broad) services.

Optimal performance comes from operational effectiveness and capital leverage. For example, Lloyds TSB in the United Kingdom, although not the largest bank in the world, until recently has been successful in consistently delivering earnings growth at equity returns of over 30 percent, culminating in shares trading at eight times book value. In contrast, no Canadian bank trades at a multiple above three. Fifth Third is one of the United States's most highly efficient banks, with a NIX ratio of only 48 percent in 1996, which at the time achieved the same market capitalization as CIBC with 85 percent fewer assets.[51] Margin pressure continues as banks focus on operational excellence and cost reduction, thereby driving down their efficiency ratios.

> IT investment in retail banking traditionally focuses on customer revenue and service, which is harder to measure and realize the value, as opposed to operational cost reduction, which can be booked and will materialize on the bottom line.

Emerging Performance Valuation

Under economic constraints, banks historically depend on financial performance measures. Research would suggest that organization-based or nonfinancial measures are becoming more popular within the banking industry as bank strategies evolve under uncertainty. Emerging valuation techniques (e.g., balanced scorecards, customer and market surveys, competitive benchmarking, scenario analysis, focus groups, decision support systems, etc.) are providing enhanced performance insights, beyond traditional financial measures. However, these measures are likely to vary significantly across banks, despite a similar economic environment. Hussain and Hoque refer to various influences on the design and use of nonfinancial performance measures within the banking industry.[52] These include:

1. **Economic constraints and uncertainty.** Including banks financial state, credit availability, market volatility, and consumer demand
2. **Competition.** Global and national players consolidating, plus new market entrants
3. **Best practices.** Linking organizational design, structure, and strategy with controls
4. **Regulatory control.** Changes to protect national interests, improve governance, and consumer confidence
5. **Accounting standards and financial legislation.** Accounting principles (GAAP) and international accounting standards (IAS) prescribing national accounting legislation that determine cost calculations and performance measures
6. **Pressures from socioeconomic and political institutions.** Such as the United Nations (UN), the World Trade Organization (WTO), and the International Standards Organization (ISO), which impact international standards and performance measures
7. **Professionals and consultants.** Driving standards, norms, and values
8. **Top management and corporate culture.** Norms that reflect senior management values and drive organizational behavior
9. **Organizational strategic orientation.** Measures that depend on organizational vision, mission, and strategies
10. **Organizational characteristics.** Driven by size, nature, and type of business, influencing performance measurement systems

Based on their banking study, Hussain and Hoque state that the influence of nonfinancial performance measures differed across banks, and that economic constraints played an important role in shaping organization-based measurement practice. The more competitive the environment, the more executives paid attention to organization-based measures to track customer satisfaction, product and service quality, and market share. However, the banks still depend on traditional financial measures of performance.

> Despite suboptimal IT value and future uncertainty, banks still depend on traditional financial measures of performance, although emerging organizational measures are considered under competitive conditions.

NA Bank Case: IT Investment Observations

The case study on NA Bank has two parts, based on a Read & Associates client engagement during 2002 to 2003. The first part, covered in this chapter, outlines IT investment valuation observations made in early 2002. Subsequently, Chapter 15 will discuss client recommendations and applied IT value network practice. Actual data has been modified to protect confidentiality, but it retains integrity in support of the IT investment observations and propositions.

NA Bank is one of the largest, full-service financial institutions in North America with 2002 average assets in excess of $100,000 million. The bank had over 20,000 employees primarily based in North America, but with some presence internationally in Europe and Asia. Bank revenue was over $4 billion, with reported earnings of approximately $250 million. Return on equity was underperforming, with an efficiency ratio (noninterest expense over sales) of more than 70 percent. This is considered high within the banking industry. NA bank declared to its stakeholders that its overall financial performance was unacceptable and changes were necessary.

The retail banking and individual wealth management businesses were performing well, especially within the credit card and mortgage business units. However, the institutional capital markets business was struggling, having been hit by a number of bad debt exposures from liquidated investments, not uncommon across many North American banks. NA Bank was focusing on shifting its business mix away from the capital and credit markets, placing more emphasis on its core retail banking and individual wealth management businesses. Its primary focus was to improve bank performance and operational efficiency, as well as to become more customer centric.

IT Spending

The internal IT and bank operations group was accountable for most of the IT investment. The IT organization was in the process of moving to a centralized operation model to drive out costs. IT functions from the business units were gradually being consolidated. Total annualized IT spending, in excess of $600 million, was allocated across the business units, with some funds allocated to corporate. Approximately half of the total IT investment was allocated to retail banking, which supported multiproduct and market channels. Retail banking IT spending represented 15 percent of revenues and 26 percent of noninterest expense (NIE). Essentially, for every dollar of retail revenue, 15 cents was spent on IT. NA Bank appeared to be spending double the retail banking industry average of 7 percent, or 7 cents per revenue dollar, although the data may not be completely comparable.[53] However, including all businesses, the bank was in line (17 percent) with the 15 to 21 percent of noninterest expense that large banks typically spent on IT;[54] although, as discussed previously, NA Bank's overall NIE expenses were high, with an efficiency ratio of over 70 percent. Retail banking's high IT spending can be explained in part by a large branch re-automation program, but it raises the question as to the overall IT amount spent. Moreover, there was no evidence to suggest that the business value of IT investments was fully determined.

Bank Baseline Survey

To evaluate organizational performance, NA Bank's IT function wanted to understand its internal client's perceptions of satisfaction and value; therefore, with the help of Read & Associates, it conducted four levels of surveys across the bank, including the following:

1. **General satisfaction survey.** This was conducted across all employees, over four quarters, surveying 5,000 employees a quarter, focusing on base IT and operational services.
2. **Event survey.** This was conducted after a service or help desk inquiry or problem was completed or resolved, polling hundreds of employees weekly with a quick satisfaction rating, across a number of service desks.
3. **Project survey and debrief.** This was completed on project closure, focusing on project success and project management effectiveness.
4. **Executive survey and interview.** This was conducted at the executive management level (VP and above), with attention on business unit alignment and service satisfaction and value.

The last two surveys are particularly relevant to the topic of IT investment valuation. An executive survey was conducted in September 2002 to establish an IT baseline of perceived business satisfaction and value. One hundred and fourteen responses to the survey were completed, producing a 44 percent response rate, from an executive target population of 260.

Similarly, a project survey was conducted in the summer of 2002 to derive the baseline level of satisfaction with strategic IT projects and project management. Strategic IT projects were defined consistently with this study. Twenty-nine completed projects were surveyed and 116 surveys were completed from different stakeholder perspectives.

IT Investment Management Observations

Key findings from the surveys revealed an absence of an IT strategic plan and a lack of business value metrics. The IT organization was perceived as heavily operational in nature, providing good service levels. However, it lacked proactive technology leadership. IT strategic planning is a central theme in conventional IT evaluation, aligning IT investments to strategic business objectives. The survey also found that governance and fiscal responsibility over IT spending and investments were lacking and business value was questioned. This was particularly evident in the evaluation of strategic IT projects. The need for an integrated IT business strategy was viewed as a high priority. Tighter alignment was deemed necessary between the business drivers and IT investments, across the overall IT portfolio. Furthermore, a new IT strategic planning and performance measurement process was requested, whereby the business units would be engaged more frequently on a quarterly basis.

Individual business unit strategies were accommodated within the IT operational plan. There was no formal or enterprise-level IT strategic planning process. An annualized operating budgeting process, a capital (project) budgeting process, and annual business unit demands or defined critical success factors determined the IT operating plan. The broader strategic planning process was business unit specific, where IT was an afterthought for budgeting completeness. IT planning was therefore more tactical or operational, focused on "better service at lower costs," driven by four operational business drivers: cost savings, control management, quality service, and delivering business unit needs. Reflecting an operational direction, IT objectives and key initiatives were focused on cost optimization, fiscal responsibility, and service excellence. In many ways, this reflected a positive IT change in direction, from a top-line focus on revenue growth, to a bottom-line efficiency focus, but there was no reference to customer-enabling initiatives (e.g., CRM) in support or alignment to the retail customer centric strategy.

Overall program and portfolio investment management was minimal at NA Bank, defaulting to individual project performance. Business unit–specific IT and business project offices tracked project performance, but there was no central program management office (PMO). Traditional project management metrics were used, such as budgets, schedules, scope, milestones, and critical success factors. Sources of tangible value were identified, and best efforts were used to measure progress. Performance dashboards were constructed. Variances were reported to individual business unit investment review boards. If interim reviews showed projects greater than $1 million with unfavorable variances greater than 20 percent, business cases were recast and reapproved.

Project investments were rationalized and prioritized at NA Bank into four categories: (1) mandatory requirements (legal and regulatory), (2) high-return strategic investments, (3) low-return strategic investments, and (4) high-return tactical investments. The capital and expense budgeting process provided an investment capacity window or envelope, which tuned priorities. Audit compliance and risk mitigation requirements justified and prioritized mandatory strategic IT investment. The business investment review boards ultimately prioritized and approved the strategic IT investments. Measurable, strategic business objectives were defined within balanced scorecards, providing tangible project outcomes and priorities. However, the surveys suggested there was a need to improve investment performance metrics and to ensure that the measures were business relevant. This was particularly evident in the evaluation of strategic IT projects.

NA Bank's principal investment justification was based on business cases using traditional accounting and financial measures—specifically, ROI, NPV, IRR, DCF, and payback period. These measures were mandatory for project values exceeding $500,000 and were selectively used (optional) for projects with a lesser value. Optional or supplementary measures were used depending on the type and level of investment. Principal business drivers and measures were cost savings, risk reduction, and incremental revenue. Measures for intangible value were rarely used. Attempts were made to convert market share, new product introduction, and new market opportunity to tangible measures. For example, new product and new market opportunities were converted to revenue streams with an expected ROI, although projections lacked rigor.

Project management received inconsistent ratings across the various project offices, in which standard processes and metrics were lacking. In addition, poor project milestone delivery and inadequate monitoring of changes to business cases were identified. Project management's best practices suggest that risk management and the quality of deliverables are critical success factors, where cost and time management are variables. In response to the strategic IT project survey, stakeholders selected timely execution, rather than risk management, as one of the critical success factors. Getting projects in on time was perceived to be more important than risk to project delivery and business operations.

Value realization consisted of a one-time postmortem review, six months after project delivery. No audit was conducted on project completion.

Complete investment value realization was not measured because it was assumed that benefits would be absorbed within future business budgets. Based on 91 completed, bank-wide strategic IT projects, between 2001 and 2003, nearly 40 percent of the projects took over three years to complete. These projects accounted for 50 percent of the total investment. Overall, a significant number of strategic IT projects and investments were exposed to uncertainty over their three-year project life cycles, subjecting risk to project success and value capture. The three-year project duration also suggested a very long timeline to deliver the business case returns, subsequent to project completion. More risk-sensitive measures should be considered in the evaluation of strategic IT projects, especially in the face of uncertainty and certainly when project life cycles extend beyond two years. A regular six-month audit over three years would ensure complete value capture and realization.

Based on the IT investment management observations of Read & Associates, NA Bank recruited a senior executive in change of IT strategic execution and service excellence to lead the creation of an IT enterprise strategic plan and to build supporting IT investment and performance management processes. Chapter 15 discusses NA Bank's subsequent implementation of the applied IT value network practice and its outcome.

This chapter has reviewed IT investment and value within the banking industry, with a focus on the North American market. Conventional approaches to IT valuation remain inadequate, as discussed through IT investment observations, questioning IT value within the banking industry, despite increased levels of spending. Part II of the book examines more effective approaches to IT value measurement and management, which, if applied, would likely increase the realizable value of IT investments. The NA Bank case continues in Chapter 15, which relates how applied IT value network practice addressed the IT investment observations, redirecting IT investments for improved value capture.

PART II

Triangulating the
Value—Somewhere Here

Triangulating is typically known for finding the coordinates relating to and the distance from an entity (e.g., a ship from the shoreline) using the law of sines, through the calculation of a triangle from two reference points. Global positioning systems (GPS) or radio waves are examples of ways of triangulating a position. Their application includes earthquake detection, virus trends, surveying, astrometry, and rocketry. Triangulating is essentially an approach to problem solving, synthesizing data from multiple sources. By applying a multidisciplinary approach to data analysis and IT investment measurement, triangulating can be successfully used for identifying IT value. Instead of relying just on financial measures—like ROI, which in Part I, we have discovered can be misleading and unreliable—we can hone in on IT investments using more than one measure of valuation. Data from different sources, whether qualitative or quantitative, corroborate value, overcoming specific flaws in any one measurement or approach.

Triangulating the IT value requires typically two to four appropriate measures, depending on the IT investment type (four "S" category model). Part I explored the types of IT investment and questioned traditional or conventional measures and techniques to determine IT value. This part discusses broader and more effective techniques and measures, applying an IT value network index. Chapter 4 defines an IT investment assessment framework, identifying six stages of evaluation. Subsequently, techniques for assessing IT investments have been extracted from a number of multidisciplinary fields, grouped into two categories. Chapter 5 explores financial-based methods and measures from decision-support as well as finance and accounting. Chapter 6 explores organization-based approaches from conventional planning, organizational management, and information economics.

Financial techniques are more structured and based on strict formulas and assumptions, whereas organizational techniques are more process driven and less definitive. When both techniques are used in an integrated and complementary approach, it is expected that there will be improvement in the quality of investment decision making. Research on conventional planning, traditional accounting, and financial IT investment measures has been generally extensive. However, new and emerging techniques have received minimum empirical research and are therefore still in a process of evolution. See the following exhibit for an overview of IT investment valuation techniques and measures.

Chapter 7 provides an IT value network index model for triangulating IT investment value. The basis premise is founded on four value lenses of evaluation: strategic, operational, stakeholder, and agility. These areas of focus triangulate various appropriate measures for IT investment value. The chapter concludes building an IT value portfolio model, which identifies IT investment stars and black holes, providing an enterprise view for more effective IT investment governance and value capture.

IT Investment Valuation Techniques and Measures

Measurement Method	Measurement Technique	Traditional Measures	Emerging Measures
Financial based	**Financial and accounting**	■ ROI/DCF/NPV/IRR ■ Budgeting ■ Business case –Cost benefit analysis ■ Investment review board ■ Audit	■ Economic added value (EAV) ■ Stock price trait ■ Value creation business case ■ Total cost of ownership (TCO)
	Decision support		■ Decision trees ■ Real options ■ IT risk management
Organization based	**Conventional planning**	■ Strategic planning ■ Operational planning ■ Program-project management	
	Organization management		■ IT governance ■ Critical success factors ■ IT balanced scorecard ■ Benchmarking ■ Service level agreements (SLA) ■ Surveys
	Information economics		■ IT investment management ■ IT portfolio management ■ Scenario planning

CHAPTER 4

IT Value Network Measurement

Organizations need a new kind of IT investment assessment approach, one designed to measure the IT value creation of the company network. Just looking at financial or accounting measures of value is a short-term focus and a lag indicator, and focusing on productivity measures does nothing to reveal the intangible value generated. New emerging decision-support methods, like real options, should be considered to complement traditional financial measures. Organization-based techniques are also required to manage and assess strategic IT investments, such as the balanced scorecard (BSC) and investment and portfolio management. Key IT performance indicators and competitive benchmarking could also be used to help triangulate IT evaluation. Most of the contemporary literature refers to one or more of these techniques or approaches, but rarely views them together to form a multidisciplinary approach; further, most discussion leaves out the stakeholder or network value view.

> Organizations need a new kind of IT investment evaluation approach, one designed to measure the IT value creation within the business network.

In assessing the value of new IT investments, it is proposed that there are six stages of evaluation, through which certain techniques or measures should be applied. Exhibit 4.1 illustrates the IT investment evaluation assessment stages, with corresponding appropriate measures or techniques, which are discussed in detail within Chapters 5 and 6. IT investments should be assessed at each stage, applying one or more primary or secondary measures or techniques per stage. IT investment evaluation assessment stages include:

1. Identifying
2. Justifying
3. Prioritizing

Measurement Method or Technique	Identify	Justify	Priority	Select	Perform	Realize
Financial-Based **12 Techniques or Measures**						
ROI/DCF/NPV/IRR		P	S	S		
Budgeting		P			P	
Business case—Cost vs. benefit		P			P	
Investment review board			P			P
Audit	P					P
Economic added value (EAV)		P	S	S		
Stock price traits		P	P			
Value-creation business case		P	P			
Total cost of ownership (TCO)	S	P	S			
Decision trees	S		S			
Real options	S	S				
IT risk management					P	P
Organization-Based **12 Techniques or Measures**						
Strategic planning	P	S	P	P	P	
Operational planning	P		P	P	P	
Program and project management					P	
IT governance	S		P	P	P	P
Critical success factors	P		P	P		
IT balanced scorecard	P				S	P
Benchmarking					S	
Surveys	P				P	
Service level agreements					P	
IT investment management		P		P		P
IT portfolio management		P	P	P	P	P
Scenario planning	S	P				

Legend: **Primary Technique** (P)   **Secondary Technique** (S)

EXHIBIT 4.1 IT Investment Evaluation Assessment Stages

4. Selecting
5. Performing
6. Realizing

Identifying Investment

IT investments are based on an opportunity or need, and a disciplined process is required to identify the investment based on strategic and operational requirements. The objective is to directionally identify and align investments to maximum firm value. Primary techniques are organizational-based—specifically, strategic and operational planning, business critical success factors, and IT balanced scorecard.

Justifying Investment

Typically, investments are justified through a business case supported by financial metrics. The objective is to determine the projected value of the investment, within degrees of confidence or accuracy. Primary techniques and measures are financial-based—specifically, value creation, business case, or cost/benefit analysis, using net present value (NPV), internal rate of return (IRR), economic added value (EAV), and total cost of ownership (TCO). Real options and risk management are excellent additions, under conditions of uncertainty.

Prioritizing Investment

Knowing the investment is justified and that a firm has constrained total investment, the question is how to prioritize based on objective and subjective measures. The objective is to determine a balanced portfolio of returns for maximum firm value, considering both short-term and long-term needs. Primary techniques are both organization-based and financial-based—specifically, strategic and operational planning, critical success factors, and IT balanced scorecard and are overseen by an investment review board, IT investment management, and corporate governance. Investment decisions are supported by a value creation business case, EAV, stock price traits, and real options.

Selecting Investment

Ultimately, the investment is selected based on an approval process and is then executed. The objective is to select investments that meet an array of stakeholder needs, ensuring an appropriate governance model that provides effective decision making for compromise and optimizing firm value. Primary techniques are mainly organization-based—specifically, strategic and operational planning; overseen by an investment review board, IT investment management, IT portfolio management, and corporate governance.

Performance of Investment

During the life of the investment, a continuous process of performance measurement should be implemented to ensure that the expected results are derived, in terms of both cost outlays and benefit capture. The objective is to ensure that approved investment is on track to deliver the stakeholder benefits, and if not, appropriately managed. Primary techniques are mainly organization-based—specifically, operational plan, program/project management, critical success factors, IT balanced scorecard, IT governance, benchmarking, surveys, service level agreements, and investment/portfolio management; along with investment review board, budgeting, and financial IT risk management.

Realizing Value from Investment

Finally, there should be a method to ensure that the expected value from the investment is captured and realized on the firm's books. In addition, there is the need to learn from the investment's management and execution experience, which should also be captured. The objective is to book the value on the firm's ledgers and improve new investment decision making. Primary techniques are mainly organization-based—specifically, corporate/IT governance, critical success factors, IT balanced scorecard, service level agreements, and investment/portfolio management, along with financial budgeting.

IT value network measurement consists of selecting the right measures, for the right investment type, at the right time. The IT investment evaluation assessment stages provide the timing framework. Chapters 5 and 6 consider the appropriate measures for categorized investment types at each assessment stage, providing application pros and cons.

CHAPTER 5

IT Value Network Measures
Financial-Based Methods

Financial-based IT investment measures or techniques are defined in this chapter. Chapter 2 challenged the norms of traditional financial-based methods to IT investment value measurement and justification, stating lost value from potential inaccuracies and inadequacies. Although fraught with problems, these measures remain popular, even with their misleading results. Therefore, to supplement conventional thinking, emerging financial and decision-support techniques and measures are also reviewed. This chapter considers the appropriate financial-based measures for the categorized four "S" investment types as defined in Chapter 1 and at each IT investment assessment stage as discussed in Chapter 4, providing application pros and cons.

> Traditional financial and accounting techniques, although fraught with problems, remain popular, giving rise to emerging financial-based methods, such as decision-support techniques for more effective investment justification.

Traditional Financial and Accounting Techniques

Most organizations use traditional financial and accounting techniques to measure or evaluate IT investments. This section defines the more popular methods.

Return on Investment

Return on investment (ROI) is a financial measure to determine and compare the gain or loss from investments, relative to the size of each investment, capital or asset. In its simplest form and on its own, ROI does not help in understanding the investment term or how long an investment is held; thus, it is typically depicted as an annual or annualized rate of return, similar to return on asset (ROA). The problem with applying ROI to new investments is that it can lead to misallocation of resources. ROI takes into account the past undepreciated investment and does not include the residual value for new investments made after the forecast period. ROI is essentially an accrual accounting return, which is inappropriately compared against an economic return of cost of capital.[1]

ROI definition. Net gain or loss divided by investment, represented as a percentage

Example. $10,000 profit from an IT investment of $100,000 equals an ROI of 10 percent

Pros:
- Quick and simple indicator of IT value
- Good for first pass, acid test, prior to further analysis

Cons:
- Gain or loss estimates often inaccurate (heuristics and historical)
- Cost of money over time not factored
- Risk on gain or loss not considered
- Investment not fully accounted
- Accrual accounting return
- Does not consider the residual value of investments

IT investments:
- General use as an early indicator for investment justification; secondary measure for prioritization and selection

Payback Period

Payback period is a business and economic term, referring to the period of time it takes to recover the initial investment or have it pay for itself. The desire is for shorter payback periods, reducing the risk of longer-term payouts. This is especially relevant with IT investments, where the trend is to break projects into chunks for faster implementation and benefit realization. Payback period is also heavily used to defend shared infrastructure investment, reducing cost of ownership over time.

Payback definition. The year when the accumulated net gain is equal to or exceeds the initial investment, represented in years

Example. $10,000 profit from an IT investment of $100,000 equal to a payback period of 10 years

Pros:
- Quick and simple indicator of investment recovery
- Good for first pass, acid test, prior to further analysis

Cons:
- Gain or loss estimates often inaccurate (heuristics and historical)
- Cost of money over time not factored
- Risk on gain or loss not considered
- Investment not fully accounted

IT investments:
- General use as an early indicator for investment justification; secondary measure for prioritization and selection
- More applicable to shared infrastructure investments

Net Present Value

Net present value (NPV) is a capital investment measure used to determine the firm's value from the contribution of an investment by summing the gain or loss cash flows generated over time. It's the standard method of appraising longer-term projects, using a discounted rate for the cost of money over time, generating the present value of investment return. Similar to discounted cash flow (DCF), where the discount rate is equal to an interest rate applied to the loan of the investment. IT investments with an NPV < 0 should be rejected.

NPV definition. $\text{Sum}^t \left(\text{annual net cash flow}/(1 + r)^t\right)$, less initial investment, where $t =$ time or year(s) of cash flows, and $r =$ discount rate (rate of return of an investment in the financial markets with a similar risk profile)

Pros:
- Strong indicator of expected return, over time
- Value creation over the cost of money
- Can be used for project comparison, assuming appropriate discounted rates were applied

Cons:
- Gain or loss estimates often inaccurate (heuristics and historical)
- Investment not fully accounted
- Singular rate used, often referred to the weighted average cost of capital (after tax), not accounting for variable risk from gain/loss streams and compounded variable risk over time (i.e., yield curve)
- Does not account for the lost opportunity cost from alternatives investments

IT investments:
- General use as a primary measure for investment justification: secondary measure for prioritization and selection
- More applicable to shared infrastructure and systems investments

Internal Rate of Return

Internal rate of return (IRR) is a capital investment measure, indicating the efficiency or yield of the investment, calculating a compounded return rate. IT investments with an IRR greater than potentially alternative investments, whether from within the business (i.e., staff investment) or outside the business (i.e., money market), should be considered, as they would add to the company value. Typically the cost of capital is the hurdle rate, which new investments are required to exceed.

IRR definition. Percentage rate at a net present value equal to zero. $\text{NPV} = \text{Sum}^t \left(\text{annual net cash flow}/(1 + r)^t \right)$, less initial investment $= 0$, where $t = $ time or year(s) of cash flows, and $r = $ IRR

Pros:
- Strong indicator of expected return, over time
- Provides the investment yield over the cost-of-capital hurdle
- Popular across financiers

Cons:
- Gain or loss estimates often inaccurate (heuristics and historical)
- Risk on gain/loss streams typically not considered or considered through only a singular discounted rate
- Investment not fully accounted
- Not applicable for mutually exclusive project comparison (NPV is better)

IT investments:
- General use as a primary measure for investment justification; secondary measure for prioritization and selection
- More applicable to shared infrastructure and systems investments

Cost/Benefit Analysis

Cost/benefit analysis originated in government institutions about 50 years ago to justify or appraise large projects. The approach is to add all related costs and benefits associated with an investment, considering alternatives, and deciding on the best option. Monetary values can also be defined for intangible returns or factored for risk (i.e., public relations impact). Formulae used for measurement would be complemented by IRR and NPV.

Cost/benefit analysis definition. Initial investment and one-time expenses are offset against the expected return, less ongoing expenses, over time.

Pros:

- Strong indicator of expected return, over time
- Comprehensive account of costs and benefits
- Considers intangible factors
- Considers options or alternatives

Cons:

- Gain or loss estimates often inaccurate (heuristics and historical)
- Risk on gain or loss streams typically not considered, or if considered through only a singular discounted rate

IT investments:

- General use as a primary measure for investment justification: secondary measure for prioritization and selection
- Applicable to shared infrastructure, systems, services, and strategic investments

Budgeting

Budgeting consists of planned expenses and revenues in support of company annual business and financial goals. The budgeting process is tied to the operation planning and, to a lesser extent, to the strategic plan, providing a measure of forecast to actual. Budget scenarios can be created based on alternative strategies, events, or plans. The annual budget can also be used to book realizable investment returns, resetting the budget quarterly or annually to reflect cost savings or revenue enhancements. Ultimately, the budget provides insights into whether a company can anticipate a profit or loss.

Budgeting definition. All forecasted and actual costs and revenue, associated to function, process, event, project, and/or investment

Pros:

- Strong indicator of quarterly and annual performance
- Variance analysis
- Well-understood accounting management technique
- Drives accountability
- Captures benefits in re-set budgets

Cons:

- Historic basis
- Inflated and protected
- Costs lag revenues or company changes
- Investment not fully accounted

IT investments:
- General use as a primary technique for investment performance and realization on the company books: secondary for selection
- Applicable to shared infrastructure, systems, services, and strategic investments

Investment Review Board

The investment review board is a governing body overseeing company investments, ensuring appropriate prioritization, selection, and performance. The board should be chaired by a company board member and should consist of executive and nonexecutive members, providing both objectivity and subject matter expertise. The board's goal is to maximize shareholder value, ensuring that investments made contribute to company value, both in the short term and the long term. Trade-offs are required within defined investment envelopes.

Investment review board definition. Capital budgets, forecast and actual, of all proposed and committed investments

Pros:
- Shareholder driven
- Objective evaluation and investment selection
- Strong indicator of quarterly and annual capital performance
- Variance analysis
- Drives accountability

Cons:
- Often not at board level
- Executive bias and emotions
- Inaccurate data and insufficient time to evaluate
- Investment not fully accounted

IT investments:
- General use as a primary technique for investment prioritization, selection, and performance: secondary for realization
- Applicable to shared infrastructure, systems, services, and strategic investments but mainly used to govern larger investments

Audit

Audits are commonly performed on company financials and internal controls, but they are also conducted on organizations, people, systems, processes, and projects. Quality audits, in pursuit of ISO 9001, are also performed to evaluate quality management systems. Audits assess information validity and reliability but are normally constrained by time; therefore, they only provide reasonable assurances that findings are free of material error. IT investments are identified by audits on internal controls and system or infrastructure (i.e., information security) risk assessments. Further, postproject auditing can ensure investment value realization. Like external auditors, internal auditors must be independent, reporting to the board or senior executives.

Audit definition. Reasonable assurances on validity and reliability for process, system, and project controls

Pros:
- Driven by governance and internal controls
- Objective, fact-based evaluation
- Recommended corrective actions
- Postproject value realization on the books

Cons:
- Insufficient time to evaluate
- Recommendation only; an executive can deflect or postpone action
- System, project, and process audits generally optional, unlike internal controls

IT investments:
- General use as a primary technique for investment realization: secondary for identification and selection
- Applicable to shared infrastructure, systems, services, and strategic investments but mainly used for internal controls and risk assessments

Emerging Financial Techniques

Although a topic of discussion, emerging financial techniques are rarely used in commerce, generally considered to be overly complex. However, such methods enhance the rigor of IT investment evaluation and justification.

Economic Value Added

Economic value added (EVA) is a corporate financial measure used to determine shareholder value creation above the opportunity cost of equity capital. Incremental IT spending should be advocated only when directly realizing increased profits. Reducing IT costs increases profits and EVA. Economic value, unlike ROI, takes into account the residual value for new investments after the forecast period. Residual value can typically account for more than 50 percent of a firm's market value. This measure focuses on shareholder value.

EVA definition. EVA equals profits generated by the investment minus an amount equal to shareholder equity (excluding minority interests and surplus capital), multiplied by the cost of capital. Alternatively, it is the net operating profit after tax generated by the investment, less the money (actual amount) cost of capital.

Pros:
- Strong indicator of expected return, over time
- Provides the investment yield over the cost of equity capital
- Optimizes the return for the shareholders
- Considers the opportunity cost of investment

Cons:
- Reflects capital market swings, as opposed to specific company performance
- Shareholder-centric, does not consider other stakeholder benefits
- Investment not fully accounted

IT investments:
- General use as a primary technique for investment justification and prioritization; secondary for selection
- Applicable to shared infrastructure, systems, services, and strategic investments but mainly used for new investments

Stock Price Traits

IT justification needs to include stock price impact or traits and necessary measurement processes, which ensure that the investment brings an appropriate risk-adjusted economic value added. Several alternative economic frameworks can be considered for IT evaluation, including an extension to the ROI model. The ROI model provides an understanding of how businesses generate profits and how a firm uses assets to generate sales, netting profits over total assets. Building on the ROI model, other metrics should be included that measure wealth creation, such as share price, competitive advantage, customer retention, and market valuation.

The IT valuation model should consider stock value, book value, and current earnings.[2] Stock value equates to the stock price multiplied by the number of shares. Book value equals the net invested capital in a firm. Current earnings are the profits generated within the current year. Exhibit 2.1 (Chapter 2) provides an example of an approach used to define the stock price traits of an IT investment, triangulating the value using financial measures and benchmarking to industry standards. Assuming more consistent accounting of IT spending, then benchmarking the ratio of IT spending to sales, general, and administration (SG&A) costs, or to information workers, could be good measures of IT performance.[3] This IT valuation approach better reflects the contribution to a firm's longer-term market value.

Stock price traits definition. Correlating direct and indirect stock price financial measures of an investment to depict the firm's long-term market value, calibrating to industry benchmarks

Pros:

- Triangulation of expected return from various financial measures over time
- Optimizes the long-term return for the shareholders
- Considers the opportunity cost of investment

Cons:

- Shareholder-centric, does not consider other stakeholder benefits
- Investment not fully accounted
- Longer and more complicated analysis
- Accuracy and comparability of benchmarking data

IT investments:

- General use as a primary technique for investment justification and prioritization; secondary for selection
- Applicable to shared infrastructure, systems, services, and strategic investments but mainly used for new strategic investments

Total Cost of Ownership

Total cost of ownership (TCO) is a form of full-cost accounting popularized in the late 1980s by the Gartner Group. The intent is to account for all direct and indirect costs over the life of the investment. Costs should include not only the initial investment and one-time project costs but all ongoing maintenance, support, business outage, security breaches, power, disaster recovery, real estate, and other associated costs. A number of methods and software tools are available to calculate and monitor costs. TCO should be included in the calculation of ROI, IRR, NPV, and EVA to ensure full costing absorption in deriving the investment economic value and investment viability.

TCO definition. All direct and indirect costs associated with the life of an investment

Pros:

- Reflects all known costs to identify true investment viability
- Accounts for direct and indirect costs over investment life

Cons:

- Cost-centric, does not consider stakeholder benefits
- Longer and more complicated analysis
- Challenge in isolating indirect costs and apportioning support costs

IT investments:

- General use as a primary technique in support of investment justification; secondary for identification, prioritization and selection
- Applicable to shared infrastructure, systems, and strategic investments but mainly used for new infrastructure and system investments

Emerging Decision-Support Techniques

Many decision-support researchers question traditional capital investment measures; as such metrics do not consider uncertainty, flexibility, and the opportunity of delay. Decision-support systems, using mathematical models, can be applied to IT investment evaluation.[4] A significant record of accomplishment has been established using management science and management information systems tools within structured or well-defined and routine business problems. Examples include financial management and budget analysis. Within unstructured or complex processes, there are no singular solutions, defaulting usually to human intuition for decision making. Consider new IT developments or strategic growth investments.

IT investment evaluation can be considered, overall, as a semistructured problem that is looking for a simple solution that can be easily applied to commerce. Aspects of this kind of problem can benefit from decision-support systems and executive information systems (business intelligence). For instance, the quality of financial measures can be improved through the application of real options, which provides for flexibility in the consideration of investment options or risk-sensitive alternatives. More complex evaluation models are being introduced, but one survey suggests that only 8 percent of firms go beyond the ROI calculation.[5]

IT Risk Management

Due to the quick pace of technology, changing economic conditions, and the volatility of market environments, IT investments and projects are inherently risk sensitive. Risks of an IT project are based on unique factors and thus are unsystematic or diversifiable. Risk management is a structured technique for managing uncertainty, whereby risks are identified, mapped, analysed, quantified, and mitigated. The objective is to minimize the risks of expected outcomes. As it relates to IT investments, risk management can factor or discount expected benefits and costs, providing a more rigorous cost/benefit analysis under uncertainty.

Traditional financial and accounting measures (e.g., NPV) do not capture the value of managerial flexibility within IT projects that have uncertain outcomes.[6] NPV typically uses one risk-adjusted discounted rate for both the upside (positive outcome) as well as the downside (negative outcome) of risk. Further, NPV provides inadequate decision consideration from investment irreversibility, uncertainty, and the opportunity of project delay. NPV is appropriate for operational or transactional IT investments, but not for strategic investments.[7] Strategic IT investments have numerous possible outcomes to factor in, each with a varied probability of occurring.[8]

Risk management definition. Quantification of risks, factoring expected costs and benefits, through: risk identification, using source or problem analysis; mapping relationships and dependencies; analyzed for severity or likelihood; quantified as a probability or discount factor; recalculating initial NPV; subsequently mitigated to reduce likelihood of occurrence

Pros:
- Adds more accuracy to NPV
- Factors cost and benefit streams based on future uncertainty
- Allows multiple discounted rates to be used for different benefit streams
- Allows multiple inflated or discounted rates to be used for different cost streams

Cons:
- Longer and more complicated analysis
- Cost of risk analysis outweighs incremental value to the business case

IT investments:
- General use as a primary technique in support of investment justification and evaluating performance over time; secondary for prioritization, selection and realization
- Applicable to shared infrastructure, systems, and strategic investments but mainly used for new strategic investments

Decision Trees

Decision trees are commonly used in decision analysis for modeling decisions and their possible outcomes. A decision tree is an effective visual and analytical technique used to compare expected values or utilities of various options or alternatives. Applying to IT investments, an optimal cost/benefit model could be created showing risk-adjusted (probabilities) costs/benefits related to various decisions. For example, a system deployment investment may or may not include a pilot. The costs and benefits of the system with or without the pilot would be compared for the optimal return.

Decision tree definition. Optimizing the cost/benefit analysis of an investment; selecting the highest, risk-adjusted, expected returns from various options or alternatives within the investment scope

Pros:
- Optimizes initial investment scope
- Factors costs and benefits based on probability of outcome
- An effective visual of options within an investment

Cons:
- Longer and more complicated analysis
- Cost of analysis outweighs incremental value to business case
- Cannot treat managerial flexibility as a separate measurable value; it must be part of a decision node

IT investments:
- General use as a secondary technique in support of investment justification, prioritization, and selection
- Applicable to shared infrastructure, systems, and strategic investments

Real Options

There appears to be strong support for a real options approach to IT evaluation, especially when IT investments are more strategic in nature, having a high up-side potential, high uncertainty, and indirect or intangible returns. Using a real options approach goes beyond the business case; it focuses the firm to assess opportunities, acquire options, nurture these options, terminate or keep options, and when the time is right, capture the value. Real options or strategic options do not replace traditional accounting and financial evaluation techniques, but they certainly can be complementary. When costs and benefits are uncertain or volatile, it can be advisable to wait for more information before committing resources, thus increasing confidence or reducing risk and determining the option value.[9] Real options are able to provide more rigor in the evaluation of IT investment projects under uncertainty.

A cost/benefit analysis example of using real option techniques would extend the decision tree analysis and the NPV model. Traditional or "passive" NPV ignores the value of management flexibility—that is, the intangible cash flows from an option. Therefore, real option techniques should treat options separately and produce an "active" NPV by adding the value of the option to the passive NPV.[10] The decision maker has a more systematic approach in considering the uncertainty of several outcomes to a course of action or option. Depending on the decision makers' view of risk, he or she can subsequently apply risk and sensitivity analysis, determining probabilities of occurrence using probabilistic or stochastic decision making.[11] Outcomes can be assessed based on the probability of success or highest added value. In Chapter 19, real options are discussed in more detail.

> **Real options definition.** In deriving an embedded option value within a cost-benefit analysis, the cash flow (tangible and intangible) subjective probabilities need to be replaced with firm or justified probabilities for the option, and then the value of the option needs to be discounted by the risk-free (not risk-adjusted) rate. The option value will change over time and can be accelerated, terminated, or postponed at points in time.

Pros:
- Considers intangible value
- Multiple discounted adjustments on different risk options, across different cost/benefit streams
- Sensitivity analysis on investment options over time
- Higher accuracy of expected returns under uncertainty

Cons:
- Longer and more complicated analysis
- Cost of analysis outweighs incremental value to business case
- Difficulty of finding a suitable risk-free discount rate for managerial flexibility

IT investments:
- General use as a primary technique in support of investment justification and prioritization; secondary for identification, selection and performance
- Applicable to shared infrastructure, systems, and strategic investments but mainly used for new strategic investments

Value-Creation Business Case

Building an optimal business case or cost/benefit analysis takes time and is often seen as a luxury, but if done well, it will accurately capture an investment's complete value. Sommer[12] proposes a wealth-creating business case that demonstrably impacts share price beyond ROI. The business case should address four elements:

1. Improvements in key financial and nonfinancial corporate assets
2. Reductions in the capital appetite of the company
3. Opportunities to increase top-line and bottom-line performance
4. Methods to improve cash flow and free up working capital

Based on an array of previously discussed financial-based measures and techniques, a value-creation business case or cost/benefit analysis should consider, depending on investment size and timeline, the following approach:

1. Tangible benefits need to be clearly defined in terms of measurable and audited value, with a margin of error:
   - Incremental revenue
   - Incremental costs savings
   - Cost of capital reduction
2. Intangible benefits need to be quantified in terms of:
   - Customer satisfaction or loyalty or trust
   - Risk mitigation
   - New products, services, and markets
   - Productivity improvements
   - Competitive advantage
   - Regulatory compliance
   - Company reputation and image
   - Flexibility and agility, speed to market, and profits
3. Intangible benefits need to be converted into a monitory value—that is, opportunity cost of not realizing, with a margin of error. Conservative risk-free estimates should be considered. Subjective opinion can be collaborated by an expert in the field, or it can be benchmarked. The intangible benefit can be defined as an embedded (into the underlying asset or investment) option that is risk free. The higher the uncertainty in the investment returns, the higher the value of managerial flexibility—and, therefore, the higher the value of the embedded real option.
4. IT investment needs to account for all costs (TCO), with a margin of error:
   - Total capital or total depreciation and residual value
   - Program or project one-time cost
   - Investment operational and ongoing costs
   - Dependent (proportional) complementary investments
   - Additional operational costs, i.e., downtime, reduced productivity
   - Redundant or replaced equipment, and application cost
   - Cost of capital
5. Cost, tangible benefits, and risk-free intangible benefits should be projected as cash flows over the depreciated life of the IT investment, or in accordance with the business case duration, for full value realization. This creates the basis to apply a risk and cost of money adjusted net present value (NPV) algorithm.
6. A decision tree could be constructed (optional), showing the interdependencies of outcomes over time and determining the compounded

probability of risk for each category of cost and benefit. There are a number of risk assessment methods to help determine probabilities, as opposed to subjective opinions. Multi-attribute risk assessment tools are gaining in popularity. Optimal configuring for IT investment is likely to require embedding a series of cascading (compound) options, balancing multiple value and risk profiles. Consider the Geske compound or nested sequence option evaluation methodology for sequential IT investments. Alternatively, consider the Margrabe exchange option for the exchange of one risky asset with another.

7. Each benefit and cost should then be separately discounted or inflated by the compounded probability of risk over the projected life of the program. Different probabilities can be applied based on alternative scenarios or applied to the high and low margin of errors. Note that the discounted rate for a downside probability will not be the same for an upside probability.

8. NPV cash flow ranges can then be calculated based on a standard inflation rate or discount rate.

9. Calculating the IRR and/or EVA range completes the cost/benefit analysis.

This process involves a lot of work, but it is worth it for very large investments or projects. Once a model has been created, it can be reused. Emphasis should be placed on key value drivers, risk assessments, and good data collection and monitoring. However, a business case alone will not be able to determine the necessary investment trade-offs for a balanced IT investment portfolio, which addresses both short-term profitability and long-term growth or organization-wide capabilities, which are discussed in Chapter 7.[13]

> Building a value-creation business case or comprehensive cost/benefit analysis takes time and is often seen as a luxury, but if done well, it accurately captures an investment's complete value.

This chapter has focused on defining and applying the right financial-based methods for measuring specific IT investment types during the six stages of IT evaluation assessment. The key message is not just to rely on traditional financial and accounting measures, but to consider emerging financial and decision support techniques, along with the application of organization-based methods, which are discussed in Chapter 6.

CHAPTER 6

IT Value Network Measures
Organization-Based Methods

O rganization-based IT investment measures or techniques are defined in this chapter. Chapter 2 challenged the norms of conventional organization-based methods as applied to IT investment value measurement and evaluation, focusing on lost value from potential inadequacies and poor execution. Like traditional financial-based approaches, these measures remain popular, even given their ineffective results. In the 1999 *Fortune* cover story, CEO failure was related to bad strategic execution, not poor vision.[1] The tools for measuring strategies and investment have not adapted to the development of the vision to create stakeholder economic value and sustained competitive advantage or network advantage.

More effective methods and measures are required to unlock and realize the IT value. Therefore, to supplement conventional thinking, we review here some of the advancements in organizational management, including critical success factors (CSFs), the balanced scorecard (BSC), and information economics, which also include scenario planning, portfolio management, and investment management. This chapter considers the appropriate organization-based measures for categorized investment types (four "S" category model as defined in Chapter 1) at each IT investment assessment stage (as discussed in Chapter 4), providing application pros and cons.

> Conventional organization-based methods for IT investment evaluation are inadequate, driving the need for more advanced emerging organizational management and information economics techniques.

Conventional Planning Techniques

Conventional planning, in one form or another, is the norm within organizations, whether at the strategic, operational, or project level. However, the quality of execution varies significantly from company to company.

Strategic Planning

Strategic planning defines a company's strategy, determining the allocation of resources in pursuit of targeted goals. There are a number of schools of thought regarding the subject of strategic planning since its commercial origins in the mid-1960s, born out of budget planning. However, it is noted that over two centuries ago there was a reference in Sun Tzu's *The Art of War* to a director of strategic planning. The design school was the first strategic planning approach, one that is still practiced today, advocating SWOT analysis (strengths, weaknesses, opportunities, and threats). An alternative model is PEST (political, economic, social, and technological) analysis. Strategic planning hit its high mark during the mid-1970s, subsequently falling in popularity over the following decade. Today, strategic planning is viewed in a more balanced way, whereby it provides a disciplined process in the context of a firm's environment. Much attention is spent on planning pitfalls, which are principally based on obsession with control. IT investment and planning should be integrated into the business strategy, not just aligned with it, and focused on achieving the company's strategic goals or objectives.

> **Strategic planning definition.** Focus is on long-term planning. There are a number of approaches, based on internal and external situational analysis of the current and future state (i.e., SWOT, PEST); defining the company vision, mission and values, targeting measurable goals and/or objectives, mapping or defining the path to reach these goals, and establishing controls.

Pros:
- Shareholder and stakeholder driven
- Company investment direction
- High-level measurable goals

Cons:
- Executive bias and emotions
- Directional, not definitive, lacking details
- Fluctuates based on market conditions
- Company controls typically limited or fluid

IT investments:
- General use as a primary technique for investment identification, prioritization, and selection; secondary for justification, performance, and realization

- Applicable to shared infrastructure, systems, services, and strategic investments but mainly used to govern strategic investments

Operational Planning

Operational planning seeks to deliver short- to medium-term milestones according to the strategic plan. Typically, the operational plan justifies the annual company budget over one to two years. Key functional or process initiatives and activities are defined, allocating resources to execute within financial budgets. Existing IT investments should be reexamined against operational goals, and new IT investments should be targeted to enhance the business capability to achieve the operational plan.

> **Operational planning definition.** Focus is on short- to medium-term execution of the strategic plan—defining objectives, identifying initiatives or activities, resourcing (people and financials), establishing timelines, setting quality standards and desired outcomes, and monitoring progress.

Pros:
- Shareholder and stakeholder driven
- Company short-term investment allocation
- Measurable objectives
- Tighter company controls on performance

Cons:
- Executive bias and emotions
- Functional or process priority trade-offs
- Resource contention
- Shifting investment allocation, dictated by quarterly plan resets
- Long-term projects can be challenged

IT investments:
- General use as a primary technique for investment identification, prioritization, selection and performance; secondary for justification, and realization
- Applicable to shared infrastructure, systems, and services investments

Program and Project Management

Programs consist of a number of separate but interdependent projects that require managing as a collective for the success of the overall business initiative. IT projects are either born out of strategic initiatives or programs or developed to meet shorter-term operational or infrastructure needs. Project planning is a discipline in detail, critically managing budget, time, scope, resources, quality, and risk. Key milestones, resources, and task dependencies are determined over time. Performance measurement should be ingrained into the project plan and performed at milestone reviews, including the assessment of outcome quality and current validity of the business case. Critical success factors and business risk needs to be considered at the project level. Upon project completion, the value should be captured or audited. Benefit realization from projects can take several years to materialize, therefore requiring more due diligence in postproject auditing.

Defining project success criteria and metrics is crucial to ensure that committed resources deliver the required business case goals and are appropriately tracked during the phases of project execution. The measures should include the various project stakeholder perspectives, where different goal priorities or different definitions of project success may exist. Therefore, in addition to the financials and schedule, other project measures should be incorporated, such as risk mitigation, change (scope) management, teamwork and satisfaction, benchmarking, technical quality targets, process compliance, and project manager review.[2]

Program and project management definition. Execution of a business initiative, defined by the strategic or operational plans, managing allocated budget, timeline, resources, scope, quality outcome, and risk

Pros:
- Execution and delivery mechanism for strategic and operational initiatives
- Standard process and performance controls
- Business value delivery at project closure

Cons:
- Failure due to inadequate business case or project success criteria and metrics
- Poor change management
- Resource contention and dependencies
- Inadequate risk mitigation
- Tracking value realization post project closure

IT investments:
- General use as a primary technique for investment performance; secondary for realization
- Applicable to shared infrastructure, systems, services, and strategic investments

Emerging Organizational Management Techniques

As new strategies evolve, performance is being assessed using nonfinancial approaches in support of traditional financial metrics. However, conventional planning does not provide an appropriate level of attention to the extended network of stakeholder interests, including customer drivers, employee engagement, supplier value chain, partner collaboration, investor expectations, and executive passion. Emerging organization-based measures and techniques, such as critical success factors, balanced scorecard, benchmarking, surveys, service level agreements (SLAs), and IT governance, provide further stakeholder insights and are being integrated into corporate metrics.[3] For instance, the conventional wisdom of the SWOT analysis and strategic planning have been effectively integrated with emerging organization-based measures such as the balanced scorecard driving execution of the plan.[4]

Critical Success Factors

Critical success factors (CSFs) have been used to assist in business planning, but only recently have they been applied to IT. CSF helps to map IT investments and projects to stakeholder requirements. Peffers and Gengler refer to a critical success chain (CSC) whereby system attributes as identified by the stakeholders define the CSFs, which, on delivery, meet the firm's goals.[5] CSFs include cash flow, customer acquisition and satisfaction, partner collaboration, quality, service and product development, intellectual capital, strategic relationships, operational sustainability, and employee attraction, retention, and productivity. A CSF example would consider the ability of an inbound marketing system to store customer preferences. Key IT projects that once were hidden or excluded in the project prioritization process are now more visible, through the aligned with stakeholder CSFs.

> **Critical success factors definition.** The intended stakeholder performance criteria and systems or process expectations, producing the greatest impact to achieve the firm's objectives

Pros:
- Stakeholder driven, beyond financials
- Identifies investment or project scope and key drivers
- Translates investment into expected measurable outcomes
- Focused on performance measurement and benefit realization

Cons:
- Conflicting stakeholder interest and priorities
- Scope creep
- Financial justification rigor lacking
- Isolating IT investment value, as part of a system or process change

IT investments:
- General use as a primary technique for investment identification, prioritization, performance, and realization; secondary for justification and selection

■ Applicable to shared infrastructure, systems, services, and strategic investments but mainly used for system and service investments

IT Balanced Scorecard

To enforce the desired behaviors in support of the strategic IT direction, there needs to be a culture of measurability and corresponding performance reward system (for the enterprise as a whole). This stretches beyond measuring financial measures and includes key performance indicators (KPIs) aligned to strategic objectives. To assist organizations in building a performance-managed culture and to link strategy to execution behaviors, Schiemann and Lingle[6] state the following four phases:

1. **Define**—strategy and objectives
2. **Design**—reliable measures and targets
3. **Cascade**—aligned measures
4. **Embed**—integrated management process

Measures must be valid, reliable, responsive to change, easy to understand, economical in data collection, and balanced. The key is to cascade aligned objectives, measures, and self-accountability down the organization.

The balanced scorecard (BSC), developed by Kaplan and Norton, has been successfully implemented in more than 200 corporations over 10 years to assist in the alignment and implementation of corporate strategy.[7] Essentially, the BSC is based on conventional strategic planning techniques, providing a tool for cascading the strategic objectives and measurements down an organization. The BSC facilitates and translates the strategy into operational terms, but executive leadership needs to be visible through an active and reinforced performance management system. In addition to financial measures, the firm's evaluation should include customer satisfaction, internal processes, and the ability to innovate. A mix of lead and lag indicators is used for performance measurement. Thus, current performance indicators, such as profitability, are measured alongside future measures of success, such as customer loyalty and product innovations. Strategic maps are good visuals for tracking key corporate themes, associated measurements, targets, and initiatives.

A generic IT BSC could comprise:

1. Key stakeholder orientation (IT internal and external customers or clients) measuring the satisfaction of IT services
2. Operational orientation (systems and shared infrastructure), measuring IT delivery processes
3. Future orientation, measuring human and technical resource capability and innovation, plus strategic alignment
4. Corporate orientation, measuring financial and economic added value created from IT

It is important to note that the use of the BSC is a continuous improvement process and not a silver bullet for strategic success.[8] The key challenge in applying the BSC to IT is to ensure that it is aligned with the overall business strategy and to keep the measures relatively simple.[9]

> "The balanced scorecard is useful in evaluating all investments, including IT."
>
> (Weill & Broadbent, 1998, p. 33)[10]

IT balanced scorecard definition. Based on the firm's strategic objectives, the IT scorecard maps KPIs according to (a) stakeholder orientation—service; (b) operational orientation—systems and shared infrastructure; (c) future orientation—strategic and agile and (d) corporate orientation—financial and economic value-added benefits.

Pros:
- Stakeholder driven, beyond financials
- Defines KPIs
- Strategic to operational alignment
- Cascading priorities down the organization
- Manages expectations and performance goals

Cons:
- Conflicting stakeholder interest and priorities
- Stakeholder orientation defaults to main customer
- Applied weighting can allow for misdirection and skewed focus
- Cascading measures may not be relevant or meaningful down the organization

IT investments:
- General use as a primary technique for investment identification, prioritization, performance, and realization; secondary for justification, and selection
- Applicable to shared infrastructure, systems, services, and strategic investments

Benchmarking

Benchmarking compares a company's current processes to defined best practices within or across industry sectors. Benchmarking was introduced by Rank Xerox to improve process quality and performance. The objective is to challenge norms and provides some objectivity in the evaluation of a company's current state. Applied to IT investment, best practice benchmarking can be useful to compare evaluation processes or methods, and financial benchmarking can assist in competitive spending and performance comparisons.

Benchmarking definition. Current-state process or financial comparison with industry best practice

Pros:
- Defines KPIs
- Objectivity and competitive performance assessment
- Directional indicator

Cons:
- Industry data not comparable (apples-to-oranges comparison)
- Inconsistent measurement methods
- Interdependent and unique variables not determined, causing misleading comparisons

IT investments:
- General use as a primary technique for investment performance; secondary for identification, justification, and realization
- Applicable to shared infrastructure, systems, services, and strategic investments

Surveys

Surveys are used for many purposes, from census to market research, and for applying quantitative and qualitative methods for data collection and analysis. Typically, qualitative questionnaires are used to assist in the determination of IT investment value. Examples include stakeholder needs assessment, stakeholder's opinions on IT service satisfaction or investment value, and project closure assessment. Administrating surveys and then analyzing and reporting on the data have become simpler through online software, which can disperse various questionnaires to targeted stakeholders within the organization and across a company's network.

Survey definition. Stakeholder questionnaires used to determine onions and views

Pros:
- Stakeholder driven
- Determines expectations
- Provides priority focus and directional view
- Strong indicator of performance
- Can define KPIs and CSFs

Cons:
- Conflicting stakeholder interests and priorities

- Valid at points in time; may be influenced or biased by recent events
- Different interpretation on questions
- Drives expectations, which may not be addressed

IT investments:

- General use as a primary technique for investment performance; secondary for identification, prioritization, and realization
- Applicable to shared infrastructure, systems, services, and strategic investments

Service Level Agreements

A service level agreement (SLA) is essentially a service contract between a service provider and a specific customer. The SLA provides a common understanding among parties of the service levels that will be provided; defining the services and their availability, operational support, help desk response times, responsibilities, consequences of nonperformance (penalties), and problem management. While most common between computing and telecommunication service providers and their customers, SLAs are increasingly being deployed within companies between the IT department and key stakeholders. An internal SLA helps align IT budgets and resources with agreed-on service provisioning, also it maintains quality assurance, objectively measures performance, and better manages stakeholder expectations. Internal SLAs can also be used to define a benchmark of investment spending and value, as compared to potential outsourcing to external service providers. Measurable service level objectives should be well defined.

Service level agreement definition. Service contract(s) between the IT department and key stakeholders or business partners

Pros:

- Stakeholder driven
- Manages expectations
- Strong indicator of service performance
- Realizable value on performance
- Alignment to budget and resources, capacity, and capability

Cons:

- Can be too rigid and inflexible
- Could expose uncompetitive internal service provisioning
- Stakeholders will have different needs and expectations across a shared infrastructure and may be prepared to pay (budget) for varying service levels, which may not be manageable

IT investments:

- General use as a primary technique for investment performance and realization

■ Applicable to shared infrastructure, systems, and service investments

IT Governance

Board governance exists to protect stakeholder interests, principally the
shareholders, by overseeing key processes and policies related to company
direction, administration, and controls. For publicly listed U.S. companies,
the Sarbanes-Oxley (SOX) Act of 2002 was a government legislative response
to accounting scandals, particularly those resulting from the collapse of
Enron, Tyco International, and WorldCom. Greater corporate governance
and internal controls were defined to build investor confidence. IT investments and risks continue to increase, promoting the advocacy of deeper
IT visibility and governance by the board. Board IT governance should go
beyond audit compliance and information security and privacy, including
investment value management. Executive IT governance should report on
cross-company IT investment and portfolio views, alerting management to
risks and expected outcomes, and tracking benefit realization against company KPIs. IT governance could be part of the program management office
(PMO) or the IT strategic office.

IT governance definition. Corporate-wide IT portfolio risk and reward
assessment and benefit tracking against KPIs, monitoring total pro-
posed and committed IT investment and spending, in addition to
traditional IT-related audit compliance on internal controls
Pros:
■ Shareholder driven
■ Independent risk and reward investment evaluation
■ Investment selection oversight
■ Strong indicator of quarterly and annual investment and spending
performance
■ Internal controls oversight
■ Benefit realization
Cons:
■ Inaccurate data and distance: insufficient time to evaluate
■ Investment not fully accounted
■ Lack of a cascading process and inconsistent reporting
■ Business challenge to tracking benefit realization
IT investments:
■ General use as a primary technique for investment prioritization,
selection, performance, and realization; secondary for identifica-
tion

- Applicable to shared infrastructure, systems, services, and strategic investments but mainly used to govern larger investments and risks

Emerging Information Economics Techniques

Organization-based techniques also include information economics disciplines, such as scenario planning, portfolio management, and investment management models. Information economics began at IBM in the late 1980s, derived from the information strategies for an information systems (ISIS) sales program. Subsequently, Oracle developed the approach to make it into an IT investment decision-making model.[11] Essentially, a weighting and point system is attributed to various projects or investments, based on respective benefits (tangible and intangible) and risks. Probabilities of success are attached to the weight and estimates, where the project or investment selected is based on the highest score. However, success of the metrics depends on subjective opinion and consensus. This bodes well for political support, but can degrade financial rigor and objective independence. Further, singular IRR or cost of risk-adjusted capital is indifferent to the complexity or the interplay of variables. No doubt for these reasons, and the constant change in technology pace, information economics is not actively or effectively deployed in most firms. However, some successful application examples are described in more detail in the following text.

IT Investment Management

Investment management is commonly used within the financial and insurance industries to maximize returns and mitigate or off-load risk. The accounting and information management division of the U.S. Government Accountability Office (GAO, formerly General Accounting Office) developed the IT investment management (ITIM) framework to assess and improve the IT investment process maturity within federal agencies.[12] The IT investment approach is based on a continuous process of three phases:

1. **Select.** Screen, rank, and select. How do you know you have selected the right project?
2. **Control.** Monitor progress and take corrective action. How are you ensuring that the projects will deliver the value?
3. **Evaluate.** Conduct reviews, make adjustments, and apply lessons learned. Have the delivered projects realized the expected value?

The framework assesses five maturity stages, similar in style to the capability maturity model for software development designed by Carnegie Mellon

University. The framework is hierarchy based, building on lower levels of maturity as the critical processes become more rigorous. Critical processes have five core elements: purpose, organizational commitment, prerequisites, activities, and evidence of performance. Each core element is composed of a number of key practices for assessment and evaluation. The ITIM is a generic framework for organizational improvements and provides a good road map for developing sound IT investment management processes. It is used in conjunction with an investment review board.

IT investment management definition. Continuous process for selecting, controlling, and evaluating IT investments

Pros:
- Stakeholder driven
- Standard process for evaluation and investment selection
- Strong indicator of quarterly and annual investment performance
- Variance analysis
- Maturity benchmarking capability
- Investment review board and PMO tool for governing investments

Cons:
- Process, measurement, and scorecard complexity
- Insufficient attention to variable risk
- Executive bias and emotions
- Inaccurate data and insufficient time to evaluate

IT investments:
- General use as a primary technique for investment prioritization, selection, performance, and realization
- Applicable to shared infrastructure, systems, services, and strategic investments but mainly used to govern larger investments

IT Portfolio Management

Portfolio management techniques are commonly used in the financial and insurance markets to manage blended investments, diversify interests, and balance risk and reward. Applying to IT, portfolio management helps the management of program or project selection by aligning IT to enterprise and business unit objectives. Shareholder value is likely to be optimized through an enterprise portfolio approach, instead of through a local optimization approach from competing standalone business units. The IT portfolio should be tailored to the firm's unique strategic objectives and is a mark of the firm's current and future currency or value.[13] Trade-offs are required to meet short-term and long-term goals. Portfolio management is typically used in conjunction with an investment review board or within the PMO. Portfolio management is discussed in more detail in Chapter 7.

IT portfolio management definition. Evaluating all current and future enterprise IT investments and projects by aligning, mapping, and measuring as a portfolio to short-term and long-term company goals or value

Pros:

- Stakeholder driven
- Standard process for evaluating and governing investments
- Enterprise focused, optimizing value across business units
- Strong indicator of quarterly and annual investment performance
- Variance analysis
- Industry benchmarking capability
- Investment review board and PMO tool for governing investments

Cons:

- Measurement and scorecard complexity
- Insufficient attention to variable risk
- Executive bias and emotions
- Inaccurate data and insufficient time to evaluate
- Business unit trade-offs

IT investments:

- General use as a primary technique for investment selection, performance, and realization
- Applicable to shared infrastructure, systems, services, and strategic investments but mainly used to govern larger investments

Scenario Planning

Scenario planning was first used in war gaming and was later applied to commerce within the oil industry when Shell successfully modeled and anticipated the 1973 oil crisis. A scenario identifies a decision, its parameters and uncontrollable variables. All possible outcomes are determined, based on a current situation and a set of evolving assumptions. Scenario simulation models can be developed with "what if" analysis. Decision trees can be used, applying financials and probability theory to event occurrence, whereby the branch of maximum value or lowest cost is determined and subsequently executed. Scenario planning requires significant time and the knowledge of "experts."[14] In considering scenarios, certain qualities are desirable; they should be relevant (to the future of the organization), plausible (identifying reasonable future outcomes), consistent (coherent with strategic direction), and surprising (challenging existing assumptions). Good scenarios consist of a few stories that a firm cannot influence but are relevant to the organizational context.[15] Scenario planning is an excellent tool for flexible long-term plans and strategic options.

Scenario planning definition. Long-term planning process to evaluate alternatives or options; based on defined problems, opportunities or decisions, known parameters, and uncontrollable variables

Pros:
- Stakeholder driven
- Supplements strategic planning
- Defines plausible investment options and alternatives.
- Investment review board and PMO tool for governing investments

Cons:
- Planning consumes significant time and cost
- Simulation tools required for detailed analysis
- Relevance of uncontrollable variables (i.e., pace of technology)
- Executive bandwidth

IT investments:
- General use as a secondary technique for investment identification and prioritization
- Applicable to shared infrastructure, systems, and strategic investments but mainly used to assess strategic investments

The key IT evaluation message is not to rely on just financial or conventional planning measures but to consider emerging organizational management and information economics techniques to determine complete IT value.

Building on Chapter 5, this chapter has focused on defining and applying the right organization-based methods for measuring specific IT investment types during the six stages of IT evaluation assessment. The key IT evaluation message is not to rely on just financial or conventional planning measures but to consider emerging organizational management and information economics techniques. All these measures will now be used to triangulate IT investment value, using the value index and value lens as discussed in Chapter 7.

CHAPTER 7

Triangulating IT Investment Value

Triangulating IT value can be successfully applied to IT investment where no one measure is relied upon. Data from different sources, whether qualitative or quantitative, corroborate value, overcoming specific flaws in any one measurement or approach. Triangulating IT investment value is the application of appropriate financial-based and organization-based measures and techniques, as discussed in Chapters 5 and 6. Selected measures or techniques, based on the investment type (four "S" category model) and stage of evaluation assessment, are defined within the IT value network index or scorecard. The value index consists of four value lenses: strategic, operational, stakeholder, and agility. (See Exhibit 7.1, which illustrates the triangulation of IT investment value.) The objective is to provide a high confidence in the total measurable value of an IT investment, increasing value accuracy during value identification and subsequently through the progression of the six stages of evaluation, as described in Chapter 4. This chapter discusses the value index and the value lens along with the concept of the IT value portfolio.

> Triangulating IT investment network value improves the accuracy of the total value proposition, where no single measure is relied upon.

Value Index and Value Lenses

The IT value network index or scorecard consists of four value lenses: strategic, operational, stakeholder, and agility. It is similar in approach to Kaplan and Norton's balanced scorecard, which focuses on four areas of organizational performance: financial, customer, operational, and innovation or learning. The IT value network index, however, is more aligned to the related value of IT investments, thus enabling the IT organization

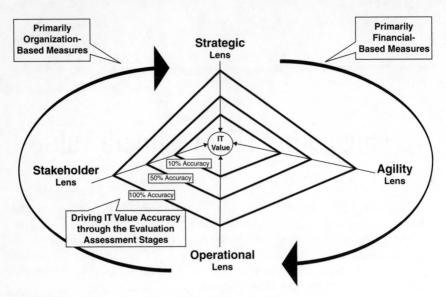

EXHIBIT 7.1 Triangulating IT Investment Network Value

to tune its portfolio to strategic initiatives, operational effectiveness, stake-holder expectations or requirements, and agile capability or options. Exhibit 7.2 illustrates the IT value network index framework, identifying the value lenses and the corresponding appropriate measures. IT investments can be assessed through each value lens, applying one or more primary or secondary measures per lens. Companies should standardize their approach to identifying the appropriate measures per lens, ensuring design simplicity for IT investment valuation. Specific metrics can be identified for each identified measure or technique within the index framework.

> The IT value network index or scorecard is composed of four value lenses: strategic, operational, stakeholder, and agility, capturing the total stakeholder economic value of an IT investment.

Strategic Lens

IT investments are required for a company's strategic initiatives, aligned to the business strategic objectives, providing competitive advantage and long-term top-line and bottom-line growth, typically over three to five years. The strategy value lens effectively aligns new and existing IT investments

Measurement Method or Technique	Strategic Lens	Operational Lens	Stakeholder Lens	Agility Lens
Financial-Based **12 Techniques or Measures**				
ROI/DCF/NPV/IRR	Primary	Primary		
Budgeting	Secondary	Primary		
Business case—Cost vs. benefit	Primary	Primary		Secondary
Investment review board	Primary	Secondary		
Audit	Primary	Primary		
Economic added value (EAV)	Primary	Secondary		
Stock price traits	Primary			
Value-creation business case	Primary	Secondary		
Total cost of ownership (TCO)	Primary	Secondary		
Decision trees	Primary			Primary
Real options	Primary	Secondary		Primary
IT risk management	Primary			Primary
Organization-Based **12 Techniques or Measures**				
Strategic planning	Secondary		Primary	Primary
Operational planning	Secondary	Primary	Primary	Primary
Program-project management	Primary	Primary	Primary	Primary
Governance	Primary	Primary	Primary	Primary
Critical success factors	Primary	Primary	Primary	Primary
IT balanced scorecard	Primary	Primary	Primary	Primary
Benchmarking	Primary	Primary	Primary	Primary
Surveys	Primary	Primary	Primary	
Service level agreements	Secondary	Primary	Primary	
IT investment management	Primary	Secondary	Primary	
IT portfolio management	Primary	Primary	Primary	
Scenario planning	Primary		Secondary	Primary
	Primary Technique		**Secondary Technique**	

EXHIBIT 7.2 IT Value Network Index Framework

and expense to capture long-term business value. The primary focus is to maximize long-term financial returns through strategic IT investments for new markets, new products, and new customer value propositions. Financial-based measures include NPV, with more emphasis on economic added value and stock price traits, building a value creation business case. Real options and risk management are necessary under uncertainty. Organization-based measures or techniques include conventional strategic planning—with stronger emphasis on scenario planning—in addition to IT balanced scorecard (KPIs), program-project management, IT investment governance, and IT portfolio management.

Operational Lens

IT investments are required for a company's operational effectiveness. They should be aligned to business operational objectives, enabling or improving budgeted top-line or bottom-line financials, typically in-year. The operational value effectively aligns new and existing IT investments and expenses to capture short-term business value. The primary focus is to optimize short-term financial returns by optimizing IT shared infrastructure and systems, in support of operational requirements and solutions. Financial-based measures include cost/benefit analysis with emphasis on ROI and equivalent measures, together with audit issue resolution. Organization-based measures or techniques include operational planning, IT balanced scorecard, project management, IT portfolio management, business critical success factors (CSFs), and service level agreements, substantiated with industry benchmarks.

Stakeholder Lens

IT investments are required to meet stakeholder requirements and expectations, aligned to the board, executives, customers, suppliers, employees, and partners, satisfying needs and critical success factors. The stakeholder value lens effectively aligns new and existing IT investments and expense to capture network business benefits. The primary focus is to satisfy stakeholder needs, by providing exceptional IT service and investment value, meeting service level expectations and improving productivity. Financial-based measures include cost/benefit analysis with emphasis on a value-creation business case. Organization-based measures or techniques include conventional planning, with emphasis on balanced scorecards, program-project management, IT portfolio management, business critical success factors, service level agreements, and surveys.

Agility Lens

IT investments are required for company agility, aligned to macro and micro options, improving company time to market and time to profit. The agility value lens effectively aligns new and existing IT investments and expense to capture flexibility and capability value. The primary focus is to build business capability and capacity, providing valued options through risk and reward assessments and quality solutioning. Financial-based measures include value-creation business case, with emphasis on total cost of ownership, real options, decision trees, and risk management. Organization-based measures or techniques include conventional planning, with emphasis on scenario planning, IT portfolio management, scorecards, and business-critical success factors.

Designing the IT Value Network Index

Triangulating the value of IT investments requires designing a standard corporate IT value network index, mapping:

1. The IT investment classification, four "S" category model (from Chapter 1):
   1. Shared—infrastructure
   2. Systems—operational
   3. Services—stakeholder
   4. Strategic—informational

2. Mapped to the four value lenses and the corresponding financial-based and organization-based measures and techniques (as discussed in Chapters 5 and 6):
   1. Strategic
   2. Operational
   3. Stakeholder
   4. Agility

> Triangulating the value of IT investments requires designing a standard corporate IT value network index, mapping the IT investment four "S" categories with the four value lenses.

Exhibit 7.3 provides an example of a standard corporate IT value network index. In the simple model, eight unique measures and techniques

EXHIBIT 7.3 Corporate IT Value Network Index Example

IT Investment Four "S" Category Model	Strategic Lens	Operational Lens	Stakeholder Lens	Agility Lens
Simple Model— Few Measures				
Shared infrastructure	Value creation business case	Budgeting	Service level agreements	Total cost of ownership
Systems	Value creation business case	Budgeting	Service level agreements	Total cost of ownership
Services	Value creation Business case	Budgeting	Service level agreements	Critical success factors
Strategic	Value creation business case, Strategic plan	Budgeting	Survey	Real options
Overall	IT portfolio management, governance, and investment review board			

(Continued)

EXHIBIT 7.3 (Continued)

IT Investment Four "S" Category Model	Strategic Lens	Operational Lens	Stakeholder Lens	Agility Lens
Complex Model— Multiple Measures				
Shared infrastructure	Cost/benefit analysis	Budgeting	Service level agreements	Total cost of ownership
Systems	NPV/IRR	IT balanced scorecard	Critical success factors	IT risk management
Services	Value creation business case	Service level agreements	Survey	Critical success factors
Strategic	Strategic plan, EAV	Program-project management	IT balanced scorecard	Real options
Overall	IT portfolio management, governance, and investment review board			

have been identified across the IT investment portfolio, four (five for strategic) for each IT investment classification. For instance, a new shared infrastructure investment would be evaluated by four measures: value creation business case (strategic lens), budget (operational lens), service level agreements (stakeholder lens), and total cost of ownership (agility lens). Thus, a comprehensive value statement would support this IT investment for justification and prioritization. In addition, an overriding IT portfolio management, governance, and investment review board approach is suggested to manage all investments. A more complex model might build to 14 unique measures and techniques, but remaining at four per investment type, plus overriding IT portfolio management and governance. The key is to identify meaningful measures and techniques, not easy measures, standardizing across the company and ensuring due diligence in accuracy an d consistency.

For each IT investment classification, the measures or techniques can change according to the *stage of IT investment evaluation*, as discussed in Chapter 4:

1. Identifying
2. Justifying
3. Prioritizing
4. Selecting
5. Performing
6. Realizing

For instance, applying the simple model, in considering shared infrastructure and system investments, the value creation business case, budget, service level agreement (SLA), and total cost of ownership (TCO) techniques might be used for an investment justification, prioritization, performance, and benefit realization. But for identification and selection the operating plan may be used.

The IT value network index standard measures should be agreed to by the senior executives, with board support. An investment review board or equivalent should govern the overall portfolio and evaluation process, as executed by the project management office (PMO) or equivalent.

> For each IT investment classification, the measures or techniques can change according to the stage of IT investment evaluation.

Stars and Black Holes

IT investments can be stars or black holes. Creating star formations, as illustrated in Exhibit 7.4, requires defining one or more measures for each value lens and creating a sliding scale from 0 to 10 and then baseline expectations or thresholds. The exhibit example may be applicable for the justification,

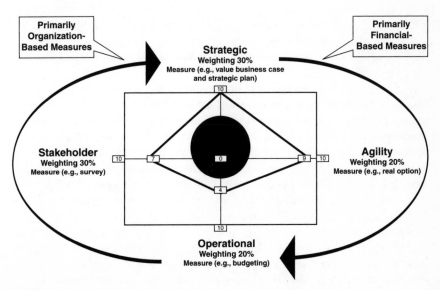

EXHIBIT 7.4 IT Investment Evaluation—Stars and Black Holes Example

prioritisation, or performance of strategic IT investments. In the illustrated example:

- The strategic lens threshold equals 10, which could represent alignment with the strategy plan, and a value creation business case with an EVA of $1 million (a point given for every $100K).
- The agility lens threshold equals 9, which could represent a real option of potentially an additional EVA of $900K (a point given for every $100K).
- The operational lens threshold equals 4, which could represent an investment budget (or annual operating budget) of $700K (reverse scale—the lower the budget, the higher the rate; 10 points for $100K).
- The stakeholder lens threshold equals 7, which could represent a stakeholder survey equivalent to 70 percent satisfaction (a point given for every 10 percent satisfaction rating or perceived value).

With higher index thresholds on the strategic and agility lenses, the base criteria is more favorable to strategic IT investments that enable long-term growth and provide a flexible capability. Corresponding weightings can then be identified. In our example, strategic and stakeholder equal 30 percent each, and agility and operational equal 20 percent each. This suggests that there is a higher importance in meeting the strategic and stakeholder thresholds.

> IT value network index and corresponding star shapes can be depicted for each IT investment classification.

IT value network index and corresponding star shapes can be depicted for each IT investment classification or for investment subgroups (e.g., telecommunications, a subgroup of shared infrastructure). For each investment type a baseline can be predefined, approved by the IT investment review board, and all measured investments can be rated and compared for selection. Clearly, only those investments that measure above the value lens thresholds should be considered. In the case of one of more measures not meeting threshold criteria, the investment review board can either reject or apply a blended IT value network index. It may be that an investment exceeds the stakeholder, operational, and agility thresholds, but comes slightly short of the strategic threshold. A blended index would accept the investment for consideration. Further, when evaluating vendors for an IT investment, they can also be compared to the baseline, facilitating vendor selection.

Black holes are easily identified, when measured IT investments fall short against most or all the baseline indexes. Exhibit 7.4 illustrates a black hole. Essentially a strategic IT investment, for instance, knowledge management, has been evaluated and does not meet any one of the measurable indexes. In our example, the knowledge management system may have an EVA of $0.5 million, a real option of only $100,000, a budget requirement of $900,000, and a stakeholder satisfaction or perceived value of 30 percent. This investment would not even be submitted for consideration to the IT investment board—more a case of "back to the drawing board."

> Stars shine bright, when measured IT investments meet or exceed index thresholds. Equally visible are the black holes, which consume investment with unsatisfactory value, unable to meet index thresholds.

IT Value Portfolio

IT portfolio management has been presented in Chapter 6 as an emerging information economics technique for improving overall value of IT investments. Here, we will provide more portfolio management insights and introduce the IT value portfolio model. In Chapter 10, we will expand to include IT value network management through portfolio governance.

IT Portfolio Management

IT is one of the single largest capital expense in a firm and must be managed like any other portfolio in terms of balancing risk and return. Earlier work by Weill and Broadbent[1] provides the basis for a strategic portfolio framework to enable managers to make optimal decisions on their IT investments, thereby sustaining competitive advantage. The IT portfolio should be tailored to the firm's unique strategic objectives, aligned to the business strategic plan. Weill and Broadbent's IT portfolio framework was categorized by infrastructure (computing and network), transactional (operational systems and support), informational (corporate management and control systems), and strategic investments (technologies from growth and competitive advantage).

> IT is one of the single largest capital expense in a firm, and it must be managed like any other portfolio in terms of balancing risk and return.

Weill and Broadbent conducted a five-year firm benchmarking study, across industries, and found that the breakdown of total IT investments averaged as follows: infrastructure, 58 percent; transactional, 12 percent; informational, 16 percent; and strategic, 14 percent. Corporate-shared IT investments typically were 64 percent of the total; the rest of the IT investment was business unit specific. The study found that the corporate IT organization increasingly owned most of the shared infrastructure investment, and the business units increasingly owned most of the transactional and strategic investments. Strategic IT investment in the hands of the business unit placed closer control on key growth options for their future business success, but such investments were prone to failure and may not bear fruit for several years.

Infrastructure consumes well over half the IT investment, which is often viewed as a cost of doing business and accordingly managed for cost reduction. A firm's operating costs are significantly affected by IT infrastructure expenses. Transactional IT investments represent over one-tenth of the total. Investments in order processing and customer service applications closely align with the business operations and can therefore be directly tied to broader business metrics; thus, they normally have a higher perceived value. Interestingly, informational IT investments consume 16 percent of the total, which is greater than core business transactional IT investment. The growth in enterprise resource planning (ERP), financial controls, executive information systems, and knowledge management is no doubt a reflection of the power of information. However, the value is often questioned, as information must be transformed into knowledge and then effectively applied for value to be derived. Strategic IT investments represents 14 percent of the total, which is a significant portion directed at future firm growth.

The benchmark study also suggested that firms with a business strategy that is based on agility and flexibility typically spend 10 to 25 percent more on IT than the industry average. By comparison, firms with a business strategy based on cost reduction would spend 10 to 20 percent less on IT than the industry average. Agility and flexibility are critical competitive factors in a world of uncertainty. Building a customer relationship management (CRM) application with predictive market analytics and thereby determining changing customer and market trends bodes well for flexible up-sell and cross-sell opportunities.

Additional studies of IT portfolio management conducted by Ross and Beath[2] suggest that as IT becomes more closely tied to business objectives, successful IT investments must consider technology scope and strategic objectives. Similar to the Weill and Broadbent approach, a framework for categorizing IT investment is proposed, identifying four types of IT investment: transformation (aligned to strategic), renewal (aligned to infrastructure), process improvement (aligned to transactional), and experiments (aligned to informational). This model is designed to assist IT management to decide which investments should be instigated and to help facilitate the selection of business cases where the total request exceeds the allotted resources.

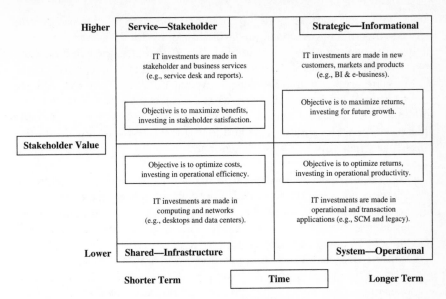

EXHIBIT 7.5 IT Value Portfolio Management—Mapping the IT Four "S" Investment Model to Stakeholder Economic Value

Trade-offs are required between types of investments, based on short-term profitability and long-term growth.

The IT value portfolio applies the IT investment four "S" category model, mapping IT investment types to stakeholder economic value and time. Categorized IT investments can be defined as either shorter-term or longer-term and with either a higher or lower stakeholder economic value. Competitive or internal benchmarking can be applied for relative positioning. Subsequently, investment trade-offs or rebalancing can occur within investment envelops or constraints. Exhibit 7.5 provides an illustration of the IT value portfolio.

> The IT value portfolio provides a framework to map IT spending, programs, projects, and assets, providing a snapshot of total IT investments relative to stakeholder economic value over time.

By mapping current IT programs, projects, assets, and spending, management can get a snapshot of key investments in their portfolio, showing relative positioning to stakeholder economic value and time. To determine stakeholder economic value, tangible and intangible values should be captured and quantified within the IT value network index. The value-created business case can be used to quantify the stakeholder economic value. The concept of value within a portfolio should be based on relative positioning between investment considerations, which accounts for the use of lower and higher labels of stakeholder economic value. True returns or stated benefits can be comparable within the same class or type of IT investment; comparisons are rarely meaningful across investment types. Time axis reflects risk over time. Relative positioning within investment types is again more important than absolute values, for appropriate investment trade-off considerations between shorter-term and longer-term, risk and reward. In the current state map, the following directional investment could be considered:

- **Shared infrastructure investments** (i.e., computing and network components) should be targeted at optimizing costs for stakeholder economic value over three months to two years. These investments should be limited to shared infrastructure renewal or consolidation and should drive operational efficiencies.
- **System investments** (i.e., operational and transaction applications) should be targeted at optimizing returns for stakeholder economic value over one to three years. Investments should be spent on well-defined process improvements for productivity increases.
- **Service investments** (i.e., stakeholder and business services) should be targeted at maximizing business benefits, for stakeholder economic value, over three months to one year. Investments should be spent on stakeholder satisfaction and critical success factors.
- **Strategic investments** (i.e., driving new customers, products, or markets) should be targeted at maximizing returns for stakeholder economic value over three to five years. Investments should be spent on future growth options and capability.

> Once the current IT investments have been consistently defined, categorized, benchmarked, and mapped against stakeholder economic value, a future-state IT value portfolio can be projected.

Once the current IT investments have been consistently defined, categorized, benchmarked, and mapped against stakeholder economic value, a future-state IT value portfolio can be projected. The future-state portfolio will be aligned to the business strategy. This exercise can be completed at the enterprise level and for each business unit, noting any disconnects between the two. Exhibit 7.6 shows an example of a projected IT investment portfolio, suggesting the following considerations:

- **Shared infrastructure investments** could be considered beyond cost optimization, if they are driving higher stakeholder economic value.

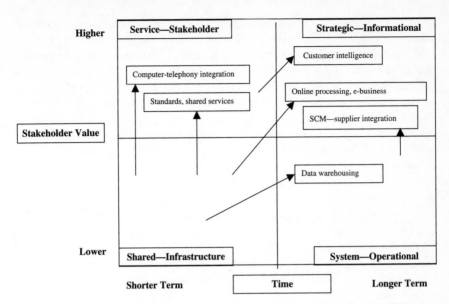

EXHIBIT 7.6 IT Value Portfolio Management—Projecting or Transforming IT Investments for Higher Stakeholder Economic Value

Consider computer/telephony integration or a standard desktop environment that improves business services and stakeholder satisfaction. Larger investments or longer-term investments may be acceptable if they provide higher returns; consider an integrated data warehouse investment to optimize application data flows. Infrastructure investments can become strategic; consider online processing capability for e-business.

- **System investments** could be considered beyond business process improvements or enhancements when a business is going through a significant transformation or reengineering. Consider a strategic investment in a new SCM application, which integrates with supplier processes.
- **Service investments** could be considered for strategic investment if they can transform information into knowledge, as in the case of customer intelligence. Customer information resides in abundance in most companies, but the information is not used intelligently. By harnessing the raw data through business analytics, customer and market trends and buying habits can be determined for effective sales campaigns.
- **Strategic investments** require critical evaluation, with a clear line of sight to the strategic plan, ensuring appropriately aligned IT investments.

The future-state IT value portfolio defines the mix of programs, projects, and assets that require investment over the next three years, based on the business and IT strategic objectives. The ultimate aim is to maximize stakeholder economic value while ensuring sufficient investment to sustain operational requirements, in this way balancing the shorter-term profitability needs with the longer-term growth expectations. The projected IT portfolio can also be benchmarked against industry averages, calculating percentages of the total, as referred to previously, for directional validation. To supplement the portfolio approach, scenario planning can assist in investment decisions. Based on a current situation and set of evolving assumptions, all of the possible business outcomes can be determined and mapped to the future-state portfolio.

> The future IT value portfolio defines the mix of programs, projects, and assets that require investment over the next three years, based on the business and IT strategic objectives, with the ultimate aim to maximize shareholder economic value in both the short term and the long term.

Star Gazing

The IT value portfolio model should be used to capture and map existing IT projects, assets, and investments to build the current-state portfolio and value statement. Subsequently, as discussed previously, the model can then be used to map and project future-state investments and projects. The IT value portfolio model provides an excellent visual for showing where IT investments are currently focused and where they need to be focused to be aligned to the company's strategic goals. The IT investment star formations defined earlier, based on the IT value network index, can be graphically mapped within the IT value portfolio model for star gazing. Exhibit 7.7 illustrates an IT value portfolio view of specific IT investments or a star constellation for review. Using some astronomy terms, star gazing might suggest the following IT investment observations:

1. **Black dwarf.** Consider a shared infrastructure investment, such as desktop renewal, proposed as an infrastructure refresh project. Like the star, this investment does not shine bright with a low incremental stakeholder value. But the value can be realized in a relative short period of time, with corresponding low risk. These stars are small in stature, less visible, and have a limited shelf life.
2. **White dwarf.** Consider a system investment, such as an order-processing application, proposed as a new off-the-shelf application to

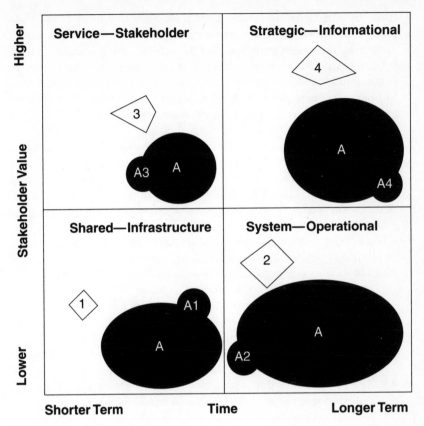

EXHIBIT 7.7 IT Value Portfolio View

replace an unsupported legacy system. Like the star, this investment shines brighter than the black dwarf with a higher stakeholder value. However, the investment size is larger and is extended over a longer period of time, subjecting returns to higher risk. These stars are relatively small in stature, with some visibility, but they are expected to burn bright over a longer period of time.

3. **Red giant.** Consider a service investment, such as a service desk, proposed for a new call center facility. Like the star, this investment shines extremely bright with a high stakeholder value. The investment size is relatively large but it extends over a short period of time. These stars can be large in stature, very visible, and can be expected to burn very bright in the short term.

4. **Blue hypergiants.** Consider a strategic investment such as a customer information management program, proposing a new custom-built system for customer analytics. Like the star, this investment shines the brightest with a high stakeholder value. However, the investment size is large and is extended over a long period of time, subjecting returns to high risk. These stars are large in stature, highly visible, and can be expected to burn very brightly in the long term.

A. **Black holes.** These are regions of space in the galaxy or portfolio where no investments can or should exist, as there is no light or brightness. IT investments or projects do not or no longer provide the required shareholder economic value over time. The size and shape of the black hole depends on stakeholder economic value expectations over time. Once a bright star, an investment can be sucked into the gravitational pull of a black hole, producing unacceptable stakeholder economic value, as illustrated in defined examples:

 A1. The desktop renewal project is projected to take longer to execute, with the same stakeholder economic value. PCs will take longer to deploy, with a risk that the technology may become obsolete.

 A2. The off-the-shelf order-processing system can actually be implemented sooner than expected, but it is now projected to have much lower stakeholder economic value. Customization costs are required for the value to materialize.

 A3. The call center facility is projected to take the same time to execute, but realizable value is much lower. A new minimum wage has been introduced into the region, increasing staff costs.

 A4. The customer analytics system will take longer to deploy, with significantly less stakeholder value. New competitive products in the market have changed the targeted customer buying habits, reducing analytical relevance.

 Supernova. In the presiding examples, these IT investments are no longer viable against the IT value network index threshold and therefore should explode like a supernova. They will be bright for a while, but will soon fade over a relatively short period of time.

> The IT value portfolio model enables stargazing, providing a helpful, if not interesting, visual representation of IT investments and their relative stakeholder economic value over time.

The portfolio roll-up of investments for each IT investment class or type provides an understanding of total amounts invested today and projected for the future. Actual and proposed investment should be monitored against allotted investment envelopes, as approved by the investment review board and subsequently monitored by the PMO. For example, a total incremental investment envelope of $50 million may be approved by the investment review board for a given year, allocated by investment class or type, creating possible investment envelopes as follows: strategic, $10 million; services, $5 million; shared infrastructure, $20 million; and systems $15 million. New investments in each investment category will have to compete within each investment envelope, based on stakeholder economic value over time. The IT value portfolio is a useful tool to govern the total enterprise IT investments, both existing and new, providing investment guidance on selecting, performance, and benefit realization. Stargazing provides a helpful, if not interesting, visual representation of IT investments and their relative stakeholder economic value over time.

This chapter has focused on triangulating the value of IT investments, through building an enterprise IT value network index, with relevant measures and techniques, to evaluate different types of IT investments. Within the IT value network index framework, the IT investment four "S" categories can be evaluated against the four value lenses. Relevant measures and techniques can change, depending on the six stages of investment evaluation. Once again, the key message is not to rely on just singular traditional financial-based or conventional organization-based measures or techniques in evaluating IT investment. The chapter concluded with the IT value portfolio model, providing a useful tool to govern both new and existing enterprise IT investments. Part III will focus on the management of IT investment value. The IT value network management framework identifies six degrees of value, from IT investment to stakeholder economic value.

PART III

Six Degrees of IT Value—There IT Is

New value-based multidimensional approaches to IT investment and evaluation are required, given the failures of traditional and conventional methods, as discussed in Part I. Value networks consist of complex relationships and transactions between social and technical resources across a business's points of presence, creating stakeholder economic value. Part III discusses the six degrees of separation from IT investment to stakeholder economic value, culminating in a framework for effectively managing IT investment value and spending, building on the IT value network measurement approach discussed in Part II.

Psychologist Stanley Milgram introduced the famous phrase "six degrees of separation," in 1967. Based on a small-world experiment, it took six steps to pass a message along a chain of acquaintances to subsequently reach a targeted person. Similarly, for IT investment there are six steps within the value network to reach the targeted IT value. "Six degrees of IT value" is a series of interrelated steps that will increase the value of existing and new IT investments. If the chain of events is broken, the targeted value becomes suboptimal. Hence, the notion of degrees of IT value network management, which is discussed in this section. The following exhibit portrays the IT value network framework, which incorporates IT value network management and measurement.

Chapter 8 provides the IT value network management context, defining value capture, value enabling, value optimization, and value realization. The subsequent chapters examine the six degrees of IT value in detail. Each degree is an extensive topic of discussion in its own right, so the focus will be on the relevance to IT value management.

The six degrees of IT value and the chapters in which they are presented are as follows:

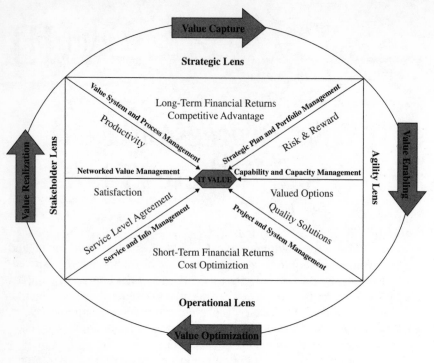

IT Value Network Framework

Chapter 9, First Degree of IT Value: Value system and process management/improvement

Chapter 10, Second Degree of IT Value: Strategic planning and portfolio management/governance

Chapter 11, Third Degree of IT Value: Capability and capacity management—IT and organization

Chapter 12, Fourth Degree of IT Value: Project management and system management

Chapter 13, Fifth Degree of IT Value: Service management and information management

Chapter 14, Sixth Degree of IT Value: Network value management

The six degrees of IT value form a cyclical framework, in which the sixth degree feeds the first degree for higher levels of IT value. IT investment can progressively be evaluated at each degree of value, utilizing the IT value network index, as discussed in Chapter 7. Specifically, this refers to evaluating or measuring IT investment through the four-value lenses, consisting of strategic, agility, operational, and stakeholder views.

IT Value Network Management

This chapter provides the underlying context to IT value network management, discussing IT value: capture, enabling, optimization, and realization. IT investment value is initially captured through strategic planning and supporting operational plans, aligned to the value chain, with input from networked value management. Value capture is managed and governed in an investment portfolio. IT value is subsequently enabled, building off value capture and through applying organizational and IT capability and capacity planning. Optimizing IT value builds off value enablement, requiring project and system management and thereby ensuring effective operational processes. IT value realization matures through value optimization and subsequently through service and information management. Ultimately, IT value is fully realized on the company ledgers and identified through networked value management; initiating a new cycle of IT value network management.

IT value network management is a set of processes, which capture, enable, optimize, and realize value from IT investment, depicted in six degrees of IT value.

Value Capture

Capturing the value of IT investments includes identifying, justifying, prioritizing, and selecting investments. This encompasses evaluation of the business processes within the value system, IT alignment to the business strategy, IT governance, and portfolio management. A disciplined process is required to identify the IT investment based on strategic and operational requirements. Typically, the IT focus is internal and lacks line of sight to external value propositions within the extended business network. Partners, alliances, vendors, suppliers, and customers should be more actively engaged in identifying IT investment opportunities. Thus, the importance of ensuring adequate stakeholder input from networked value management across the business or value network.

Subsequently, investments are justified through a value-creation business case and capital/expense budgeting process. Part II discussed in depth various measures and techniques to triangulate the value through the IT value network index. The objective is to determine the value of the investment, assessing risk and reward, over time. Knowing the investment is justified and that a firm has constrained total investment or investment envelopes, priorities should be assigned through IT value portfolio management. Ultimately, the investment is selected based on an approval process, governed by an investment review board.

Value Enabling

Enabling the value of existing and new IT investments builds off value capture decisions, considering the underlying enterprise capability and dependency enablers along with the capacity and resource constraints. Value options should be considered to provide capability and capacity flexibility or agility, as discussed in Chapter 1. Chapter 2 discussed the criticality of identifying and enabling conditional prerequisites that are needed to unlock and realize the full shareholder value. Complementary investment in IT in organizational capital makes a difference to performance outcomes. These enabling or dependency investments include decentralized decision-making systems, self-directed teams, job training, organizational design (OD), business process improvement, and internal communication.

Managing the portfolio of IT investments and assets includes dealing with financial and organizational constraints. Envelopes of investment will be based on financial indicators and performance. Organizational culture, organizational development, talent availability, and resistance to change are critical and often constraining modifiers. The portfolio challenge is to maximize value, based on a firm's current and future capability and capacity, managing critical constraints. Real or value options based on futures and current constraints provide added value alternatives. This is particularly relevant in the attempt to leverage the business network capability and capacity beyond the firm. Vendor or partner agreements should be effectively managed, as often they represent constraints or potential options. Creating the optimal or agile technology and organizational platform enables IT value for effective execution. Subsequently, project and system management capability, capacity, and performance will determine the effectiveness of the execution.

Value Optimization

Optimizing the value of existing and new IT investments focuses on IT execution or deployment. The management effectiveness of IT operations and existing IT investments and assets directly correlates with the effectiveness of new IT investment execution. In other words, IT project deployment depends on the effectiveness of the processes, people, and technology within the IT organization. Often new IT projects are executed despite the state of the underlying system management. Building new capability with the wrong skills, ineffective tools, inconsistent procedures, on top of a broken foundation leads to disaster. Yet it happens—no wonder so many projects crash, exceeding budget and timelines.

System management includes the processes, people, and technology in support of the shared infrastructure, systems, and services. Program and project management is applied to new IT investment, but it is dependent on the effectiveness of system management. Building off value enablement, through effective system and project management, the objective is to optimize and deliver the IT investment value. System optimization can be realized through lowering the overall IT cost of ownership, compared with industry benchmarks. An optimal project is judged to be one that is on time, on budget, and delivers quality deliverables to the business case with mitigated business risk. Performance management and quality assurance are critical components of optimization, meeting negotiated service level agreements and critical success factors, which are instruments for communicating IT value. Vendor or partner agreements need to reflect business service commitments, with sufficient flexibility to accommodate change.

Value Realization

Realizing the value from IT investments amounts to nothing short of booking the value on the firm's ledgers. The value-creation business case, as discussed in Chapter 4, is instrumental in defining where program-project value will be captured and subsequently realized. Operational budgets can provide a clear view of baseline projections and value realization adjustments, from project and system gains. In some cases, material gain can be clearly identified (e.g., head-count reduction) and so accounted for in new budget projections. However, this gain can often be dissipated or dispersed in support of other departmental needs. Transformation from IT investment to booked returns takes time, through the benefit-realization approach discussed in Chapter 2; therefore, there is a need to derive shorter-term stakeholder value. This is accomplished through service management and information management.

Stakeholder economic value is achieved through delivering the business case, but also through meeting service level agreements, providing knowledge, and satisfactorily delivered IT capability. Therefore, managing the networked value should consider a continuous process of performance measurement and tracking, surveying stakeholder satisfaction, and ensuring that stakeholder expectations are transformed into expected results. Ultimately, there should be a sustainable process to ensure that the expected value from the investment is captured and realized on the firm's books. Furthermore, there is also a learning value from IT investment management and execution, which should also be captured. Audited value becomes the final proof point, providing independent validation of realized and booked IT value.

The IT value network management framework consists of four elements of IT value: capture, enabling, optimization, and realization. The following chapters examine the six degrees of IT value within this framework.

CHAPTER 9

First Degree of IT Value

The first degree of IT value network management is concerned with IT value capture, focused on the firm's value system and process improvement. A key focus within the business should be on core competencies and the added value processes that provide competitive advantage, shedding less-valued capabilities and building new strengths on key fundamentals. The first degree identifies and justifies IT investment opportunities within the value chain and value system, aligned to process improvement or reengineering opportunities within the firm and across the firm's business network. In the second degree of IT value, identified IT investments in support of process change are prioritized, based on the business strategy. The concept of six degrees of value embodies a cyclical framework in which the sixth degree, networked value management, feeds the first degree for higher levels of realized IT value.

> The first degree of IT value network management is concerned with IT value capture, focused on the firm's value system and process improvement. IT investments are identified based on enhancing competitive advantage from changes to the firm's processes, across the business network.

Value System

Popularized by Michael Porter in the mid-1980s, the value chain consists of a series of activities that adds customer value to a firm's products or services, whether through differentiation or lower cost to competition. The objective is to offer the customer, buyer, or client a level of value that exceeds the cost of these activities, thus providing the firm a profit margin. The value system goes beyond the firm's value chain, including the firm's business network

Firm's Value System

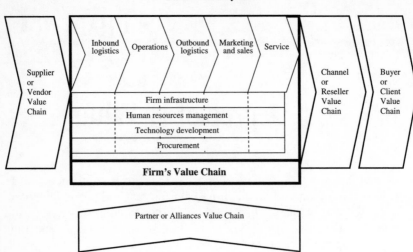

EXHIBIT 9.1 Porter's Generic Value Chain and Value System

of customers, partners, vendors, and alliances. Opportunities for process improvement or reengineering should be identified within the extended value chain and value system, targeting higher stakeholder economic value and showing IT system dependencies. Chapter 19 discusses the firm's value system in more detail; for now the focus is on IT investment value capture. Exhibit 9.1 illustrates an adaptation of Porter's generic value chain and value system, incorporating a partner and an alliance value extension.

The value chain key activities include:

- **Inbound logistics.** Receiving and warehousing of raw materials or supplies and subsequent distribution to manufacturing or operations
- **Operations.** Transformation of materials and supplies into finished products and services
- **Outbound logistics.** Receiving and warehousing of finished products and subsequent distribution to the buyer or intermediate channel
- **Marketing and sales.** Identification of customer, buyer, or client needs and the subsequent generation of sales
- **Service.** Support of the customer, buyer, or client after the product or service is sold

Key activities are supported by:

- **Firm infrastructure.** Real estate, legal, internal controls, organizational culture, and the like

- **Human resource management.** Organizational development and employee recruiting, hiring, training, development, compensation, and recognition
- **Technology development.** IT shared infrastructure, systems, services, and strategic investments
- **Procurement.** Vendor management and purchases of materials, supplies, equipment, and machinery

Capturing IT value requires blueprinting the firm's value chain and value system within the firm's stakeholder business network, depicting process interrelationships and IT dependencies. Cascading process views or levels determine the firm's business model, culminating in value statements throughout the value system. Overlaying the IT shared infrastructure, systems, and services to the value system maps process dependencies to current IT investments. Projecting a future-state value chain or necessary process changes for competitive advantage subsequently provides insight into potential new IT investment opportunities. Mapping IT investments to the process blueprint reveals critical dependencies and embedded IT value.

IT investment dollars can be mapped to the current and future process map, providing insights to underinvested or overinvested processes, highlighting those strategic or added value processes that require additional or reallocated IT investment. Determining or capturing the value of IT investments will be based on measurable process improvements, working in collaboration with all business stakeholders. Integrating processes with IT systems throughout the firm's value system can provide substantial competitive advantage. Vertically integrated firms typically benefit from one-time information flows or one-stop processing from supply to buyer. IT management should be familiar with a firm's value chain and value system, in terms of IT dependencies and integration challenges, and should coach business executives on opportunities to provide enhanced competitive advantage through IT.

> Capturing IT value requires mapping the firm's current and future IT investments to key processes within the firm's value chain and value system, showing embedded IT value and dependencies for process improvement.

Process and System Improvement

Champions of business process reengineering (BPR) Hammer and Champy maintain that BPR is required for fundamental rethinking and radical redesign of business processes to achieve significant performance improvement. Since the late 1980s, BPR has evolved from tackling changes to the entire end-to-end value chain or complete enterprise resource planning (ERP) system, to more manageable selective process redesign opportunities.[1] Large BPR failures in the early 1990s drove firms to focus on targeted high-value process improvements and to outsource low-value processes. Customer interfacing and new product introduction processes are examples of core valued processes for a company seeking competitive advantage through time to market and customer service. Outsourcing manufacturing and possibly operations might be worth considering if external providers can perform at lower costs to the firm.

One of the biggest challenges to a firm is scoping the process for redesign, especially when processes are interdependent or dependent on the underlying IT system. The default is to target functional processes such as human resources or sales, carving out processes into silos. Thus, the value chain can be suboptimized as a whole, due to value leakage between silos or functions. Consider a sales process that has been redesigned in the absence of service or product development process dependencies. The selling process is optimized, but the product may not meet customer needs and service may not meet customer expectations. Further, assuming the process for redesign is appropriately scoped, inclusive of process dependencies, the supporting IT system may be a constraint. Legacy systems may not be able to adapt or evolve. Vanilla off-the-shelf applications may provide only part of the solution. Custom builds may lack integration capability.

Essentially, process redesign should be examined together with system capability. Often ERP solutions advocate industry best practice, negating the need for process redesign unless they are justifiably unique in providing competitive advantage. Customization or point solutions for unique firm processes can be cost-prohibitive—not just the initial investment and integration costs but from ongoing support and cost of ownership. Today, more companies are adopting vanilla applications for transaction systems (i.e., financials, item processing) or operations systems (i.e., supply chain management), as depicted by the success of such large ERP providers as IBM, SAP, and Oracle. Customization occurs when the value outweighs the long-term cost, and invariably amounts to no more than 10 to 20 percent of the total system footprint. However, customer interfacing processes and knowledge management processes can provide considerable unique value to a firm. Therefore, customized Web-enabled point-solutions continue to grow, hopefully based on a service-orientated architecture (SOA) and focused on unique process design for competitive advantage. IT management needs to become more process orientated, collaborating with key stakeholders to capture the synergy and integrated value of combined process and system simplification and optimization. IT systems and business process redesign should be evaluated together using the IT value index, capturing the value from the strategic, operational, stakeholder, and agility value lens. Process culture is discussed in Chapter 19.

> IT management needs to become more process orientated, collaborating with key stakeholders to capture the synergy and integrated value of combined process and system simplification and optimization.

The first degree of IT value network management is concerned with IT value capture, whereby IT investments are initially identified and justified. However, due to the cyclical nature of the six degrees of IT value, the first degree can also be an extension of the sixth degree and thus of IT value realization. In other words, stakeholder economic value materializes through the implementation of process and system improvements. Chapter 10 discusses the second degree, strategic planning and portfolio management governance, continuing with IT value capture. Identified process improvements are aligned to the firm's strategic plan for prioritization and selection.

Second Degree of IT Value

L ike the first degree of IT value network management, the second degree is concerned with IT value capture, but with a focus on IT strategic planning and portfolio management governance. The firm's strategic objectives and initiatives are defined for a three-to-five-year period, identifying investment priorities over the next three years. Process and system improvements identified within the value system, as defined in the first degree, would be aligned to the strategic initiatives for prioritization. The IT strategy should be aligned to the business strategic direction, and through portfolio governance IT investments are prioritized and ultimately selected. Yet in Chapter 1, we discovered that formal IT strategic planning was adopted by only 60 percent of firms,[1] citing a number of impediments in its deployment.[2] Subsequently, only a quarter of planned strategic IT investments were deployed.[3] Capturing total IT value requires integrating the IT strategy with the business strategy and governing IT investments through portfolio management.

> The second degree of IT value network management, like the first degree, is concerned with IT value capture, but with a focus on IT strategic planning and portfolio governance, whereby IT investments are identified, prioritized, and selected for stakeholder economic value.

Strategic Planning

Chapter 2 suggested the need to integrate the IT strategy into the corporate business strategy, effectively aligning and prioritizing strategic initiatives and associated IT budgetary outlays.[4] Hierarchies of objectives and budgets are related to performance controls, and hierarchies of strategies and initiatives or programs are related to action planning.[5] Chapter 6 defined some tools or methods to assist in the strategic planning process, including

SWOT analysis (strengths, weaknesses, opportunities, and threats) and PEST (political, economic, social, and technology) analysis. There are a number of approaches to strategic planning, based on internal and external situational analysis of the current and future state (i.e., SWOT, PEST). Alongside the business model, these are useful for defining or tuning the company's vision, mission, and values, targeting measurable goals, mapping or defining the path to reach these goals, and establishing controls.

Business strategies are either structured, normative, and rational or behaviorally oriented. The reality is that companies apply a blended approach, especially in times of uncertainty and change, implementing a mix of evolving strategies.[6] The formal planning process typically is driven from a structured process of environmental analysis, internal analysis, and strategic goals. However, in practice, political and organizational dynamics strongly influence this formal process. The desired result should be well-defined strategic objectives and clearly scoped initiatives, which drive change, whether through new customers or products, business process change, organizational change, activity or volume change, or a new way of doing business.

IT is often described as an enabler to company performance, deployed in support of these business-driven changes and indirectly correlates to captured shareholder economic value. However, our counterargument maintains that IT initiatives go beyond enablement and constitute a business strategy unto themselves, directly contributing to stakeholder economic value. Consider an online business, where the Internet is the channel to market, the principal product is a search engine, the infrastructure scales for volume and is leveraged for added value hosting, online tools capture free content supplied by the customers, and the consumer value proposition is a new way of doing business—in short, Google. However, maximizing IT value will be realized when it is fully integrated with other complementary investments, such as new strategies, new business processes, and new organizations.

Leadership in IT application is seen by many companies as a strategic imperative.[7] Integrating the IT strategy with the business strategy is the most important step in capturing and managing the value of strategic IT investments. IT strategy encompasses both information systems (IS) and technology. However, there is an important difference. IS strategy is more associated with information, services, and system requirements in delivering the business objectives, a strategy that is driven by business demand or needs. On the other hand, technology strategy (sometimes called IT) is focused on specific technologies that support or deliver the applications, driven by IS requirements.[8] Technology enables the business, but IS can drive the business.

Information within the IT domain is often overlooked as a strategy unto itself. The past 60 years should be called the data age rather than the information age, as data remains unlocked or latent in terms of realizable value.[9] Data is often not transformed into information or knowledge creation; it sits collecting in databases. Technology infrastructure in support is often misdirected when data storage and recovery priorities and investment outweigh data consolidation, analytical tools, and business intelligence. Information/data ownership never seems clear, although it should be in the hands of the process or functional owners. In reality, it often defaults to the stewardship of the "I" in the CIO. Information can also be isolated within functional silos and therefore is not leveraged across the enterprise. Information maps should be created that align to decomposed business process and the enterprise value chain. Data can then be optimized or rationalized through relational databases and workflow integration. Better information behaviors and value capture will lead to improved business performance, creating visible intellectual capital and valued intangible assets.

Exhibit 10.1 illustrates a path to integrate the business and IT strategy, identifying IT investments or programs/projects based on strategic initiatives. Company vision, mission, and values shape the corporate goals, which define the business strategy. Measurable strategic objectives subsequently define key strategic initiatives, which in turn define key business and IT programs or projects. The relationship between strategic objectives to strategic initiatives is typically one to many, but it can be many to one. A customer service initiative or strategic business CRM program can be created in support

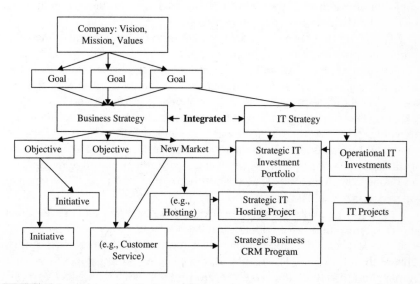

EXHIBIT 10.1 Integrated Business and IT Strategy

of a strategic objective of increasing sales and in support of another strategic objective to penetrate new markets. In the illustrated example, hosting capability and services could be another strategic initiative in support of the new market objective, where the principal strategic program or project is led by IT.

IT programs essentially generate increased tangible and intangible value, from the likes of customer service improvement, application interoperability, human knowledge, supply chain improvements, business process efficiencies, and business cycles. When considering the broader perspective of IT's contribution to company performance, it is critical to consider other associated company investments. For instance, significant investment in people and change management is required for new technology solutions to be effectively implemented and deployed. Training and education are essential for technology application and utility.

Integrating the IT strategy with the business strategy requires the CIO to be at the CEO table in shaping the future, not behind the scenes waiting three to six months to respond to and subsequently align to corporate directives. IT is often in a lag situation, merely supporting and not defining future direction. The IT strategy needs to be embedded into the corporate and business unit strategies, becoming mainstream in achieving corporate goals, not just enabling. Consider the opportunity, as discussed previously, within the value chain, where process redesign and system optimization merge to achieve a strategic objective. A supply chain strategic initiative to achieve a cost reduction objective would be better served when both process simplification and IT system rationalization are considered together, not process first and then system in response.

The IT investment portfolio subsequently captures the full value of all programs, projects, and investments that touch IT. These usually account for the majority of all corporate investments outside the business infrastructure (e.g., real estate). IT investments must meet the changing business unit needs as well as the enterprise needs, clearly showing priorities and interdependencies. The strategic plan cannot be set in stone, but must be living and dynamic.[10] IT investments need to be leveraged fully across the business units and optimized for the enterprise. Strategically aligning IT investments to the enterprise and business units takes extensive executive involvement and consensus. Once this is achieved, the real work starts, as the key is to operationalize the alignment.

Crystallizing and cascading the IT objectives and program metrics down the IT organization drives operational accountability and value capture. To assist in defining the appropriate objective and program metrics and to ensure that the whole IT organization is aligned to the business priorities, Kaplan and Norton's balanced scorecard process (BSC) is an effective tool.[11] The BSC helps to facilitate the strategy and translate it into IT operational terms, as discussed in Chapter 6; it is an emerging organizational management technique for value capture. Continual and sustained executive support through communication, performance measures, and incentives is required to embed the enterprise direction and achieve expected alignment. If these are not in place, alignment will diverge, IT value will dissipate, and organizational performance will become suboptimal. Benko and McFarlan[12] state that if there is greater organizational alignment, companies are able to fly in formation more effectively, comparing them to geese traveling 70 percent farther in a "V" formation.

> Integrating the IT strategy with the business strategy for IT value capture requires the CIO to be at the CEO table in shaping the future, not behind the scenes waiting three to six months to respond and subsequently align to corporate directives.

Portfolio Governance

As discussed in Chapter 7, capturing stakeholder economic value can be maximized through an enterprise portfolio approach instead of through a local optimization approach from competing standalone business units. Trade-offs are required to meet short-term and long-term goals across the business, managing risk and reward. A company should consider classifying its IT investments into the four "S" category model and comparing them with industry benchmarks to see if there are major variances that would suggest a competitive advantage or disadvantage—or just a statement on overall IT investment effectiveness. Benchmarking, as discussed in Chapter 6, is meant to be directional or relative and not to be overanalyzed, prompting questions and further analysis. Once the IT investment portfolio's current and future state has been defined, accommodating the strategic direction, a migration plan can be established to rebalance the portfolio. This is no easy task, as in-flight investments will need to be reassessed, potentially canceling projects. There is only a finite amount of IT investment available, and it must be appropriately prioritized for short-term and long-term needs. The IT value portfolio approach will identify relative IT investment stars and black holes for selection consideration.

Establishing an executive investment review board or committee is necessary for strategic alignment and governance, where leaders from the business and IT can make the hard trade-offs with respect to investment prioritization and selection. This investment governance is also extremely useful to ensure standard investment policies and decision making across individual business units and functions, for the good of the enterprise and overall shareholder economic value, thus minimizing the politics of local optimization. By ensuring that business executives are fully engaged in IT investment decisions, the likelihood of capturing maximum shareholder economic value improves. An investment review board or council is recommended for firm-wide program governance, reporting to a company board committee.[13] The company board should be more engaged in ratifying investments for shareholder economic value. Exhibit 10.2 provides an example of an enterprise investment portfolio governance model.

Business programs should be owned by an executive sponsor, accountable for the business case and value capture. When there is a strong IT investment component or large IT project within the business program, it's not uncommon that the business executive will explicitly or implicitly delegate the accountability to an IT executive. This can be fraught with problems, causing execution issues in the program delivery and value capture. IT led programs, sponsored by the CIO or IT executive, could be jointly owned by the IT executive and a business executive, providing a broader sponsorship base and acknowledgment or stakeholder economic value. Consider establishing steering committees for larger programs, consisting of impacted executive IT stakeholders, to ensure support and appropriate governance.

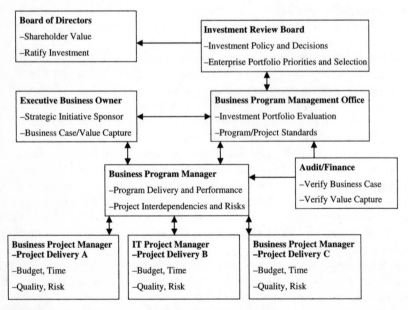

EXHIBIT 10.2 Enterprise Investment Portfolio Governance

In support of the investment review board and executive business sponsors, there should a business program management office (BPMO), which provides program and project standard practice and evaluation. It is important that investment decisions be based on independent and quality metrics, which may not be the case if individual business units or functions are assessing their own programs. The BPMO establishes standards for project management and reporting on programs, conducts performance reviews, collates the investment portfolio maps, completes the benchmarks, tracks the value realization, and advises the investment review board. Audit and finance should be engaged, validating business cases and ratifying value captured.

As discussed in Chapter 7, a number of useful measures and techniques can be applied by the BPMO to manage the investment portfolio. The IT value network index and the IT value portfolio approach can assist in identifying and comparing investment value, identifying stars and black holes. In support of portfolio management, there are a number of prevalent software vendors (e.g., Prosight) to assist in stargazing. The BPMO can also benefit from the processes advocated by the IT investment management (ITIM) framework, applying a select/control/evaluate model, assessed at five maturity stages. Each core element within the model consists of a number of key practices for investment assessment and evaluation.[14] Further, financial-based methods, specifically capital and operating budgets, are key investment tracking methods.

The BPMO could also apply real option techniques for strategic IT investments, managing risk and reward. Real option analysis is a more systematic approach in considering the uncertainty of several outcomes to a strategic option; it functions by applying risk analysis, determining probabilities of occurrence, and applying probabilistic or stochastic decision making. Outcomes can be assessed based on likelihood of success or highest added value. Similarly, scenario planning can assist in investment decisions, by determining and assessing the investment parameters and uncontrollable variables. All possible outcomes are determined, based on a current situation and set of evolving assumptions. Scenario simulation models can be developed, with "what if" analysis. Such advanced techniques can be used to facilitate IT investment prioritization and selection, maximizing potential IT value.

> Capturing stakeholder economic value can be maximized through an enterprise portfolio governance approach, instead of through a local optimization approach from competing stand-alone business units or functions.

The second degree of IT value network is concerned with IT value capture, whereby IT investments are identified, prioritized, and selected. Through strategic planning and enterprise portfolio governance, IT investments are aligned to the corporate strategic objectives and in support of operational priorities. Chapter 11 discusses the third degree, transitioning into IT value enabling, through effective capability and capacity management.

CHAPTER 11

Third Degree of IT Value

The third degree of IT value network management is concerned with IT value enabling, with a focus on enterprise capability and capacity management for IT systems and infrastructure and for the IT organization and people. The IT executive should provide technology solutions to the business and be engaged in investing and managing the systems and the shared infrastructure capability and capacity. As discussed in Chapter 1, underlying IT investments need to be agile to accommodate future business opportunities and solutions. Further, Chapter 2 discussed the criticality of identifying conditional prerequisites that must happen in order to enable complete shareholder economic value. Such conditions include the IT organization and its people's capability and capacity for change.

> The third degree of IT value network management is concerned with IT value enabling, with a focus on enterprise capability and capacity management, both for IT systems and infrastructure and for the IT organization and its people. IT investments are required to enable agility for current and future business solutions.

IT Systems and Infrastructure Capability and Capacity

The business stakeholders continue to demand agility, requiring speed to market and profit through quality IT solutions. However, technology is moving ever faster, to the point that an IT executive invariably struggles to keep up, focusing on immediate domain expertise and following key trends, as outlined in Chapter 1. Further, enabling the value of new and existing IT investments requires managing the portfolio of IT investments and assets, where the current-state systems and shared infrastructure contain capacity limitations and overall technology constraints. The challenge within the portfolio is to maximize stakeholder economic value, based on a firm's current and future capability and capacity and through managing critical constraints.

The key is to build an IT architectural strategy, based on best practice and proven technology standards, embedding flexibility and value options. Often the current-state architecture consists of a collection of hardware assets, licenses, system diagrams, and perhaps data flows, with no meaningful order or hierarchy. Mapping technologies onto an overall enterprise process map provides visibility to known IT investments and their dependencies in support of business processes. Architectural IT blueprints should be defined from various enterprise and business unit perspectives—namely, data/information (and security), interface/communication, systems integration, and underlying computing and networking.[1] A portfolio inventory, based on IT asset management, ensures version control and supportability, identifying investment technology life cycles and cost of ownership.

Subsequently, future-state architectural blueprints can be defined based on best practice and technology standards, with a migration plan to close the gap or transition from the current state. Blueprints should consider value options for flexibility, identifying open technology options for longer-term agility. These IT blueprints should also be used as a filter on new business-driven technology solutions, ensuring that enterprise solutions and point solutions are carefully considered within the overall enterprise portfolio and architecture. What might seem a cost-effective point solution to meet a specific business requirement could be costly to integrate and support from an enterprise perspective.

Capability and capacity management of applications or systems within the business environment is challenging, especially if systems cross functional, regional, and business unit boundaries. Layer this with international cultural issues, language differences, time zone changes, or simply operational variations, and the level of difficulty is compounded. Let us also not forget the demanding business stakeholder, expecting agility and requiring a timely solution to meet the changing business environment. Standardizing applications in complex environments for agility requires enterprise resource planning (ERP), a familiar term as advocated by large application vendors SAP, IBM, and Oracle. Enterprise-wide system deployments need to be mapped against future-state architecture blueprints and aligned to the firm's value system and business processes, as illustrated in Exhibit 11.1. An extended ERP value system encompasses the relationships, transactions, and information flows across the firm's business or value network.

Customer relationship management (CRM) systems align to customer-facing processes; supply chain management (SCM) systems align to vendor-facing processes and operational and logistic processes. Enterprise

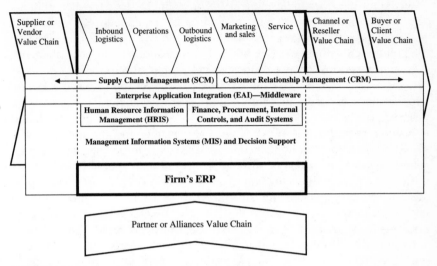

Firm's Extended ERP

EXHIBIT 11.1 Enterprise Resource Planning (ERP)

application integration (EAI) or middleware provides the information and transaction bus between systems, integrating with human resource information management (HRIS), finance, and procurement-related systems. Ultimately, stakeholder economic value materials in value exchanges within the value system or business network, which can be tracked and evaluated by management information systems (MIS) and decision support systems. Managing the ERP environment is no easy task, one that calls for ensuring that application incidences and versions are compatible and supportable within an integrated environment. However, if it is done well, it can significantly enable business value, providing quality solutions in an agile environment.

Capability and capacity management of the underlying shared infrastructure is equally challenging as the speed of technology change quickens. Storage growth, data normalization, and server virtualization are driving complexity, especially when all three are juggled at the same time. Network quality of service (QoS) struggles with data and voice packet priorities and bandwidth issues. Data center space and power requirements continue to grow or require reconfiguring, especially to accommodate business and disaster recovery expectations. Information security vulnerabilities change weekly. In most cases, the shared infrastructure is transparent to the business community, until an element crashes; then the witch hunt starts. Decisions should be made on longer-term technology standards for cost of ownership reduction, while managing incremental investments to sustain operations and short-term additions to meet new business requirements.

A shared infrastructure requires a computing and networking architectural blueprint, with more discipline being applied to IT asset management. Too often, desktops, servers, routers, switches, and the supporting operating systems are not kept up to date and lack current version or patch releases. Supportability exposure and information security vulnerability create business risk. Exposure is increased with interoperability issues between shared infrastructure and applications, when incompatible and unsupported versions are operational or implemented. These risks can be mitigated through sound IT asset or inventory management. Further, capability and capacity are variables influencing the cost of doing business. In most cases, the quality of the shared infrastructure should be tied to agreed service level agreements (SLAs), where the business acknowledges the budgeted capability and capacity. Capital allocations must be reasonably constant and aligned with depreciation to ensure that the shared infrastructure is refreshed and effectively updated to meet current and future requirements or thresholds.

Value options can be created to help manage the capability and capacity of systems and shared infrastructure, enabling future business value. (Reference real options, as discussed in Chapter 5.) In conditions of outcome uncertainty, like long-term business growth or technology pace of change, more emphasis should be placed on negotiated options within the business network. Supplier, vendor, partner, alliance, channel, and customer agreements should provide for agility. Too often intercompany contracts or SLAs are overly structured to protect well-defined commitments. Instead, such agreements should provide for strategic intent and partnership flexibility. They should not be focused just on operational due diligence in such matters as service levels, compliance, warranties, and penalties.

Strategic intent could consider mutually agreed long-term shared goals, shared risk and reward, and the nature of symbiotic relationships. Vendor, partner, and customer management should deal with these critical relationships and should not be just transactional in nature. Valued options between stakeholders provide flexibility in bipartisan arrangements, adapting to changes in the market and industry and ensuring a win-win situation over the life of the relationship. Such options can be implemented to overcome capacity and capability constraints at various points in time, ensuring responsiveness to business requirements. Consider a vendor loaning a server or router or increasing maximum bandwidth to overcome a short-term customer constraint without lengthy renegotiation of current contracts. Such added value will be paid back to the vendor through longer-term agreements and fair value exchange.

Architectural IT blueprints, enterprise resource planning (ERP), and asset management, with value options, are necessary to effectively manage the capability and capacity of systems and shared infrastructure, thereby providing flexibility and speed to market and so enabling stakeholder economic value.

Organization and People Capability and Capacity

Complementary investments to IT in organizational capital makes a difference to performance outcomes, as discussed in Chapter 2. These investments, sometimes classified under change management, would include decentralized decision-making systems, self-directed teams, job training, organizational design, business process modification, and internal communication. Further, organizational culture, organizational development, talent management, and resistance to change are critical modifiers and often a constraint in realizing complete IT value. For instance, underinvesting in the capability and capacity of people, who are instrumental to adopting business change, will leave value on the table because implemented IT solutions won't be effectively deployed or realized.

Company vision, mission, and values provide a strategic beacon, as discussed previously, determining the company's charter. The company's organization structure should be designed to deliver its charter and stated goals. Intracompany and intercompany relationships and interdependencies should be clearly defined within the firm's business network. Often, an internal focus precludes opportunities for building value options with partners, customers, and vendors. Identifying capabilities and competencies outside the firm can complement or supplement the internal organization, providing flexibility without increasing fixed costs. The virtualized workforce was discussed in Chapter 1. Managing internal and external partnerships or relationships should be a major concern for the IT executive.

Defining centers of excellence within the firm focuses on building internal capability on core competencies for competitive advantage. External centers of excellence provide a virtual capability on a just-in-time or incremental basis. In reality, the firm's management structure and organization continually evolve; this may be based on a new business model, market changes, company maturity, a move to centralize or decentralize, or just politics. The CIO needs to consider how best to align the IT organizational capabilities with the business, while keeping the integrity of the delivery groups. IT governance must also tackle the issues of ownership, accountability, and responsibility, to which management may be indifferent, to the frustration of the person trying to deliver a service.

Human resource planning ensures that tomorrow's skills and capabilities are available in the right place at the right time, while attending to the needs of today's staff. How to get the best out of the best is always a challenge, especially when there is more work assigned to fewer staff, constrained by available talent or financials. The key is to acquire, build, motivate, and retain critical and scarce skills. IT staff who possess these skills are vital for the company's success and should be treated as human investments, not just labor assets. The IT professional is sometimes treated as a necessary evil and often misunderstood. Talent attraction and recruitment should be focused on building core internal competencies, while utilizing outside contractors for noncore or supplementary resources. Motivating and retaining staff requires close attention to reward, recognition, development, and career planning, all essential tools to enable IT value. Ultimately, resource management becomes the biggest challenge, enabling a capability to meet demand and prioritizing against business benefits and organizational constraints.

Beyond skill development, organizational alignment, and competency centers, the IT executive needs to embrace and engage change management. As discussed earlier, IT investments will not realize their complete business value without significant complementary investments in organizational capital. Typically, new business-related IT investments require training and communication interventions, but in many cases they also require investment in job redesign to accommodate revised processes and accountabilities. Further, when business processes are impacted, procedure and possible policy changes are required. The level of stakeholder impact needs to be appropriately assessed, given any material change to business operations. New system and shared infrastructure investments must include change management, whether just for communication or training or for organizational design. Engaging change management experts earlier in the project scoping is essential to ensure comprehensive stakeholder consideration.

> Beyond the pursuit of organizational alignment and competency centers, the IT executive needs to be a master of internal and external partnerships and to embrace change management, enabling IT value through complementary investments in organizational capital.

The third degree of IT value network is concerned with IT value enabling, to ensure that IT and complementary investments are considered to meet enterprise capability and capacity requirements, managing constraints as necessary. Chapter 12 discusses the fourth degree, transitioning into IT value optimization, through project and system management.

CHAPTER 12

Fourth Degree of IT Value

The fourth degree of IT value network management is concerned with IT value optimization, with a focus on program and project management along with systems management. Optimizing the IT value from IT investments is the fundamental responsibility of the senior IT executives, through the delivery and support of cost-effective quality IT solutions. Chapter 2 highlighted lost value from poor project management practice. Project management should aim to optimize the value of planned IT solutions, delivering quality outcomes that achieve the business case. Systems management considers value optimization through the ongoing support and maintenance of system applications and shared infrastructure. Further, there is a significant interdependency between project execution and the supporting systems management capability and competence; inadequacies in the latter can seriously hinder the success of project delivery.

> The fourth degree of IT value network management is concerned with IT value optimization, with a focus on program and project management along with systems management, from which quality outcomes and cost-effective solutions are expected for stakeholder economic value.

Program and Project Management

Programs deliver strategic or operational initiatives, and projects deliver programs or initiatives in themselves, depending on size and complexity. Program and project management was discussed in Chapter 6 as a conventional planning technique for IT investment evaluation. Project management is expected to deliver quality outcomes, as defined by the business requirements, optimizing the deployment of company resources. The additional added value in applying project management is realized through risk

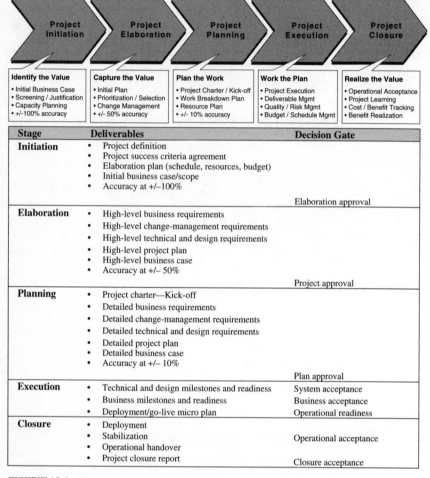

Project Initiation	Project Elaboration	Project Planning	Project Execution	Project Closure
Identify the Value	**Capture the Value**	**Plan the Work**	**Work the Plan**	**Realize the Value**
• Initial Business Case	• Initial Plan	• Project Charter / Kick-off	• Project Execution	• Operational Acceptance
• Screening / Justification	• Prioritization / Selection	• Work Breakdown Plan	• Deliverable Mgmt	• Project Learning
• Capacity Planning	• Change Management	• Resource Plan	• Quality / Risk Mgmt	• Cost / Benefit Tracking
• +/–100% accuracy	• +/- 50% accuracy	• +/- 10% accuracy	• Budget / Schedule Mgmt	• Benefit Realization

Stage	Deliverables	Decision Gate
Initiation	• Project definition • Project success criteria agreement • Elaboration plan (schedule, resources, budget) • Initial business case/scope • Accuracy at +/–100%	Elaboration approval
Elaboration	• High-level business requirements • High-level change-management requirements • High-level technical and design requirements • High-level project plan • High-level business case • Accuracy at +/– 50%	Project approval
Planning	• Project charter—Kick-off • Detailed business requirements • Detailed change-management requirements • Detailed technical and design requirements • Detailed project plan • Detailed business case • Accuracy at +/– 10%	Plan approval
Execution	• Technical and design milestones and readiness • Business milestones and readiness • Deployment/go-live micro plan	System acceptance Business acceptance Operational readiness
Closure	• Deployment • Stabilization • Operational handover • Project closure report	Operational acceptance Closure acceptance

EXHIBIT 12.1 Project Management Life Cycle

mitigation for flawless execution, within budget and schedule. Exhibit 12.1 portrays a project management life cycle, depicting five key stages.

1. **Project initiation.** This involves identifying the business value, through scoping the initial requirements and developing an initial cost/benefit or value-creation business case at +/−100 percent accuracy (stated as a financial contingency). Before significant organizational resources are committed to the project, an executive investment review board should screen the initial business case justification for validity and capacity to

execute. Typically, a project definition is submitted with the plan along with a predicted elaboration cost. A project success criteria agreement should be documented between the PMO and the executive sponsor to ensure project baseline metrics and to manage stakeholder expectations. The executive review board will reject, approve, or ask for further information at the elaboration approval decision gate.

2. **Project elaboration.** This involves capturing the business value, through a high-level business case and an initial project plan, at +/− 50 percent accuracy. Contingency on estimated costs should be reduced to a level within 50 percent. Business, technical, and change management requirements are produced, supporting the business case costs and benefits. The level of detail is a factor of elaboration time, resources, and cost. There is no point spending money on a project that during elaboration falls short on stakeholder economic value. Therefore, these documents are not detailed but should be sufficient to provide confidence for executive decision making, relative to other projects and the investment envelope or constraint. The executive review board will reject, approve, or ask for further information at the project approval decision gate.

3. **Project planning.** This involves planning the work through detailed project planning and a rigorous business case, at +/− 10 percent accuracy. Contingency is now down to 10 percent of total project costs. A project charter is produced to kick off the project, ensuring comprehensive stakeholder engagement and responsibilities. The project moves through detailed planning with appropriate due diligence on business, technical, and change management requirements, culminating in accurate costs for business case validation. The project plan is appropriately resourced, with a detailed work breakdown structure. The executive review board will reject, approve, or ask for further information at the plan approval decision gate.

4. **Project execution.** This involves working the plan through milestone delivery, managing scope, resources, budget, schedule, and risk. Technical or design milestones include modeling or system design, configuration or development, various testing steps, infrastructure, and implementation. Business milestones include business process redesign, policy and procedures, deployment readiness, and change management, including communication, training, and organizational design. Decision gates occur at technical system acceptance, business acceptance, and finally at deployment or operational readiness. Project change management is administered for scope, budget, and timeline changes. The investment review board should review project milestones against the project success criteria on a regular basis. A dashboard will aid the investment review board in making sound decisions across the

portfolio and in deciding whether to cancel, accelerate, deaccelerate, descope, delay, or continue as is with project execution.

5. **Project closure.** This involves realizing the value, through project delivery and postproject cost/benefit tracking. On deployment and after system stabilization, the project moves to closure and the end product is handed over to operations or production support. The operational acceptance decision gate formalizes the completion of deployment and stabilization. The project is formally closed at the closure acceptance gate. The project success criteria are reviewed for completion, and learning is captured for continued PMO best practice. The business owner or sponsor now owns the deliverables or end product and should be held accountable for benefit realization, as tracked against reset annual budgets. Subsequently, portfolio reviews should be conducted quarterly or annually to track realization of the benefits.

Programs and projects often fail because of the challenges of identifying the right measures and subsequently collecting and analyzing the right data. Chapter 6 discussed the importance of defining project-critical success factors, setting appropriate stakeholder expectations, and managing against agreed metrics. Resources and time are required for evaluation, but the effort will pay back several-fold in stakeholder economic value. Business, technical, and process measures are needed to evaluate a program and project. Through the governance of the business project management office (BPMO), IT programs and projects should be managed against critical success factors or multidimensional measures. These include:

- Cost/benefit value capture, as defined in the business case
- Achieving the business specifications, as defined in the business requirements document
- Ensuring that the organization is ready to adopt change, as defined by the change management document
- Delivering to quality technical specifications, as defined by the technical requirements document
- Project management to PMO best practice methodology and processes
- Achieving milestone deliverables and quality assurance
- Mitigating risk, whether project specific or related to business operational impact
- On time or schedule
- On budget or investment
- Resource and team management
- Accurate communications and reporting
- Stakeholder expectations and satisfaction

It's important to define relevant and measurable project success criteria, aligning team members and optimizing resources as tracked during project stages. The measures should be sensitive to the different stakeholder perspectives, given that criteria weighting or priorities will vary. Advanced approaches to IT project management are related to understanding and assessing the risk of a project. For example, adopting the Childs and Triantis framework for R&D spending, a firm can forecast expected IT spending through time for an optimally executed IT project. In applying the risk model, a firm can decide whether to accelerate, shelve, or abandon projects, providing investment flexibility.[1] Through sequential investment, collateral learning from one project can prevent the need to invest in another project. There is a constant need to assess current project performance and new project opportunities. The IT value index and the IT value portfolio, as discussed in Chapter 5, aid investment decision making and investment performance, providing the BPMO with tools for comparing project returns.

> For project success, it's important to define relevant and measurable project success criteria up front, aligning team members, optimizing resources, and managing stakeholder expectations.

System Management

Systems management considers value optimization in the ongoing support and maintenance of system applications and shared infrastructure. Enterprise system management holistically considers the relationship and dependencies of all IT investments in support of business operations. Through best practices, the following should be optimized for effective IT value delivery:

- **Asset management.** An inventory of hardware and software assets is performed, providing a complete view of the embedded IT base. The inventory should profile each asset, identifying the stage in the technology life cycle—current, mature, or end of life cycle. The total cost of ownership (TCO) should be stated, including initial capital cost, depreciation, residual value, and support costs. Supplementary or complementary investments or costs should be included, such as power consumption, potential business downtime, and ongoing training requirements. The intent is to cost-optimize the asset base, projecting necessary future refresh or replacement investments.
- **Performance management.** This involves viewing system and shared infrastructure performance from an operational and business

perspective. IT operational performance can be benchmarked for productivity, considering processing statistics or cost-based assessment (e.g., IT cost per employee or IT costs per sales revenue). Business transaction management is relatively new, but it represents a potential approach to determine business performance. Aligned to business processes, transactions can be measured for speed to execution, availability, scalable volume, and accuracy. User activities can be monitored, providing insights for system improvements. Ultimately, service level agreements (SLAs) manage performance expectations and performance.

- **Application management.** This focuses on system administration, problem management, and controls. Application administrators provide necessary access privileges, job scheduling, and operational routines for day-to-day production management. Problem management identifies underlying causes of application incidents and issues. Control management includes version control, release management, and change control. Rigorous application change management controls should ensure that new functionality, new patches, or new versions are safely migrated or released into the production environment, minimizing business downtime. License agreements should be monitored for user and server limitations and relevance across multiple incidences. Application performance management should consider business expectations that focus on availability, responsiveness, and capability.
- **System development life cycle (SDLC).** Whether to buy or build is always a dilemma. Vanilla or off-the-shelf software is now providing more and more capability and agility, based on industry best practice. Commercial developments have significantly evolved and are providing flexibility in configuration to business processes, minimizing the need for customization. When a unique business operation provides a competitive advantage, there is often good reason to develop applications or unique point solutions to what would seem a standard problem. Although building from scratch has its risks, it can be mitigated by a sound SDLC approach, whether applying a standard waterfall approach or a rapid application development (RAD) method.
- **Data center and computing management.** This includes fault detection and resolution, capacity management, and utilization monitoring from the desktop clients to the back-office servers. Client management includes the desktop and laptop environments, from image control and office productivity tools to the help desk. Concurrently, server management considers application and data computing horsepower. Storage management specifically considers data servers, including backup and restore procedures. Server availability monitoring and metrics provide visibility for proactive response to points of contention or failure. Overall data center management includes the application and data servers

as well as environmental conditions such as power, space, security, and recovery capability.

- **Network management.** This includes fault detection and resolution, capacity management, and utilization monitoring of the telecommunication voice and data network. The open systems interconnection (OSI) systems management overview (SMO) provides the FCAPS standards for network management, referencing, as follows:
  - **Fault management.** Detecting, isolating, and correcting malfunctions within the telecommunications network
  - **Configuration management.** Network settings, version control, and scalability
  - **Accounting management.** Financial monitoring and transaction or usage billing
  - **Performance management.** Node or component monitoring and delivery of service level agreements
  - **Security management.** Regulatory compliance, network vulnerability, identity, access, and risk mitigation strategies
- **Security management.** In a broad sense, this encompasses the protection of assets, information, people, and the organization. Policy, procedures, directives, guidelines, and standards are applied to mitigate risk of threats or vulnerabilities. The information security mandate is to secure the data, retaining confidentiality, integrity, and availability. Increasing data losses are rapidly driving security protection inward, from the network perimeter, through application access, to database encryption. Protection of the crown jewels requires many defense systems, down to the final security level of the data itself.
- **Vendor management.** This is often overlooked, but it should include both contractual and relationship management aspects. Within the business network, vendors can become partners, providing incremental value exchanges. Managing service level agreements against contracts is a must, but managing the relationship based on strategic intent is desirable. Flexibility and complementary capability provides agility to respond to changing business and market conditions. Outsourcing arrangements raise the ante, as vendor dependency increases within the firm's value chain. With the popularization of managed services, hosting, and application service provisioning, vendor management becomes a primary necessity for value management.
- **Business continuity and recovery.** This involves planning and rehearsing for business-impacting disasters. Business continuity planning is a primary business process function, dealing with replacement or backup of business practice, as required. Disaster recovery is typically associated with IT system and shared infrastructure backup and recovery procedures and capability. The biggest challenge to most IT

organizations is the cost of hot backup and production replication. Essentially, duplicating production environments in recovery sites or data centers can double the associated IT bill. Thus, many firms balance risk and cost, locating their development/QA environments in a location separate from their production environment, providing some recovery capability.

Enterprise system management holistically considers the interrelationship and dependencies of all IT assets, optimizing lights-on operations, which also enables optimal project delivery.

The fourth degree of IT value network management is concerned with IT value optimization, ensuring effective project management and systems management processes and competencies. Chapter 13 discusses the fifth degree, transitioning between IT value optimization and IT value realization, through service management and information management.

Fifth Degree of IT Value

The fifth degree of IT value network management is concerned with the transition from IT value optimization to IT value realization, with a focus on service management and information management. Business stakeholders are more interested in what services IT can deliver or processes it can support, as opposed to the underlying system applications or infrastructure capability. Further, these services and processes provide information and knowledge in a collaborative network, driving stakeholder economic value. In Chapter 1, information on demand and real-time business intelligence were highlighted as key IT investment trends and drivers of intellectual capital; lost intangible value was also discussed in Chapter 2. Business value realization starts to materialize when service level agreements are met, projects deliver on the business case, business solutions are delivered to business requirements, and information is liberated for improved decision making.

> The fifth degree of IT value network management is concerned with the transition from IT value optimization to IT value realization, with a focus on service management and information management; this is where stakeholder economic value materializes through business solutions, service delivery, and liberated information for intellectual capital across the business or value network.

Service Management

As we transition from value optimization to value realization, we turn our attention to service management. The firm's operational capability can be described as the sum of its processes and stakeholder services. Therefore, optimizing IT value is derived from enhanced service and processes, providing business solutions throughout the firm's value system, including customers, suppliers, and partners. Customer relationship management (CRM) or supply chain management (SCM) should be considered as process and service solutions and not categorized as enterprise resource planning (ERP) applications.

The information technology infrastructure library (ITIL) is a customizable framework of best practices for the provisioning and management of IT services. Driven by quality and process improvement, the U.K. Office of Government Commerce (OGC) defined and developed the ITIL framework, which has been internationally popularized since the late 1990s. In June 2007, the ITIL guidelines were refreshed. ITIL v3.0 considers an integrated service life cycle approach to service management, as opposed to its predecessor v2.0, which was organized around processes for IT service delivery and support.[1] ITIL v3.0, service management practices initially includes five core text volumes:

1. **Service strategy.** Focused on marketing opportunities for service design in meeting internal and external customer requirements. Critical areas considered in this text include service portfolio management and financial justification.
2. **Service design.** Based on strategic direction. Services and supporting processes are designed. Critical areas considered in this text include capacity management, availability management, continuity management, and security management.
3. **Service transition.** Implementation of new or modified services into production. Critical areas considered in this text include configuration management, release management, change management, and service knowledge management.
4. **Service operation.** Activities required to operate and maintain or support services, as defined by internal and external customer service level agreements. Critical areas considered in this text include request or demand fulfillment, incident management, problem management, and event management. The latter is a new process addition to ITIL v2.0; it covers managing information-related matters (logs), warnings (alerts), and critical events (trigger incidents).
5. **Continual service improvement.** Focused on the quality of service through the process of continual improvement. Critical areas considered in this text include service measurement, service level management, and service reporting.

ITIL v3.0 provides guidance on how to optimize and realize the business value of services, focusing on ROI and financial justification. The intent is that firms will mature in process improvement, thereby reducing costs of service provisioning and support and improving quality and business value, thus ultimately optimizing realizable IT value. Targeted improved performance will be achieved as required by the various internal and external customer service level agreements (SLAs).

Transitioning from an IT system to a stakeholder service culture requires a service mentality, changing the way the IT organization delivers valued business capability and solutions. IT executives need to embed and institutionalize a service mentality across the IT organization. Service management processes must be defined and implemented. Services should be designed within a service catalog based on the service strategy, providing stakeholders with a visible and meaningful shopping list. A service catalog defines generic and unique service components that support the overall business and are then packaged according to specific internal or external customer requirements, building solution sets with corresponding SLAs. Packaged or bundled services are deployed effectively in the telecommunications industry, where consumers can benefit from higher-value propositions in signing up for mobile phone, land-line phone, Internet, desktop computing, and entertainment services. See Exhibit 13.1 for a service catalog design example. An SLA is defined for a power consumer, identifying three packaged service categories: telecommunications, computing, and entertainment. Services are also tightly coupled with processes, whereby the service is often the process itself (i.e., help desk) and whereby quality outputs are the measures of performance. Process playbooks can be useful supporting documents, defining customer processes, procedures, and required services.

The service catalog could include the following attributes for each service component:

Initial—index

1. Service category
2. Service description

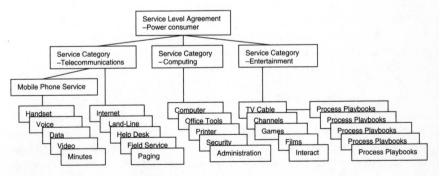

EXHIBIT 13.1 Service Catalog Design

3. Service owner
4. Customer or client segment
5. SLA reference
6. Process playbook reference

Secondary—body

1. Measures
2. Performance
3. Utilization, frequency, or timing
4. Costs or resources
5. Delivery channel
6. Evoking service

The objective of an SLA is to manage and maintain the quality of services delivered to an internal or external customer. This is achieved through a continuous cycle of agreeing, monitoring, and reporting on service level performance. Managing customer expectations is critical throughout the process, in which continuous communication is required to ensure awareness and understanding. When service levels are applied internally, the process is no different from an external service. However, a number of elements are usually excluded from the agreement—specifically warranties, remedies, intellectual property, legal compliance, confidentiality information, security, and possibly compensation. This does not negate the importance of due consideration.

Building an IT organizational service culture also requires the design and implementation of a service-oriented architecture (SOA), enabling the underlying system and shared infrastructure to liberate valued services. As discussed in Chapter 1, in designing a SOA, there can be considerable debate as to whether to drive an enterprise-wide initiative based on standard business processes and data schematics or to employ a more bottom-up approach focused on specific system integration challenges. Perhaps the compromise is to meet in the middle, focusing on an enterprise service bus (ESB), with attention to service definitions, integration, quality of service, SLAs, security, message processing, modeling, communication, ESB management, and infrastructure intelligence.

Based on an SOA, Web services are becoming increasingly popular, breaking complex systems into reusable service components that provide business value and are considered a business priority. In addition, Web services are task specific or process centric, stateless or independent, loosely coupled but having a stable interface, coarsely grained or infrastructure friendly, all of which are distributed across multiple tenants and consumers. The challenge is to separate core legacy functionality across multiple tenants or systems to create a service interface that can be reused across multiple platforms. Thus, intermediary or aggregate services become important interfaces to basic business logic or data Web services. Basic services can be wrapped together with legacy functionality and other Web services or service interfaces. The death of large, monolithic ERP applications could well be insight, given the advent of managed service providers (MSP) and an IT service-oriented culture.

> Transitioning IT from a technology to a stakeholder service culture optimizes stakeholder economic value, but necessitates a fundamental change in the IT organization; it requires building a service mentality, implementing service management processes, and considering a service-oriented architecture (SOA).

Information Management

Data is typically underutilized, possessing latent potential; often, it is not transformed into information or knowledge creation. Intangible assets, generated by IT, can provide an explanation for excess returns, producing higher market valuation. But the tools for managing and measuring intangible value and intellectual capital have not kept up with the vision to create value. Better information behaviors will lead to optimized business performance, realizing measurable intellectual capital and valued intangible assets. Exhibit 13.2 shows the building blocks required for business or value network intellectual capital.

The business network intellectual capital is the accumulative stakeholder intellectual capital derived within the enterprise sphere of influence. This capital increases the firm's market value through appreciated intangible assets, yielding measurable intellectual rights or property; thus, a principal driver for stakeholder economic value. Venture capitalists continue to demonstrate the importance of intellectual capital, valuing firms at multiples much higher than the underlying tangible asset base would support. This was particularly prevalent in the dot-com boom during the mid- to late 1990s. However, with the exception of research and development and acquisition accounting, intellectual capital rarely appears on the firm's books. Subsequently, an unexplained disparity materializes between the firm's market value and its book value, and that disparity leads to speculative valuation or market behavior. Ultimately, intangible value is discounted, lost, or not accounted for, which can negatively affect a firm's decision making with regard to IT investment and business value.

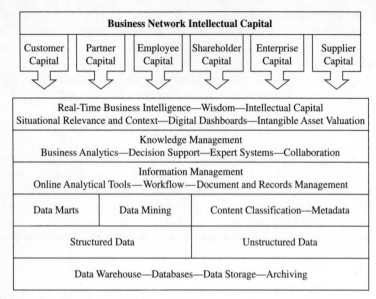

EXHIBIT 13.2 Business or Value Network Intellectual Capital—Building Blocks

Information management in the broad sense is the catalyst for intellectual capital and is essentially the key transformational path from latent and fragmented structured and unstructured data, providing an enterprise integrated view of potential business value. Yet many firms have failed to master an integrated enterprise approach to information management. This is ironic, given that the first letter in IT as well as the second letter in CIO is indeed "I" for information. The challenge begins when, as in most companies, no one seems to own the data. Process owners exist, system or technology owners exist, but no data owners exist. Falling between the divide, data becomes invisible and lost in databases. Although the IT organization should be the custodian of data standards and fundamental data management technology, the business process owner needs to step up and own the data itself. By commanding a better understanding of data flows and work flows, the business owner can effectively align data to process and subsequently optimize. Data mining, domain-specific data marts, and online analytical tools provide the means to effectively organize structured data; while content classification (using metadata) and document and records management improves the usability of unstructured data.

Managing information has become far more complex, requiring a rigorous process for capturing, organizing, maintaining, storing, retrieving, and archiving structured and unstructured data or content. The increasing growth of digitalized information flying around the network brings a need to be more discerning. Knowledge management was introduced as a discipline in the mid-1990s, providing a methodology to align information to organizational goals. Understanding the knowledge required to achieve stated goals (e.g., performance improvement, customer loyalty, or organizational learning) implies the need to determine what we know and how we know it, as well as what we are missing. Asking the right questions involves identifying the right information to build knowledge for action. Applying business analytics, decision support, expert systems, and effective collaboration methods and tools enables meaningful filtering and synthesis for effective decision making. Further, knowledge transfer is critical in enabling timely decision making, ensuring that the right person has the right information at the right time. Knowledge mapping across the business network is discussed in Chapter 19.

Real-time business intelligence requires applying enterprise knowledge to a given time-sensitive situation. Digital dashboards provide real-time views of business metrics as events occur. Just-in-time information, or knowledge at a point in time, requires real-time access and collaboration across the business network. Network value analysis is discussed in Chapter 19, which explores stakeholder relationships, collaboration, and value exchanges. In the context of IT value network management, the key is to convert the intangible knowledge asset to measurable intellectual capital and stakeholder economic value. Such conversion is clearly evident in subscription services, where fees are paid for knowledge and information. Online search tools, research agencies, forums, bulletin boards, and aggregated or domain sites all provide valuable stakeholder services, which generate revenue. Educational services are further examples of real-time knowledge, providing just-in-time certifications or content with situational relevance. Conversely, consider the likely eventual death of the printed newspaper, outdated and obsolete at the time of publishing, thus diminished in value.

Ultimately, the premium over and above the cost of knowledge that the stakeholders are willing to pay is the value of intellectual capital. This is evident in the premium price for a service provider that a firm is willing to pay, where the provider is perceived to have a higher level of knowledge or implementation experience than rivals. Similarly, this is the reason a firm will pay more for shared infrastructure flexibility or for applications that have a high degree of configuration options. The embedded knowledge or capability of interoperability, integration complexity, ubiquitous standards, or best practice commands a premium value. IT organizations that have institutionalized best practice, implemented evergreen technologies, or provided agile platforms for changing business needs increase intangible value and, accordingly, stakeholder intellectual capital. Calculating the intangible asset relies on stakeholder values and measures around future options, similar to those found in the financial futures markets. Embedding the value into the business case was discussed in Part II, with respect to the value-creation business case and real options. Value options are discussed further in Chapter 19.

> The tools for managing and measuring intellectual capital and liberating latent data have not kept up with the vision to create value; intangible assets, generated by information management and business intelligence, can provide an explanation for a company's excess returns, producing higher market valuation.

The fifth degree of IT value network management is concerned with the transition from IT value optimization to IT value realization, driving stakeholder economic value through service management and information management. Chapter 14 discusses the sixth degree of IT value—networked value management for realized IT value.

Sixth Degree of IT Value

The sixth and final degree of IT value network management is concerned with IT value realization through network value management. Value realization is most evident when IT returns are booked on the company ledgers or budgets are reset to accommodate benefits. Audited value becomes the final proof point, providing independent validation of realized booked IT value. However, shareholders continually evaluate IT performance and value, especially as IT investment takes time to transform onto the books and to market share price, as discussed in Chapter 2. Network value management is a continual process to identify and realize stakeholder economic value, through managing business-critical success factors, satisfaction, and expectations.

> The sixth and final degree of IT value network management is concerned with IT value realization, through network value management; in additional to booked returns, stakeholder economic value is gained through managing business-critical success factors, satisfaction, and expectations.

Networked Value Management

The value-creation business case, as discussed in Chapter 5, is instrumental in defining where the value will be captured and subsequently realized. However, IT value can take time to materialize and may require transformational approaches—for example, the benefit realization model, discussed in Chapter 2. Subsequently, IT executives need to manage stakeholder expectations and continually realize value in the eyes of the beholder; hence, the need to provide stakeholder economic value in the shorter term.

Stakeholders formally and informally evaluate IT performance against expected returns, service level agreements, business solutions, project delivery, operational capability, availability, flexibility, and—if nothing else—perceived value at points in time. Therefore, the IT executive needs to continually assess the IT shared infrastructure, systems, services, and strategic investments; effectively measuring and communicating IT impact on the business network stakeholders is essential. Part II discussed numerous measures and techniques to evaluate IT investments, including surveys. To understand expectations and perceived stakeholder economic value, it is wise to continually perform internal and external stakeholder satisfaction surveys and to organize focus groups to identify areas of improvement as well as areas of delight, thereby improving performance through a process of discovery and alignment. Performance measures for both tangible and intangible values need to be supported by key stakeholders and be sustainable. In fact, perceived stakeholder value is real value, which needs to be captured up-front and delivered at points in time. Chapter 19 explores stakeholder value expectations and perceptions in more detail.

The art of surveying requires understanding the stakeholder landscape—or, in other words, the business or value network. Chapter 19 also explores value network analysis for identifying members and relationships. Networked value management builds on network value analysis to define member "loyalty" or satisfaction drivers. Aligning to the firm's strategic goals and key performance indicators (KPIs), the balanced scorecard cascades business objectives down the organization, defining functional critical success factors (CSF). Satisfaction business drivers can be extrapolated and subsequently validated through focus groups and surveys; IT investment is evaluated against these drivers, measuring perceptions of satisfaction and value. In addition, external stakeholders should be engaged in a similar "light" process to establish satisfaction drivers within the business network. Extending the reach across the business network provides a line of sight to perceptions of value from key stakeholder groups, like customers, suppliers, partners, and even the board. Thus the full potential of IT investment is captured and managed to realization. Network value management is essentially a value loyalty business model for IT investment. Building loyalty drives realizable value.

Network value management is a continual process to identify and realize the stakeholder satisfaction drivers and expectations. Stakeholders should be categorized by common business drivers, considering external members (i.e., supplier, partner, customer segments, shareholders) and internal functions (i.e., sales, marketing, finance) or by organization level (i.e., executives, management, employees). Focus groups and supporting surveys determine the IT investment baseline performance, measuring satisfaction and perceived value. Stakeholders are informed of baseline performance and mutually agreed on targeted actions and improvements. Continuous performance review and stakeholder communication should be conducted, deploying timely surveys and follow-up briefings as appropriate. The intent is not to survey to death, especially as surveys will be used by other functions or groups, but to target value opportunities and dissatisfiers. Surveys should be valued by the stakeholder as meaningful and purposeful, in which responses are acknowledged and actionable. Firms could consider a hierarchy of targeted surveys and focus groups, potentially including:

External focus

- An annual board focus group to capture and realize board IT value
- An annual shareholder focus group to capture and realize shareholder IT value
- An annual customer focus group to capture and realize customer relationship satisfaction and IT value
- An annual supplier or vendor focus group to capture and realize supply chain and operations satisfaction and IT value
- An annual partner focus group to capture and realize partner satisfaction and IT value
- An annual industry focus group to capture and realize benchmarking, best practice and IT value

Internal focus

- An annual executive survey or focus group to capture and realize IT strategic alignment and value
- An annual functional survey or focus group to capture and realize IT operational capability and value
- A quarterly employee survey or an event-based service or help desk survey to capture and realize IT service satisfaction
- A project closure survey to capture and realize IT project management satisfaction and value

Stakeholder satisfaction is a state of mind at a particular point in time; therefore, due care is required in the interpretation of responses and quantitative methods should be applied for evaluation rigor. Satisfaction responses can be misleading if underlying expectations or perceptions of value are not well understood. Average performance can generate a high satisfaction rating if expectations are low or a low satisfaction rating if perceptions of value are high. Further, the timing of focus groups or surveys is critical, as stakeholder responses will reflect more recent events or experiences in relation to prior expectations. Therefore, conducting surveys at annual events or after major events (i.e., strategic review) may provide a more balanced perspective.

The design of the survey and supporting communication should support the context and assessment period. Online survey capability has significantly advanced, providing an effective means to build, administer, and analyze responses. Stakeholder survey feedback can be consolidated on a digital scorecard, supported by business analytics, providing IT investment predictive or directional views, thus capturing IT investment opportunities as well as IT value realization.

The circle of satisfaction argues that investment in employees will drive employee satisfaction, which in turn will drive customer satisfaction through service quality. IT investment must be maintained in staff training, development, career progression, reward, and recognition. A corporate or IT service culture should be promoted. This is to ensure that staff are motivated and competent in meeting stakeholder expectations, driving satisfaction, and maintaining value loyalty. As discussed previously, a service catalog is a useful tool to measure and communicate service value. Remember, there are always alternatives. If the internal IT shop does not deliver to stakeholder expectations or deliver value, external IT service providers or outsourcing could be considered—or, in the worst case, an alternative CIO. Adapted from the net promoter concept, the ultimate stakeholder question could be: "How likely is it that you would recommend our IT to a friend or colleague?"[1]

IT value loyalty cannot be managed just by focus groups and surveys; the underlying or true expectations and perceptions need to be uncovered through building strong partnership relationships. The network value management process includes the alignment of IT executives to business executives to foster strong partnership relationships. Aligning executives typically follows functional domains—that is, IT application/system owners are paired with functional process owners and external vendors, or IT service owners are paired with business operations owners and external service providers. The CIO will be aligned to the CEO and senior executives, both within and external to the firm, including board members.

Strong partnerships will be based on trust, where IT executives will need to manage expectations and pursue effective communications with paired business stakeholders. The remit should include clear accountabilities around network value management, with regular updates on IT investment performance and value realization. Specifically this involves balanced scorecard, SLA(s), satisfaction rating, project management performance, information management and dashboards, capability evaluation, and financial (cost/benefit) statements. Essentially the IT executive becomes an account manager for each stakeholder relationship, facilitating IT and business decisions to achieve stakeholder economic value. IT value loyalty goes beyond traditional concepts of internal customer and employee satisfaction; it calls for reaching out over the business network to capture and realize value from suppliers, partners, end customers, shareholders, and the board of directors.

> Networked value management goes beyond internal IT satisfaction surveys; it requires building IT value loyalty and trust over the business network, continually delivering stakeholder value in parallel with material benefit realization on the books.

The sixth and final degree of IT value network management is concerned with IT value realization through networked value management. Part IV applies the IT value network best practice. Actual client engagements are discussed, identifying company challenges, the IT value network solution, and stakeholder economic value impact.

PART IV

IT Value Network Clients—Did IT, Got IT

B etween 1997 and 2009, the IT value network framework and approach has been successfully applied to many Read & Associates clients across the Americas and Europe. The IT value network management and measurement techniques and models have been tuned and enhanced during this period, accommodating lessons learned and changing times. The IT value network has been deployed during the highs of the Internet boom, the lows of the Internet crash, and, currently, during the challenges of a recession and banking crisis. New approaches to measuring and managing IT investment, beyond traditional financial and conventional planning techniques, are more applicable for realizing IT value in today's environment than ever before. Organizations need a new kind of IT investment management system, built to maximize stakeholder economic value over the business or value network, delivering both hard dollars and intellectual capital. Part IV reviews the IT value network practice as applied to four client cases, drawing on methods and models discussed in Part II and Part III.

IT value network has been deployed, improving stakeholder economic value within the following four clients:

- **NA Bank (anonymous).** Result—improved IT value capture through the second degree of IT value: IT strategic planning and portfolio management. The IT strategy was aligned to the business priorities and IT investments were subsequently redirected for higher strategic value.
- **Nortel Networks (Nortel).** Result—IT value enabling, through the third and second degree of IT value: IT reorganization and IT strategic planning. Improved IT capability and alignment was provided to enable the new "Webtone" (data and voice convergence) company direction, to make a "right-hand turn."

- **Indigo Books and Music (Indigo).** Result—IT value optimization, through the fourth and second degree of IT value: establishing a project management office and portfolio management. A PMO (project management office) was built to improve the success of project governance, execution, and delivery.
- **NA Credit Union (anonymous).** Result—IT value realization, through all six degrees of IT value, cycling IT value network management twice. A bank integration and banking system conversion from a merger of two credit unions was successfully completed.

Each client case study will consider the company challenge, the IT value network solution, and its subsequent impact on stakeholder economic value. Networked value management, the sixth degree of IT value, was also applied to all clients to achieve initial or baseline satisfaction and value and was subsequently employed to determine the impact of new IT value network practice. Benefit realization materialized in the case of all four clients.

CHAPTER 15

NA Bank

The NA Bank case study is in two parts, based on client engagement during 2002 to 2003. The first part was covered in Chapter 3, outlining early-2002 IT investment valuation observations. Subsequently, this chapter discusses applying the practice and impact of the IT value network value measurement and management implementation. Actual data has been modified to protect confidentiality, but it retains its integrity in support of the applied practice.

NA Bank is one of the largest, full-service financial institutions in North America, with 2007 revenues in excess of $6 billion and a growth of 50 percent since the IT investment study was completed four years earlier. The bank has over 20,000 employees primarily based in North America, but with some presence internationally in Europe and Asia, serving over 6 million customers.

Challenge: Strategic IT Investment Alignment

Following the 2001 Internet crash and the subsequent economic downturn, NA Bank's 2002 return on equity was underperforming. In addition, NA Bank's efficiency ratio (noninterest expense over sales) was over 70 percent. This is considered high within the banking industry. NA bank declared to the stakeholders that the overall financial performance was unacceptable and changes were necessary.

Total annualized IT spending, in excess of $600 million, was allocated across the business units and at the corporate level. IT spending was a key influence on the efficiency ratio. Despite this high level of expenditure, there was no evidence that the business value of IT investments was fully determined. Key stakeholders were starting to question the IT value. NA Bank's CIO was also concerned that the IT spending or investment was not effectively aligned to the bank's strategic direction.

NA Bank was underperforming, with noninterest expenses over sales (efficiency ratio) exceeding 70 percent; changes were required. IT was a large expenditure with undetermined value, requiring more effective alignment to the bank's strategic direction.

Solution: The IT Value Network

With no baseline stakeholder satisfaction ratings or value metrics in place and lacking an IT investment portfolio view, NA Bank commissioned Read & Associates in March 2002 to conduct an extensive strategic IT investment assessment, which consisted of the following elements.

Networked Value Management: Sixth Degree of IT Value—Stakeholder Baseline Satisfaction Assessment

The initial approach was to baseline IT stakeholder satisfaction and perceived value to provide directional IT performance improvements. The following actions were completed in the spring of 2002:

- An IT executive survey was conducted to establish an IT baseline of perceived business satisfaction and value. The survey was administered by an independent party to preserve anonymity. One hundred and fourteen responses to the survey were completed, producing a 44 percent response rate from an executive target population of 260. Follow-up executive interviews were conducted to gain further insights.
- Project surveys were conducted to derive the baseline level of satisfaction with strategic IT projects and project management. Strategic IT projects were defined consistently with this study. Twenty-nine completed projects were surveyed, and 116 surveys were completed from different stakeholder perspectives. Subsequently, project closure briefings were conducted to provide additional insights.

Strategic Plan and Portfolio Management: Second Degree of IT Value—Portfolio Management Assessment

The current-state IT investment portfolio was assessed at the end of 2002, and the future-state portfolio was projected for 2003. The following activities were conducted:

- An assessment of NA Bank's IT investment decision-making process; a questionnaire was conducted between September and November 2002.

The survey respondents included seven executives representing the business, IT, and finance functions. Each executive was selected based on his or her decision-making roles with regard to managing the IT investment management process.

- A financial portfolio analysis of the bank's total IT investments from 2001 to 2003 was conducted, with a focus on retail banking and to some extent on individual wealth management. Retail banking included the following business interests: retail branches, Internet banking, and commercial banking.

The IT Value Network: Summary Findings Reported to Senior Executives

Based on the executive IT satisfaction and value feedback, project surveys, and IT portfolio analysis, the following findings were reported to senior executives.

THERE WAS NO IT STRATEGIC PLAN AND ENTERPRISE INVESTMENT PORTFOLIO VIEW TO DRIVE ENTERPRISE SHAREHOLDER VALUE IT investments tended to be tactical, supporting the business unit objectives. Individual business strategies were accommodated within the IT operational plan. There was no enterprise-level strategic planning process. An annualized cost budgeting process, a capital (project) budgeting process, and annual business unit demands or defined critical success factors determined the IT operating plan. The broader strategic planning process was business unit specific; IT was an afterthought for budgeting completeness. IT planning was therefore more tactical, focused on "better service at lower costs," driven by four operational business drivers: cost savings, control management, quality service, and delivering business unit needs. The IT organization was operationally focused, driving at cost reduction and service excellence. IT strategic planning is a central theme in conventional IT evaluation—aligning IT investments to strategic business objectives. The need for an integrated IT-business strategy was viewed as a high priority. Tighter alignment between the business drivers and IT investment, overall IT portfolio, and related measures were all deemed necessary.

IT investments were evaluated at the project level, and not as a complete portfolio for optimal bank-wide value. NA Bank had an informal, corporate project review board focused on individual business unit project performance, but there was no overall IT investment management or portfolio management. A business unit "bottom-up" approach defined strategic projects, which had to work within a "top-down" enterprise investment envelope (capacity based). Here, the pace of investment was subsequently managed. The ability to execute change and other organizational constraints was taken into consideration, in addition to external mandatory compliance requirements. The focus was on individual project review. NA Bank had various business and IT project management offices and recognized that it needed to consolidate. IT investment realization requires a business program management office (BPMO). This office should be accountable for project and investment performance measurement. A PMO establishes standards for reporting on business programs and IT projects, conducts performance reviews, collates the IT investment portfolio maps, completes investment and competitive benchmarks, tracks the value realization, and advises the corporate investment committee.

INSUFFICIENT FUNDS WERE SPENT ON STRATEGIC IT INVESTMENTS, DUE TO OPERATIONAL INVESTMENT LEVEL AND QUESTIONABLE VALUE During 2001 to 2002, IT spending was biased toward transactional or operational investments, which significantly exceeded industry benchmarks. NA Bank IT spending was classified according to Weill and Broadbent's IT portfolio. Based on 2001 and 2002 data, NA Bank appeared to be spending significantly more than the industry norm on bank transactional technology in support of bank operations (37 percent of total IT compared to an industry norm of 13 percent). Furthermore, despite the high overall spending, NA Bank could possibly be underinvesting in strategic IT investments (overall, 4 percent of total IT, compared to an industry norm of 13 percent). The data reinforced the finding that the IT organization was heavily focused on operational matters. Competitive benchmarking would likely indicate that base technology operational spending was uncompetitive, consuming higher levels at the expense of strategic and informational investment.

IT investments were mostly focused on noncustomer-facing processes. The study found that there was no reference or significant IT investment in customer enabling initiatives such as CRM in support (or alignment) of the retail and individual wealth customer-centric strategy. Historically, banks have driven a top-line focus on revenue growth, as opposed to a bottom-line efficiency focus. In an economic downturn, NA Bank's focus reflected cost concerns; however, this focus subsequently exposed misalignment of IT investment with the retail banking strategic direction. This would have a material impact on longer-term revenue growth and shareholder returns, especially as NA Bank was redirecting energy away from the wholesale and institutional business to the retail and individual wealth-management businesses.

Strategic IT investment value realization was incomplete and not audited subsequent to project delivery. Without demonstrable benefit realization, strategic investment justification is challenged, diverting investments to shorter-term operational opportunities. Investment value realization requires the measurement and tracking of projects throughout their life cycle as well as for several years after project completion, capturing the total investment value. NA Bank conducted only a six-month project postmortem, and the complete investment value was never determined over the subsequent years of value creation. Investment returns were not audited. Between 2001 and 2002, 91 strategic IT projects were completed bank-wide. Almost 40 percent of the strategic IT projects took over three years to complete, committing 50 percent of the total investment. Overall, a significant number of projects and levels of investment were exposed to uncertainty and risk over the three-year lifespan, threatening project success, value capture, and returns. The three-year duration also suggests a significant delay in deriving returns. By applying a more rigorous value realization process, NA Bank would become fully aware of the contribution of strategic IT investments. The bank could then apply learning and benefit realization to the justification of new investments.

STRATEGIC IT INVESTMENT BUSINESS CASE METRICS AND PERFORMANCE MEASUREMENTS WERE INADEQUATE IT investment business case or ROI models were inadequate and inconsistent. Executive feedback cited the necessity of improved basic business measures. NA Bank's principal investment justification was based on business cases using traditional accounting and financial measures—specifically, ROI, NPV, IRR, DCF, and payback period. These measures were mandatory for project investments exceeding $500,000 and were selectively used (optional) for projects with a lesser value. Sources of tangible value (intangible value was not included) were identified, and best efforts were used to measure these benefits. However, business cases lacked rigor and projected questionable long-term benefits. More advanced IT value network measurements—for example, stock price traits, portfolio management, scenario planning, benchmarking, and decision support systems (real options)—were not used. These techniques received a high level of interest in the potential application, but improved basic measures were deemed of greater importance. See Exhibit 15.1, NA Bank IT strategic investment value assessment.

Risk reduction in strategic IT investments and project execution were deemed necessary. NA Bank recognized that it needed improved risk management for IT investments and project delivery. Typically, strategic IT projects had a life span of three years, with outcome uncertainty. Traditional application of DCF is more appropriate for operational or transactional IT investments than for strategic investments. Investing for growth options rather than cash streams is an important factor for justifying strategic IT investment. Real options methods can incorporate risk management metrics within traditional financial measures, thereby, accounting for uncertainty and flexibility over the investment's life. By applying real options to business cases, NA Bank could have a higher potential of enabling the upside value, while limiting the downside or risk of no value.

EXHIBIT 15.1 NA Bank IT Strategic Investment Value Assessment

NA Bank Practice	NA Bank Techniques Applied	Techniques Not Used
Identifying strategic IT investments	SBU strategic planning Operational planning IT governance Balanced scorecard (Audit—to some extent) (Surveys—to some extent)	Stock price traits Total cost of ownership Real options Critical success factors Benchmarking Scenario planning
Justifying and prioritizing strategic IT investments	SBU strategic planning Operational planning Balanced scorecard IT governance ROI/NPV/DCF Standard business case Audit Business investment review board Balanced scorecard Surveys	Value-creation business case Real options Economic value added Stock price traits Total cost of ownership Decision trees Risk management Critical success factors Benchmarking Portfolio management Scenario planning
Selection and performance of strategic IT investments	SBU strategic planning Operational planning IT governance Balanced scorecard ROI/NPV/DCF Budgeting Standard business case Governance Business investment review boards IT and business program office Critical success factors Service level agreements	Portfolio management Scenario planning Real options Decision trees Benchmarking Risk management Audit Economic value added Stock price traits Total cost of ownership Value-creation business

Realizing strategic IT investments	SBU strategic planning
	Operational planning
	IT governance
	Budgeting
	Surveys
	Balanced scorecard
	IT and business program office
	  and project management
	Business investment review
	  board
		Audit (realization of value)
		Risk management
		Critical success factors
		Benchmarking
		Portfolio management

Project management performance measurement was inconsistent and nonstandard. Traditional project management metrics were used, such as budgets, schedules, scope, milestones, and critical success factors. Performance dashboards were constructed. Variances were reported to individual business unit investment review boards. If interim reviews showed projects greater than $1 million with unfavorable variances greater than 20 percent, business cases were recast and reapproved. However, project management received inconsistent ratings across the various project offices, highlighting nonstandard processes and inconsistent metrics. In addition, poor project milestone delivery and inadequate monitoring of changes to the business case were identified. A centralized business program management office (BPMO) would standardize and optimize project management performance.

Risk management was also indifferent within project management. Project management best practices suggest that risk management and the quality of deliverables are the critical success factors, where cost and time management are variables. In response to the strategic IT project survey (completed in 2002), stakeholders selected timely execution rather than risk management as one of the critical success factors. Getting projects in on time was perceived to be more important than risk to project delivery and business operations. Risk analysis could also be performed at each project stage or milestone review to provide periodic evaluation. By applying this technique, NA Bank would be in an effective position to decide whether to accelerate, shelve, or abandon projects, thereby gaining investment flexibility.

> Determining IT investment baseline performance through satisfaction and value surveys and IT portfolio analysis provided NA Bank with a transparent current view for future IT investment considerations.

Impact: IT Investment Redirection for Higher Value Capture

Based on the IT value network study and recommendations, the following practice was implemented toward the end of 2002 by the NA Bank's IT organization.

New IT Strategy Aligned to the Business

NA Bank recognized that it needed an IT strategy that was integrated at the enterprise and business unit levels. When this approach is adopted, strategic

IT investments are likely to be focused more on business strategic initiatives (e.g., customer-facing initiatives) and less on transactional or operational projects. Based on the study, NA Bank subsequently appointed a senior vice president of IT and Operations strategic execution and service excellence, who facilitated the creation of an enterprise-wide IT strategy that was better positioned for business alignment and competitive advantage. Exhibit 15.2 illustrates an IT value network tool that helped align IT strategic investment with the retail banking objectives; correlating with key business attributes, transformation objectives, and targeting business value (i.e., stock traits—see Exhibit 5.1 in Chapter 5 for more details).

NA bank had implemented balanced scorecards, but they were internally focused. Therefore, the IT balanced scorecard did not reflect the business strategic objectives and business measures. IT organizations should be strategic partners to the business and should define their balanced scorecard as a business within a business, linking the IT scorecard to the business objectives and measures. A business-aligned balanced scorecard was subsequently implemented, providing more meaningful strategic IT investment measures for value creation. The scorecard and biannual performance reviews were cascaded down the IT organization to ensure enterprise and business unit alignment.

Standardized Project Management, Performance Measurement, and Investment Governance

Centralizing the various NA Bank IT and business project management offices was recommended, but it was determined that the business units were too independent to centralize around one enterprise business project management office (BPMO). However, an initiative was launched to standardize project management methodology and performance measurement. The retail banking PMO took the lead and built a standard practice and tool kit, providing a best practice for subsequent reuse in the other business units. Best practice included the definition of improved project performance measures, application of project management methodology standards, improved business case change management, and improved accountability of milestone delivery. Further along in the implementation, NA Bank did place increased rigor on postproject reviews but felt that value realization was solely accountable in the business and would be reflected in the budgets of subsequent years.

In addition, based on the recommendations, a corporate IT investment review board oversight was formalized, transitioning from an informal business unit investment review. The corporate IT investment review board now included key business stakeholders, across the business, with a remit to govern IT investments by prioritizing and selecting strategic IT investments and

EXHIBIT 15.2 NA Bank Strategic IT Investment Alignment to Retail Banking Objectives

IT Strategic Investment	Attributes	Retail Banking Transformation Objective	Retail Banking Business Value
Customer relationship management (CRM) and branch automation	Customer service focus Cross-sell Up-sell Customer analytics Multichannel integration	Enhanced retail markets customer service process Refresh retail branch sales process	Increased revenue Increased market share Improved customer loyalty
Enterprise resource planning (ERP)	Human capital focus Employee satisfaction Consolidated financial controls	Enhanced human resource process Improved financial process and controls	Improved net income Improved economic profit Reduced operating risk
Mortgage e-business platform	Online transaction focus Transactional efficiency Re-engineer processes	New e-business model for origination, approval, and servicing mortgages	Incremental revenue Increased market share Lower operating costs
Credit card platform	Risk mitigation Early fraud alert Exposure profiling	New credit card risk and fraud system	Reduced fraud and financial risk Customer loyalty Capital reduction
IT application rationalization	Application standards focused Middleware—connects Re-use and object coding	New application support processes Process and application streamlining	Lower operating costs

(Continued)

EXHIBIT 15.2 (Continued)

IT Strategic Investment	Attributes	Retail Banking Transformation Objective	Retail Banking Business Value
IT infrastructure optimization	IT operational focus One common standard Cost of ownership Interoperability	New IT operational support processes Computing and networking streamlining	Lower operating costs
Information security	Customer and company protection focus Risk mitigation Regulatory compliance	New information security and privacy processes New operating risk processes	Capital reduction Risk reduction
Vendor management	IT vendor focus Procurement efficiency Less IT suppliers	Enhanced IT procurement	Lower operating costs Economic profit
Outsourcing	IT partnership focus Reduce in-house sourcing Focus on core competencies	Revised IT provisioning and support model	Lower operating and net costs

managing significant project and investment variances. Through adopting an enterprise approach, potentially higher returning investments in one business unit would be selected over lower-performing projects in another business unit. Improved corporate investment governance would drive enterprise shareholder value, determining maximum returns across business unit domains.

Redirection of IT Investment

Capital investment is a good indicator of a company's future direction, as discussed in Chapter 7. Classifying current IT investment and mapping within a portfolio model provides a good visual for projecting future investment and balancing the portfolio, as depicted in Exhibit 7.6. (Chapter 7). The Weill and Broadbent portfolio classification model was applied to NA Bank's proposed 2003 IT project capital investment. Referencing Exhibit 15.3, on aggregate from 2001 to 2003, NA Bank IT projects totaled 100, culminating in a total investment of $500 million. The total amount of IT investment was reasonably consistent between 2002 and 2003 at $150 million per year. However, the trend depicted larger investments in fewer IT projects.

Proposed 2003 IT project investment significantly reduced the emphasis on lower-value transactional or operational projects, compared to the past

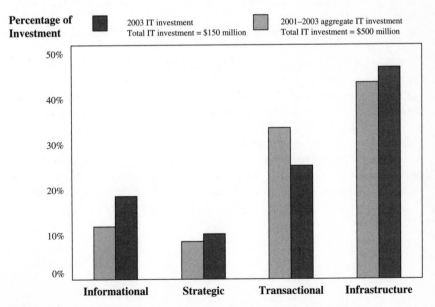

EXHIBIT 15.3 NA Bank Enterprise Portfolio—Total IT Project Investment

three-year aggregate, down from 34 to 26 percent of the total investment. But the amount was still significantly high, as it included the replacement of the mortgage and credit card legacy systems. Informational IT investments increased from 12 to 18 percent of the total investment, accomodating initiatives such as collaboration and new ERP systems. Strategic IT investments slightly increased from 9 to 10 percent of the total investment, for customer-facing strategic initiatives, such as a customer profiling project. Infrastructure investments slightly increased from 45 to 47 percent of the total investment, driven by a large IT network and computing optimization program and an information-security project.

Through more effective strategic planning, investment governance, and project management, 2003 IT capital spending increased in favor of informational and strategic investment at the expense of transactional or operational investment, thus redirecting IT investment to higher-value business programs. Strategic IT investments were expected to significantly increase over the next few years, focused on CRM—that is, one-to-one marketing, customer information management, and multichannel integration in support of the retail banking and individual wealth-management strategic direction. Time will tell whether the higher-value programs realized their actual value.

> Through an aligned enterprise IT strategy and improved IT investment governance, NA Bank redirected IT investment to higher-value informational and strategic programs.

The IT value network framework enabled NA Bank to establish an IT investment performance baseline. The sixth degree of IT value, networked value management, advocates measuring business satisfaction and IT value, thereby defining areas of performance improvement. Subsequently, based on stakeholder feedback, NA Bank focused on the second degree of IT value, IT strategic planning and portfolio management governance. With better insight and transparancy, a new NA Bank enterprise IT strategy was developed, with appropriate investment governance and project management, enabling the redirection of IT investment for higher value capture.

CHAPTER 16

Nortel Networks

Northern Electric was founded in 1895, when Bell Telephone Company (now Bell Canada—BCE) spun off its manufacturing operations. Renamed in 1976, Northern Telecom's breakthrough came in the mid-1970s, when it provided leading-edge digital technology (DMS telephone switches) to the public carriers. In 1998, the company was once again renamed Nortel Networks (Nortel), and it has since become a multinational telecommunications equipment manufacturer. Nortel become an independent company in 2000, when BCE distributed the majority of its stake to the shareholders, at which time annual revenues were over $20 billion. In 2007, Nortel's operations consisted of four strategic business units (SBUs): Carrier Networks, Enterprise Solutions, Metro Ethernet Networks, and Global Services, employing over 32,000 staff globally. Nortel's 2007 revenue was $10.95 billion, which was significantly down from its high point at the turn of the century. Nortel's head office is in Toronto, Canada.[1]

Challenge: Speed of Market Change

The 1990s was an exciting growth period for Nortel. During the 1990s, global staff grew from 49 thousand in 1990 to approximately 80 thousand in 1999. Revenue grew from $6.8 billion in 1990 to $21.3 billion in 1999. The key turn of events was the explosive growth of the Internet, from the mid- to late 1990s. Metcalfe's law kicked in, driving exponential networked value to corporate and individual personal computer connections.

Nortel had to address this data growth opportunity and impending data/voice convergence. In 1998, the CEO, John Roth, publically announced that Nortel would need to complete a "right-angle turn" and aggressively move from being a telecommunications supplier to a "Webtone" solution

---

[1] IT Value Network: Nortel Networks Case. (2009, January). Nortel Networks Corporation. *Printed with permission.*

provider. The intent was to provide customer-centric integrated voice and data solutions, with a focus on reduced company operating costs and improved profitability. Nortel needed to become an agile customer-focused company with speed in product delivery; it referred to calendar quarters (three months) as Web years. Within months, Bay Networks, an industry leader in worldwide IT networking, was acquired for over $7 billion. Nortel's corporate culture and organization was about to radically transform.

Nortel's IT organization had to change in support of the company directional change, especially as it aspired to become Nortel's best customer. In other words, it would be the lead advocate of its own solutions, leading the way in proving in the value of Nortel's products. Previously, the IT organization had been primarily a support operation to the strategic business units (SBUs), aligned to both product groups and global regional markets. The challenge was to transition from a fragmented support organization to one with a strategic added value capability, aligned to support process excellence and customer engagement.

In addition, the IT organization needed to implement new data technologies recently acquired (i.e., Bay Networks), migrating to "Webtone" solutions for its strategic businesses. In 1997, Nortel's global IT infrastructure was already supporting: more than one million Web URLs, a quarter of a million Web pages, 80,000 personal computers, 130,000 e-mails per day, 87,000 voice calls per day, 6.7 billion data packets per month, and 4,300 gigabytes per month on the global intranet backbone. Nortel had a large global infrastructure capability; by continuing to internally implement its new integrated technologies and deriving benefits from them, it would provide confidence and motivation to potential Nortel customers.

> The 1990s was an exciting growth period for Nortel, requiring a right-angle turn toward becoming a "Webtone" solutions provider, delivering data/voice convergence.

Solution: The IT Value Network

In mid-1997, Nortel's CIO announced the intention to reorganize the firm's IT organization and to realign its IT strategy to enable a new capability in support of Nortel's pending "right-angle turn." The IT value network framework was applied, with a focus on the third and second degrees of IT value.

Capability and Capacity Management: Third Degree of IT Value—IT Reorganization

The initial IT value network approach was focused on the third degree of IT value, creating an integrated IT organization aligned to the new business structure. The intent was to consolidate and centralize the IT organization, aligning IT investment governance with the new business organization, and to enable a new IT strategic direction.

Strategic Plan and Portfolio Management: Second Degree of IT Value—IT Strategic Planning

With a more effective IT organizational alignment, the focus turned to the second degree of IT value, realigning the IT strategy to meet the business's "right-angle turn." The intent was to move from a fragmented IT support organization to one with a strategic business capability, offering valued business services. In addition, the intent was to become the lead customer advocate of the benefits from implementing Nortel's new voice/data technologies and architecture.

IT Value Network Deployment

The first step in reorganizing IT was to consolidate or repatriate the various IT shops across the company, which had been born within the business to support its rapid growth. Nortel's IT organization was called Information Systems and focused primarily on providing system support and regional IT infrastructure services (i.e., server and desktop support). A parallel organization existed, called Global Enterprise Services (GES), that had been established within the Enterprise SBU, providing data network support to all the SBUs and offering added value network services to North American customers. In August 1997, the company merged these two organizations to provide better leverage, synergy, and voice/data integration. The new IT organization was called Information Services (IS) to better reflect a new added value proposition, serving the SBUs and customers. The intent was to build a professional services organization that would deliver customer value and provide competitive advantage.

Information Services had doubled in size, now managing $890 million annual investment and spend and required complete reorganization. The IT value network approach consisted of a series of joint planning sessions with SBUs and IT executives. Nortel was also moving to a process focus and had recently appointed senior executives to lead specific processes—sales and marketing, supply chain management, product development, and human resources (see Exhibit 9.1-value chain). Subsequently, a dual-portfolio organizational model was selected that aligned to IT capability or service and to business client management. The Information Services organization was aligned to the following business clients or partners:

Strategic business units (SBU)

- Public Carrier Networks
- Enterprise Networks
- Wireless Networks
- Broadband Networks
- Nortel Technology—R&D

Regions

- Caribbean and Latin America (CALA)
- Europe
- Asia Pacific
- (*Note*: North America was integrated into the SBU)

Enterprise processes

- Supply chain management
- Sales and marketing
- Product introduction
- Corporate services—HR and finance

Information Services appointed executive client managers to the SBU, global regions, and process owners. The remit was to manage client IT needs and total IT investments/spending. Client managers typically had a CIO title, to reflect the seniority of the position and to elevate its status to assist the business with customer engagements. Nortel CIOs were talking to customer CIOs about Nortel solutions and value add capability. Each executive also had an IT capability portfolio to lead and manage. For example, the IT VP and CIO for sales and marketing and CALA was the client manager to the sales and marketing process owner as well as to the Caribbean and Latin America region. In addition, the IT VP had IT capability ownership for sales and marketing solutions and CALA IT regional services. The client manager role included:

- **IT business consultant.** To partner with the business units to ensure that Information Services was aligned to the strategic corporate goals
- **Business analyst and service enabler.** To collaborate with the business clients to define business requirements and ensure delivery

excellence through the Information Services solution or capability providers

- **Process leadership.** To implement common operating processes across the business, aligned to IT directives, standards, and tools
- **Service quality.** To communicate and review CSAT (client satisfaction) performance, to address IT business requirements, and to create actions for continuous improvement
- **Investment management.** To act in partnership with the business and to manage and govern the IT investment for corporate added value
- **Change agent.** To enable the "right-angle turn" as a catalyst for "Webtone" solutions

An Information Services client management council was established to ensure that IT was meeting client needs and collaborating across the portfolios. For instance, if the IT VP of sales and marketing and CALA required network services for his clients, he would need to negotiate with the IT VP of enterprise networks to determine service level and cross charges. This client management council was, in fact, an IT governance body, which advised the corporate executive president's cabinet on IT strategic investments and overall spending.

With the Information Services organizational structure aligned to the new Nortel, attention turned to aligning the IT strategy to the corporate "Webtone" strategy and enabling the "right-angle turn." Following the IT value network strategic planning approach depicted in Exhibit 10.1, a series of offsite meetings was conducted with the Information Services client managers and respective business clients or partners, producing a new IT strategy that is reflected in Exhibit 16.1. The strategy was subsequently ratified by the corporate executive presidents' cabinet. The Information Services strategy consisted of the following layers of Nortel value:

1. **Deploying and evolving a world-class, standards-based IP network, demonstrating the Nortel "Webtone" value proposition**
   - Enhanced service and reliability through increased manageability and scalability, at desirable price points
   - Ubiquitous access to Nortel information, from anywhere to anywhere
2. **Establishing a common infrastructure operating environment, one that is responsive, reliable, and secure**
   - Delivering service excellence, improving CSAT, and doubling employee productivity
   - Oracle worldwide database license found to save $30 million (instead of licensing project by project)

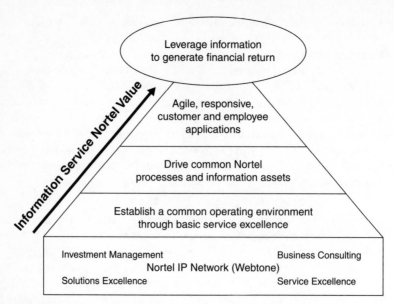

EXHIBIT 16.1 Nortel Information Services Strategy—1998

3. **Driving common business processes and information assets, creating a single, easy-to-deal-with Nortel**
   - Global system deployment—Baan enterprise supply chain management (SCM); Oracle finance; Clarify customer relationship management (CRM) in support of sales and marketing. (See Chapter 11, Exhibit 11.1, Enterprise Resource Planning (ERP).)
   - Global integration of systems, for seamless information flow
4. **Developing and delivering e-business agile solutions for customer and employee benefits**
   - PowerNET online order management system, in just four months, drives $10 million revenue monthly in CALA
   - ServiceWeb customer service tool provides 24-hour, real-time product support and software patches
5. **Leveraging information for financial return**
   - Most knowledgeable sales force, through customer information management and collaboration, via Sales.com
   - Build corporate memory, competitive intelligence, and, therefore, competitive advantage

The Information Services strategy was fully integrated into the business strategy and aligned to the business goals, raising the visibility of IT strategic value. The IT organizational transition from a fragmented support operation to a strategic business capability was successfully completed by mid-1998.

The IT culture changed from being technology support–based to business service–focused. Appropriate IT investment governance and portfolio management was established through the client management council and the corporate executive president's cabinet.

Nortel's Information Services responded to the challenge by transitioning from a fragmented support organization to become client-service driven; it collaborated with the business to form an integrated business-IT strategy, delivering Webtone solutions.

Impact: IT Reorganization and Improved Capability for Value Enabling

An Information Service communications office was established, managing overall investment value and stakeholder value proposition. Client satisfaction (CSAT) surveys were conducted across the company's employee base and at the executive level. From 1997 to 1999, the level of business satisfaction with IT services and value increased by 50 percent, achieving 86 percent satisfaction. During this time, the annual IT investment doubled to $1 million to meet exponential company growth, despite a successful $60 to $80 million annual IT cost-saving program. Information Services consolidated various business IT departments, including the R&D SBU network infrastructure, and absorbed acquired company IT functions, thus increasing its overall IT investment level. This consolidation allowed for baseline savings and contributions to Nortel's bottom line, while maintaining strategic IT investments. To ensure business accountability for IT spending, a rigorous cross-charging mechanism was implemented; 60 percent was allocated directly to the business P&L based on service consumption, and 40 percent was allocated to corporate services in support of enterprise goals (i.e., SCM).

IT strategic investments were recommended by the Information Services client management council and governed by the corporate executive president's cabinet. These investments were aligned to strategic business goals and were required to produce a positive net present value (NPV), with a return on asset (ROA) of between 16 to 19 percent. Investments under $100,000 required a payback within one year, while higher investments required a payback within two years. Investments higher than $500,000 were also required to produce a sensitivity analysis on projected cash flows, with a corresponding risk assessment focused on outcome uncertainty (see Chapter 5, "IT Value Network Measures: Financial-Based Methods, Emerging Decision Support Techniques").

To keep stakeholders informed and aware of the IT contribution to the "right-angle turn," various communication vehicles were deployed, including the successful "Pit Stop" and "Cyber Café." The Pit Stop consisted of a quarterly newsletter with regional exhibits, focused on employee productivity tools. The program was also attached to annual sales conferences, providing customer information management (i.e., Sales.com), laptop productivity, sales tools, and training. The idea was for sales individuals to pull up to the Pit Stop as a one-stop shop for quick support, and then get back on the road, as depicted in Formula One racing. The Pit Stop was voted by industry analysts as a leading example of innovation, in support of a global sales force. The Cyber Café was an Internet café as commonly seen today, but at that time it was a new concept, providing employee productivity support.

The Information Services reorganization and partnership with the business enabled a highly valued client-service and customer-responsive IT organization, with significant business and stakeholder impact, as discussed in the following subsections.

Organizational Boundaries Dissolved

Organizational boundaries dissolved, as process-driven standardized systems were deployed across the SBUs and regions. Supply chain management was streamlined, with a global deployment of Baan SCM, and outsourced manufacturing plants. Vanilla Baan (minimum customizations) was implemented in the CALA region within six months, accommodating an aggressive Brazilian growth business with $500 million revenue. Customer relationship management was standardized around the newly acquired Clarify software company. Finance standardized globally on Oracle. Information Services partnered with Matra Nortel Communications, a French joint venture, to deploy a $20 million Nortel technology infrastructure. In addition, the Information Services business process support services (BPSS) centers of excellence were frequently engaged for customer implementations in which process improvements and change management were required for technology deployments.

Product Development and IT Collaboration

Nortel product designers collaborated with Information Services for rapid technology testing and modification, utilizing the internal IP network. The speed of developing and provisioning market-driven solutions significantly improved, leading competition in many sectors, including broadband networks and wireless solutions. For example, Nortel acquired BNI (Broadband Networks, Inc.) in December 1997, and within three months, in partnership with the Wireless SBU, Information Services had integrated the new Reunion wireless access product into the Nortel IP network.

Seamless Information Flow and Knowledge Transfer

Information flow and knowledge transfer moved seamlessly and rapidly across the business interests, improving decision making and customer responsiveness. Global sales and marketing organizations standardized on an internally built collaborative system called "Sales.com," providing product and marketing information to the global salesforce. Sales.com was in fact designed prior to Netscape going public in the summer of 1995; in 1998 it was successfully deployed to over 15,000 employees, providing 37,000 information assets and culminating in an audited $56 million annual cost savings. This Web-based, customer information management application, designed and developed by Information Services, received company and industry recognition for excellence and shareholder value.

IT Largest Nortel Customer and Advocate

Information Services became one of Nortel's largest customers and true customer advocates, facilitating and supporting customer engagements, and proving-in technology solutions and business benefits. For example, the IT VP CALA conducted an annual CIO conference to enlighten Nortel's South American customer CIOs of successful technology deployments and business benefits.

Significant IT Satisfaction Gain

Information Services client satisfaction (CSAT), an annual business partner survey, improved by 28 percent from 1997 to 1998. The level of business satisfaction with IT services and value subsequently increased to 86 percent satisfaction in 1999.

IT Shareholder Value

During the late 1990s to 2000, Information Services reorganization, along with subsequent IT strategic alignment to the "right-angle turn," enabled significant Nortel value. Nortel market capitalization during this time hit a high of $370 billion, an amazing growth from just under $10 billion in 1995.

In an interview with Nortel's current (2008) CIO, Steven J. Bandrowczak, it was stated that the IT organizational and strategic principles remain similar to the past success model. Steven had joined Nortel in July 2007 and was interviewed in mid-September 2008. Strong IT partnerships with the business remain critical, ensuring an integrated IT and corporate strategy. IT portfolio management is essential for enterprise investment management. Service excellence continues, through a common ITIL service model, delivering business services to the employee base. Business simplification through process solutions continues, driving application rationalization. The major difference is the current focus on costs during challenging times. The remit is, therefore, to improve the expense ratio and to drive incremental revenue for improved return on investment. Since 2007, a project management office and a project portfolio review board manage and govern Nortel's strategic IT projects, with a focus on a one-year payback. Subsequently, strategic projects were cut back from 200 to 50, driving $80 million benefits in year. Nortel's IT organization continues to pursue a business value realization approach to the IT portfolio, aligned to shareholder value.

Information Services become Nortel's best service provider and customer. From 1997 to 1999, the level of business satisfaction with IT services and value increased by 50 percent, achieving 86 percent stakeholder satisfaction, as organizational boundaries dissolved, knowledge transfer improved, business collaboration increased, and new products were implemented.

The IT value network framework enabled Nortel Information Services to move fast in adapting to market changes and the company's "right-angle turn." Through IT reorganization and strategic IT alignment, Information Services improved its capability for value enabling. The third degree of IT value, capability and capacity management, was enhanced through consolidation and reorganized in support of the new company direction. Subsequently, the second degree of IT value, IT strategic planning and portfolio management governance, aligned IT investment and leveraged information capital for higher financial return. Finally, the sixth degree of IT value, networked value management, realized higher levels of business satisfaction and IT value.

CHAPTER 17

Indigo Books & Music

Headquartered in Toronto, Canada, and founded in 1996, Indigo Books & Music, Inc. (Indigo) employs 6,700 staff, serving over 250 stores across Canada. Its merger with Chapters, Inc. in 2001 created the largest book reseller in Canada, under the brands of Indigo, Chapters, and Coles. Merchandise includes books, music, gifts, and toys, with a new "green" product line launched in 2008 and Shortcovers (digital books) launched in 2009. The company generated revenues of $875 million CDN in 2007 and has been voted one of Canada's Top 100 Employers in 2005 and 2006.[1]

Challenge: Project Management

Project management had become a significant challenge during the early summer of 2006, culminating in a few of the large strategic projects that significantly exceeded budget and schedule. Indigo's leadership team acknowledged that improved project management was indeed a priority, when delays in these projects started to impact the business, through increased operational risk and quality concerns. Specifically, three troubled strategic projects were hindering the ongoing success of the business operations:

1. **Online order management system (OMS) in support of Indigo's significant e-business revenues.** The selected technology platform was proving to be unreliable and inadequate, generating major costs and schedule overruns. Key stakeholders were concerned because:
   - Incremental IT cost to complete the project was $2.2 million above the original budget.
   - Business owners were very dissatisfied with product functionality and stability.

---

[1]It Value Network: Indigo Books & Music Case. (2009, February). Indigo Books & Music, Inc. *Printed with permission.*

- Long-term technology direction was questioned, driving a projected high cost of ownership.
- Business and project risk was deemed unacceptable.
- The business case was subsequently challenged.

2. **Product catalog and database (iPROD) in support of Indigo's merchandizing and inventory.** The selected technology platform was proving to be unreliable, with significant integration challenges that questioned its ongoing viability.

3. **Warehouse management system (WMS) in support of Indigo's distribution and logistics center.** The selected technology platform was proving to be unreliable; it required extensive stabilization and integration validation.

With an aggressive company growth projection in support of both retail store and online revenues, these projects were critical for the company's ongoing success and profitability.

> Indigo's leadership team acknowledged that improved project management was a priority, when a few large strategic projects significantly exceeded budget and schedule, raising quality concerns and operational risk.

Solution: The IT Value Network

Indigo brought in new IT leadership, and the incoming CIO, Michael Serbinis, commissioned Read & Associates in July 2006 to review these projects and subsequently to build a business project management office (BPMO). The project management assessment considered processes and techniques from the fourth and second degrees of IT value.

Project and System Management: Fourth Degree of IT Value—Online Order Management System Evaluation

The first step was to apply the fourth degree of IT value, encompassing a complete review and audit of the OMS project. Interviews with key stakeholders, project team, and the vendor were conducted. A comprehensive review of all project documents and supporting project management practices was also completed.

Strategic Plan and Portfolio Management: Second Degree of IT Value—Project Management Office (PMO) and Portfolio Management Assessment

OMS project management findings were validated with a broader review of other strategic projects, including WMS and iPROD. Subsequently, the second degree of IT value was applied in building a new PMO practice and portfolio governance model.

IT Value Network Deployment

An OMS problem route cause analysis was completed, as illustrated in Exhibit 17.1, and the project management deficiencies were validated across other projects. The following project management summary findings were subsequently reported to the senior executives:

- **Planning was insufficient.** Projects were managed with an operational mentality and required more proactive planning.
- **Project management leadership or governance was lacking.** The company was not good at complex projects, especially across functions.
- **There was no consistent project management methodology.** No standard templates, tools, or processes were implemented.
- **Focus was more on time and budget at the expense of quality and risk.** The business operations were exposed.
- **Risks not mitigated.** Risks were understood but poorly mitigated.
- **Business functional requirements documentation was inconsistent or lacking.** Scope lacked clarity.
- **Resource management was inadequate.** Resource allocation and management showed weakness.
- **Project roles, responsibility, and accountability were not clearly defined.** Project managers had different titles and roles.
- **Milestones were not managed.** Milestones and key deliverables were not managed effectively.
- **Project tracking, monitoring, and reporting were insufficient.** There was no standard format and comprehension was lacking.
- **Project communication and coordination was absent.** No formal review process was in place.

Read and Associates's recommendation was to create a new corporate business PMO responsible for planning, managing and executing all company projects. Under the direction of Michael Serbinis (CIO) and in collaboration with the VP Strategic Planning, Dan Leibu, a portfolio and BPMO governance model was built based on Chapter 10, Exhibit 10.2. Within the governance model, accountabilities were defined, as illustrated in Exhibit 17.2. An executive committee was created to govern the enterprise investment portfolio and to oversee the BPMO value model, with the remit that included:

- **Business strategy and IT architecture:**
  - Ensuring that investments are aligned to the strategic business plan

Description

Examples

Category	Description	Examples
Leadership	Issues caused by overall project charter and project drivers/constraints/priorities	▪ Significant customization ($2M services on $0.6M software) ▪ Selection of unreleased product ▪ Pressure to achieve holiday release leading to shortened schedules ▪ Failure to hold vendor to delivery commitments ▪ Failure to revisit business case during April re-plan
Project Management	Lack of project management discipline, particularly with respect to establishing and tracking project milestones, gates, deliverables, and risk	▪ Work-stream team leads not assigned ▪ Complete resource plan not created and resources not committed ▪ Detailed project plans not created ▪ Driven by schedule/budget and not quality deliverables and risk management ▪ Business owners not engaged until July ▪ End June over 60% of overall schedule spent just on Online Dev/Test, 12 weeks left on the rest—overlapping dependencies (testing) ▪ No formal change control process for scope management
Scope Management	Scope missed during requirements analysis or lost during transition between teams/phases	▪ Significant reliance on third-party consulting to produce initial RFP ▪ Inadequate production of detailed business requirements, functional specifications, technical requirements, or architecture ▪ Limited review of solution outline and design documents delivered by vendor ▪ Significant scope gaps discovered in UAT and in Aug./Sept. ▪ Significant scope change requests—PCRs
IT Delivery	Underestimated effort to meet commitments	▪ Data migration, reporting, and QA effort underestimated ▪ Thorough review of architecture was not completed ▪ Limited review of solution outline and design documents delivered by vendor ▪ Inadequate management of interfaces between Indigo and vendor code ▪ Insufficient testing during functional test cycle and incomplete data set used
Vendor Delivery	Vendor inability to deliver against commitments	▪ Delivery of code was only 80% through testing, two weeks after original date ▪ Core product has numberous gaps (e.g., agent-level reporting, e-mail opt-out) ▪ Implementations poor in many areas (e.g., corporate orders, breaking out of the box functionality during customization) ▪ Weak project management—staffing of resources during vacations, management of interfaces with Indigo code ▪ Poor execution on a number of areas, (e.g., performance testing, data migartion)

EXHIBIT 17.1 Indigo Project Management: Problem Route Causes—Online Order Management System (OMS)

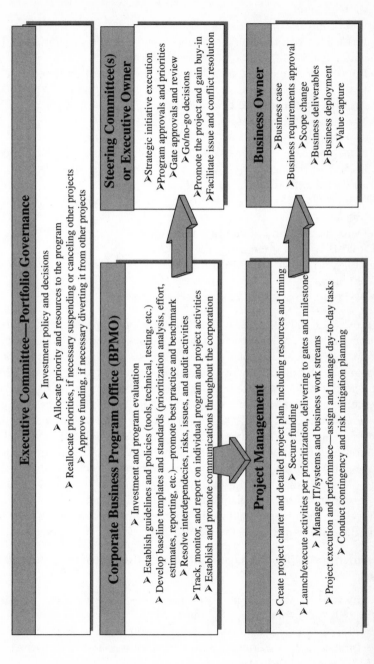

Executive Committee—Portfolio Governance

➤ Investment policy and decisions
  ➤ Allocate priority and resources to the program
  ➤ Reallocate priorities, if necessary suspending or canceling other projects
    ➤ Approve funding, if necessary diverting it from other projects

Steering Committee(s) or Executive Owner

➤Strategic initiative execution
➤Program approvals and priorities
  ➤Gate approvals and review
    ➤Go/no-go decisions
➤Promote the project and gain buy-in
➤Facilitate issue and conflict resolution

Business Owner

➤Business case
➤Business requirements approval
  ➤Scope change
  ➤Business deliverables
  ➤Business deployment
    ➤Value capture

Corporate Business Program Office (BPMO)

➤ Investment and program evaluation
  ➤ Establish guidelines and policies (tools, technical, testing, etc.)
  ➤ Develop baseline templates and standards (prioritization analysis, effort, estimates, reporting, etc.)—promote best practice and benchmark
  ➤ Resolve interdependecies, risks, issues, and audit activities
  ➤ Track, monitor, and report on individual program and project activities
  ➤ Establish and promote communications throughout the corporation

Project Management

➤ Create project charter and detailed project plan, including resources and timing
  ➤ Secure funding
  ➤ Launch/execute activities per prioritization, delivering to gates and milestone
    ➤ Manage IT/systems and business work streams
  ➤ Project execution and performnace—assign and manage day-to-day tasks
    ➤ Conduct contingency and risk mitigation planning

EXHIBIT 17.2 Indigo Investment Portfolio and PMO Governance

201

- Activities conceived as a finite set of opportunities filtered through the strategic filter
- **Investment management:**
  - Process of determining how much investment/spending should be made against different types of business needs
  - Portfolio management of risk versus reward and short-term versus long-term investments
- **Program and initiative evaluation:**
  - Assessment of business priority, value, change, risk, options, and benchmark
  - Management of resources against supply, demand, and competing business priorities
- **Value realization:**
  - Monitoring of ongoing value being created against the portfolio of initiatives
  - Demonstrable and audit book value
- **Capability management:**
  - Ability to deliver based on the state of organizational capacity and readiness
  - Ability to plan against financial constraints

In October 2006, the BPMO was launched, to improve Indigo's ability to successfully execute an increasingly complex enterprise-wide portfolio of projects. The mandate of the BPMO was to improve project planning due diligence and effectively deliver projects in order to maximize business benefit and manage risk. A project management life cycle was designed and implemented, as depicted in Exhibit 12.1. PMO tools, processes, and policies were subsequently built, based on industry project management best practices, which included rigorous business cases, detailed documentation, defined roles and responsibilities, task and activity management, resource management, cost control, and proactive risk management. The BPMO, consisting of a PMO director and initially four staff, reporting into Dan Leibu, vice president for strategic planning, under the CIO remit.

Specific organizational principles were defined to identify and realize the business value from effective portfolio and project management:

Investment portfolio management (called the Funnel)—"identify the value":

- **Principle 1.** Realization of business benefits across the company, through the management of initiatives or programs as an integrated portfolio, reducing the risks of benefit duplication or omission
- **Principle 2.** Prioritizing and allocating resources according to the enterprise's strategy and capability

- **Principle 3.** Resolving program and project conflicts by reference to the program management governance
- **Principle 4.** Monitoring progress and results, reporting to the executive investment committee
- **Principle 5.** Continually reassessing expected benefits and adjusting or evaluating options within the portfolio, to support the evolving business strategy

Business project management office (BPMO)—"realize the value":

- **Principle 1.** Monitoring all active and proposed projects within a single overall project management framework, coordinating project interdependencies
- **Principle 2.** Valuing individual projects against the benefits they are expected to yield
- **Principle 3.** Executing projects through risk mitigation and quality deliverables, appropriately managing time and budget
- **Principle 4.** Ensuring that gate approvals are established and deliverables appropriately signed
- **Principle 5.** Determining project teams and allocated team members, identifying time commitments and management approvals

The formation of the BPMO constituted a significant change to Indigo's conventional operational focus, introducing heightened attention to planning, resource allocation, milestone reviews, and accountabilities. Still, the enterprise speed of adoption of the PMO methodology was remarkable, with significantly increased project management demand across the company.

> Indigo managed at a fast operational pace and needed to step back and review the firm's total investment against the short-term priorities and longer-term direction, which was achieved through the implementation of portfolio governance and project management best practice, capturing and optimizing stakeholder economic value.

Impact: Project Management Office for Value Optimization

Through implementing a BPMO and applying portfolio and project management best practices, as advocated in the second and fourth degrees of IT value, Indigo was successful in optimizing stakeholder economic value, from investment justification to project delivery.

PMO Effectiveness

Indigo's BPMO celebrated its first anniversary in November 2007, having applied project management best practices to 50 enterprise projects, totaling an investment of over CAN$25 million. Twenty of these projects (CAN$7 million investment) had been closed within the year. These projects were delivered within 5 percent of targeted budget and schedule as a weighted average, compared to the previous year, where projects managed counted less than 10 in number, with significantly higher variances. The executive committee had optimized the enterprise portfolio value and governed effective project management, enabling business benefits.

Chimera: On Time, On Budget

The first strategic project to go through the whole Indigo project life cycle was OMS, known as Chimera, the three-headed monster, migrating the current OMS legacy system to a new technology platform. Chimera was implemented in September 2007, exactly 12 months from the previous failed attempt. In October 2006, the OMS project was reset, based on the IT value network project assessment and audit. The vendor agreement was canceled and new in-house technology development was initiated, providing the following benefits:

- Alignment to enterprise architecture and technical direction
- Complete control of code base
- Lower total cost of ownership (TCO) and better long-term supportability
- Earlier delivery of primary business benefits and phased options for other business benefits
- Total incremental operating cost of CAN$0.5 million, with benefits of $5.1 million, over five years
- Excellent incremental IRR (129 percent)
- Lower risk on project delivery, given the incremental nature of work

Chimera (OMS) came in on time and on budget, at half the cost of the previously rejected technology solution. The projected annualized $1 million benefits started to materialize in October 2007.

PMO Networked Value Management

To determine the stakeholder satisfaction and value of BPMO, in October 2007 a 360 "touch point" stakeholder survey was conducted across all Indigo functions, attaining approximately 50 responses. Based on this networked value management feedback, the BPMO was well supported across the company, providing significant business value through effective project delivery. Structured and consistent project management had improved project execution, to the extent that priorities, resources, quality, and risks were soundly managed. Reporting and communication provided visibility and transparency to project progress and issues. Cross-functional coordination and mediation had alleviated the amount of time functional managers spent on projects, thereby improving decision making. Above all, the senior leadership team had provided sustained support, ensuring excellent governance and rigor to the project life cycle process.

Areas of improvement were also identified, including PMO capacity concerns, project managers' varying capabilities, project team roles and responsibilities, PMO tool tuning, business education, and further portfolio management. In response to the 360 "touch-point" survey feedback and subsequent focus groups, the following three refresh changes were introduced in the first quarter of 2008.

PROJECT LIFE CYCLE FRAMEWORK Minor revisions to project stages, deliverables, and gates were introduced, increasing the up-front focus on elaboration planning. An organizational change management requirements deliverable (CRD) was added to ensure comprehensive consideration to training, employee impact, organizational design, and communication. A project success criteria (PSC) value agreement was introduced, comparable to a service level agreement (SLA), constituting a contract between the PM and business owner or executive sponsor, outlining project management expectations and success criteria. Finally, "light" projects were managed through a consolidated life cycle, collapsing elaboration and planning stages into one planning stage and gate to accelerate smaller projects.

PROJECT TEAM EFFECTIVENESS Team meeting effectiveness was targeted, driving project ownership and team cohesiveness, commitments, accountabilities, and improved decision making. Project team roles and responsibilities were clarified, differentiating between enterprise and light (small) projects. Project Server 2007 was implemented for project management automation and resource management visibility. Business education and awareness were enhanced, through "lunch and learns" and a PMO Web site. The Web site became the single source of truth, with a SharePoint-enabled document portal, comprising project overviews, weekly status reports, project deliverable templates, all project documentation along with other PMO best practices collateral. Finally, project manager skills and business knowledge were enhanced through a facilitation skills course for project team mediation and accountabilities and through business engagement to ramp up project manager process or domain knowledge.

FUNNEL—INVESTMENT PORTFOLIO MANAGEMENT EFFECTIVENESS Funnel revisions were introduced to ensure consistent project and program classification and justification, subsequently raising the bar on project entry. Communications were enhanced to ensure that all stakeholders understood the Funnel expectations or prerequisites as well as project status and conditions. Finally, portfolio management was enhanced to include investment envelope views by investment types, organizational impact, head office and retail resource capacity planning, improved accuracy on financials (Opex/Capex/Costs/Benefits/IRR), system architecture impact reviews, and benefit realization assessment.

PMO Value Optimization

The BPMO refresh changes were effectively deployed in 2008 to the satisfaction of stakeholders. In the fourth quarter 2008, the BPMO had grown to 10 project managers and coordinators, managing $40 million investment, with 70 percent being invested in 12 strategic projects. The BPMO managed an array of business and IT projects, including kiosk, new store openings, SAP upgrade, storage area network, customer information management (CRM), customer loyalty, scan-based trading, toy expansion, workforce management, server virtualization, and home office expansion. The PMO is a key component of the IT value network management process, which enabled and optimized Indigo's business value. Indigo's senior executives were key advocates and ratified the following messages:

1. The BPMO has provided significant business value, contributing to improved project delivery through the deployment of project management best practices. Within the first anniversary, half of the PMO's 40 managed projects have been delivered, within 5 percent of target, on time, and on budget, representing a significant improvement from the previous year.
2. Across the company, project stakeholders have adopted the BPMO standard processes and tools, resonating with the effectiveness of a consistent and structured approach to project management. Further, reporting and communication have provided increased visibility and transparency to project progress and issues, especially across functions.
3. Stakeholders have higher expectations of the BPMO in growing the franchise and supporting Indigo's strategies, specifically in regard to a variety of enterprise portfolio views, facilitating decision making on investment priorities, capacity planning, and organizational impact and readiness.

> The newly created Indigo business PMO provided significant stakeholder economic value through effective portfolio governance and project delivery; within the first year, 50 percent of the 40 managed projects had been delivered within 5 percent of target, on time, and on budget.

The IT value network framework assisted Indigo to improve value capture and drive value optimization through portfolio governance and effective project delivery. The second degree of IT value, portfolio management, aligned and governed company investment in support of the business strategy. The fourth degree of IT value, program and project management, was driven by a newly created BPMO, deploying best practice in project planning and execution. Finally, the sixth degree of IT value, networked value management, realized higher levels of business satisfaction and value, with respect to the BPMO and delivered project benefits.

CHAPTER 18

NA Credit Union

NA Credit Union is a North American (NA) credit union, offering its members a full range of retail banking services—specifically, retail branches, commercial business centers, online banking, individual wealth management, and credit products and services. Credit unions are cooperative financial institutions owned and controlled by their members. NA Credit Union is one of the largest in North America, managing billions of dollars of member assets, on par with an average U.S. bank. Like many credit unions, the company's vision is to provide outstanding service to its members, making a difference to the communities it serves. Actual data has been modified to protect confidentiality, but it retains integrity in support of the applied practice.

Challenge: Credit Union Merger

In the mid-2000s, NA Credit Union was created through the merger of two credit unions, both having a long history of serving their local communities. The challenge was to integrate the banking operations, processes, and systems under one organization within 15 months. NA Credit Union is the story of two great financial institutions coming together to build a better bank for the communities and members it serves. The challenges it faced included:

- The existence of two, if not more, of every type of technology used to deliver service to members and employees
- The existence of two, if not more, of every type of process used to deliver service to members by employees
- Being uniquely positioned to rationalize and optimize its technology and related processes through integration
- The need for NA Credit Union to make immediate business decisions, related to the following:
  - Member policy, rights, and satisfaction
  - Account conversion

- Branch review and brand experience; product and service mapping and alignment
- Kiosk offering ATM and POS support
- Back-office conversion; check clearing; centralized lending
- Head-office transition; call center integration
- Board and financial reporting; legal compliance and documentation
- Credit and risk management
- Network convergence; Internet and Intranet consolidation
- PC platforms; e-mail consolidation
- Online banking consolidation
- Data center consolidation
- Business continuity and disaster recovery
- HR organization; employee policy
- Banking platform selection

A critical decision, made up-front, was to retain one of the core current operating systems or banking platforms of the merged credit unions and migrate or convert the other credit union members from an old legacy system to the retained platform. This early decision shaped the approach to bank integration and conversion, focusing critical business decisions around the retained system's capability and constraints. Subsequently, significant analysis was required in considering differences between the two credit unions and alignment considerations, as outlined in the business decisions above. Meanwhile, over the projected transitional year, NA Credit Union would have to operate two sets of processes and technologies, creating considerable pressure on internal IT and head office resources.

> NA Credit Union, the creation of a merger, was significantly challenged by having two or more of every type of process and supporting technology; critical decisions had to be made quickly in pursuit of bank integration and a single banking platform.

Solution: The IT Value Network

NA Credit Union's newly appointed CIO in charge of the bank's technology and operations (T&O) commissioned Read & Associates to assess and organize all the work necessary for a successful bank integration and banking platform conversion. The initial assignment, planned for six weeks, was in fact extended to include three phases, over 15 months. Phase 1's objective was to clearly identify the required programs and projects for prioritization and selection, including an assessment of T&O's capability and capacity to execute these projects. Phase 2 required the implementation of a rigorous and consistent project management practice, initiating project planning and execution. Phase 3 included tracking and monitoring project execution, managing interdependencies and risks, with the expectation of a successful bank integration and banking platform conversion. The IT value network management approach utilized four degrees of IT value.

Strategic Plan and Portfolio Management: Second Degree of IT Value—Bank Integration Portfolio Management

The second degree of IT value was applied to build the merger portfolio; it involved identifying all necessary programs and projects for bank integration and banking platform conversion. Program and project prioritization and selection were determined, and interdependencies and risks were identified.

IT Systems, Infrastructure and Organizational Capability and Capacity: Third Degree of IT Value—T&O's Ability to Execute Projects

Once the approved portfolio of programs and projects was determined, attention turned to the third degree of IT value. The T&O organization's capability and capacity were evaluated as to its ability to deliver on the portfolio by identifying gaps and resource needs. In parallel, T&O's infrastructure capability and capacity were also evaluated as to its ability to accommodate and enable the banking platform conversion in support of the bank integration.

Project and System Management: Fourth Degree of IT Value—Project Management Organization and Practice

With an approved portfolio and T&O capability and capacity in place, the next step was to apply the fourth degree of IT value. This required building a rigorous project management methodology process and governance practice. Subsequently, bank integration and conversion projects were planned and executed.

Network Value Management: Sixth Degree of IT Value—Realizing Bank Integration and Banking Platform Conversion

The final phase was to realize bank integration and banking platform conversion, transitioning from the fourth to the sixth degree of IT value. It consisted of:

- Monitoring and tracking program and project execution to achieve successful bank integration and banking platform conversion

- Managing project interdependences and risks and ensuring appropriate project sequencing and resolving project resource conflicts along with risk mitigation
- Conducting a postintegration IT satisfaction survey through networked value management

IT Value Network Deployment

Phase 1 of the engagement started in April and initially consisted of a six-week assessment of the current state and an initial portfolio build, identifying all the necessary programs and projects for bank integration and banking platform conversion, including interdependencies and risks:

Week one. Program and project catalog template build and initial data collection. The objective was to obtain a first pass on the program and project portfolio and reach agreement on a consistent data collection methodology. Existing project data was collected and analyzed, in addition to interviewing key IT and operational heads of departments. A PMO workshop was held with project managers for input and alignment.

Week two. Complete program and project identification and initial cataloging. The objective was to obtain a complete program and project portfolio view, based on functional 100-day plans and current projects and to account for any data quality gaps. The executive leadership team was interviewed, as were IT and operational functional heads.

Week three. Complete program and project classification, based on business drivers and stakeholder commitments. The objective was to align the project portfolio to business objectives, drivers, and priorities. A strategic plan and business cases did not exist; by default, the alignment and classification was based on the 100-day plans, stakeholder (member and employee) promises, and the five-year business plan for the merger. The executive leadership team was interviewed again to ratify functional programs and priorities.

Weeks four and five. Complete project status, resource allocation, risk assessment, interdependencies, and expected benefit realization. The objective was to complete the program and project catalog and portfolio. Details depended on the available data. Most programs were in the prework investigative stage and had not been appropriately scoped. Therefore, data was based, at best, on estimates and a number of assumptions. Business owners, as appointed by the executive leadership team, were interviewed to collect data.

Week six. Present the program and project portfolio summary data and findings to the executive leadership team for inclusion in the merger planning process. The objective was to provide fact-based data for executive program prioritization, selection, and decision making. Preparation for an early June leadership offsite working session was also included, to enable a quick-start program and project planning and execution launch.

The initial proposed program and project catalog and governance was fragmented, amounting only to a collection of functional thoughts and activities. This scattered array of efforts required migration to a structured portfolio organization, as depicted in Exhibit 18.1. Subsequently, identified programs were easily reduced from 48 to 43 and potential projects from 294 to 175. Although not part of the PMO activities, a number of more operational tasks were identified as consumed key resources that were required for the integration or conversion programs. The number of projects placed a heavy load on the organization's resources and state of readiness. There were also many program interdependencies and critical timelines, drawing attention

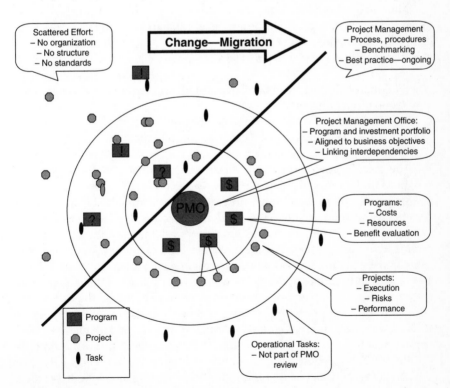

EXHIBIT 18.1 NA Credit Union Portfolio Migration from Scattered to Structured

to complex sequencing and scheduling. Key interdependencies are depicted in Exhibit 18.2.

The retained banking platform was central to many integration programs, including branch reinvention programs (i.e., ABM POS), bank retail operations programs (i.e., call center integration), and back-office convergence programs (i.e., centralized lending). Business process reengineering, product offering, and standard member interactions had to be defined to ensure an effective evolution of the banking platform. The sequencing of the bank integration programs and projects was a pivotal activity, especially given the backdrop of significant business transformation, staff relocation, and centralization of functions (i.e., corporate office transition). Subsequently, phasing of the banking platform build and evolution was also critical for success, ensuring minimal development during data conversion; this effort also had to be synchronized with the build-out of the underlying IT infrastructure. Various supplementary IT projects were required to support the bank platform migration (e.g., increasing the data center's capacity) and in support of bank integration (e.g., the new call center system and desktop upgrade).

After two months shaping the portfolio, the projected level of work remained too high and further project scrubbing and prioritization was necessary. Based on the merger's five-year plan and stakeholder commitments, the following portfolio scorecard was designed to filter projects:

- Banking platform conversion—bare minimum required for integration
- Regulatory compliance
- Member commitments, loyalty, and attrition
- Employee commitments, satisfaction, and retention

The final portfolio selection was based on timing, with priority on programs and projects to be completed by December. The cross-functional integration programs were reasonably distributed across the business value drivers, with some weighting toward member needs. This was viewed as appropriate, given the critical importance of member satisfaction and service levels during the integration challenge. Weighting toward cost and risk control was also applied while delivering member service. A high-level T&O capability and capacity plan was developed, identifying gaps and resource needs. At the end of June, after three months' work, the executives approved the final portfolio recommendation, a reduction to 16 programs and 48 projects. Final projected investment was over $10 million, with approximately 20 person-years of work to be completed within 12 months.

Phases 2 and 3 of the assignment focused on the PMO project methodology, planning, and execution. Only one-fifth of all programs were in detailed planning, emphasizing the need for speed to business scope and project charter. A major concern was T&O resource availability and expertise. Based

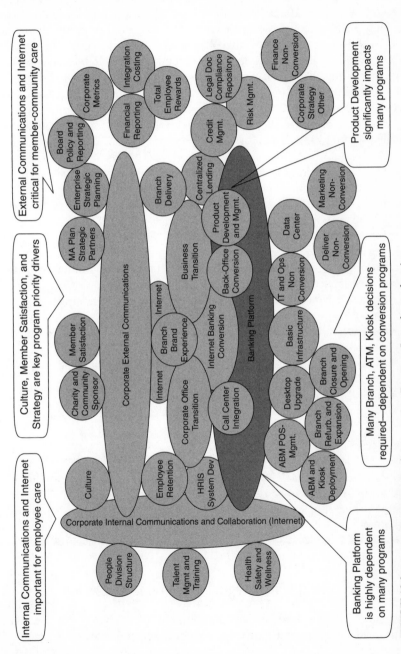

EXHIBIT 18.2 NA Credit Union Bank Integration Program Interdependencies

External Communications and Internet critical for member-community care

Culture, Member Satisfaction, and Strategy are key program priority drivers

Internal Communications and Internet important for employee care

Product Development significantly impacts many programs

Many Branch, ATM, Kiosk decisions required—dependent on conversion programs

Banking Platform is highly dependent on many programs

Corporate Internal Communications and Collaboration (Internet)

Corporate External Communications

Banking Platform

Corporate Metrics

Integration Costing

Board Policy and Reporting

Financial Reporting

Total Employee Rewards

Legal Doc Compliance Repository

Finance Non-Conversion

Enterprise Strategic Planning

Branch Delivery

Credit Mgmt.

Risk Mgmt.

Corporate Strategy Other

MA Plan Strategic Partners

Centralized Lending

Product Development and Mgmt.

Member Satisfaction

Business Transition

Back-Office Conversion

Data Center

Marketing Non-Conversion

Charity and Community Sponsor

Internet

Branch Brand Experience

Internet Banking Conversion

IT and Ops Non Conversion

Deliver Non-Conversion

Corporate Office Transition

Call Center Integration

Basic Infrastructure

Culture

Employee Retention

HRIS System Dev

Desktop Upgrade

Branch Closure and Opening

ABM POS-Mgmt.

Branch Refurb. and Expansion

ABM and Kiosk Deployment

People Division Structure

Talent Mgmt and Training

Health Safety and Wellness

215

on the gap analysis, key resources were hired—in addition to securing contractor and vendor support—and allocated to project teams. A corporate project management office (PMO) governance model was established, as depicted in Exhibit 10.2 (Chapter 10), overseeing all bank integration and banking platform conversion programs. An integration steering committee was established, which met biweekly. A consistent project management process was implemented, with standard template deliverables and weekly status reporting. Various "go/no-go" checkpoints were scheduled throughout the transition timeline, with regular progress reports being made to the NA Credit Union Board.

The high-level banking platform conversion timeline was communicated to all stakeholders. It called for:

- Program and project charters and detailed plans to be completed by the end of August
- Integration business decisions, exceeding 100 in number, to be finalized by the end of September
- Business requirements to be defined and documented by early December
- System design and data mapping to be defined and documented by the end of January
- System enhancement development and testing to be completed by the end of February
- Infrastructure upgrade and capacity increase to be implemented by the end of March
- Data migration (tens of thousands of members) with final mock conversion to be completed by the end of May
- Employee training to be conducted by mid-June
- Banking platform conversion to be completed by the end of June

By applying structured portfolio management and capacity planning, within three months from announcing the merger, NA Credit Union was in a position to start executing critical programs and projects for bank integration and banking platform conversion, governed through the PMO.

Impact: Successful Bank Integration for Value Realization

Through applying four of the six degrees of the IT value network framework, NA Credit Union was able to plan and execute a series of programs that culminated in the successful integration of bank operations and banking system conversion. Subsequently, Read & Associates were employed to recycle on the IT value network framework and implement the remaining two degrees of IT value, to maximize stakeholder economic value.

Bank Integration and Banking System Conversion Realization

The overall guiding principle for the banking platform or system conversion was to minimize member impact while mitigating all risks to achieve an "on time and on budget" banking integration. On July 4, 15 months from the merger announcement, NA Credit Union delivered its banking services on the new integrated banking platform. The bank integration and banking platform conversion was a success, delivering on time and within budget. Portfolio management and rigorous PMO program and project tracking ensured that the banking platform conversion and the ultimate bank integration were accomplished to the stakeholders' satisfaction. Value realization was achieved; a new NA Credit Union was built, delivering superior service to its members.

Networked value management was subsequently measured through various satisfaction surveys. Both members and employees rated high scores in what seemed a seamless transition from the state of "two of everything" to an integrated "state of one." The technology and operations (T&O) organization conducted an annual executive survey before and after the banking platform conversion, surveying the key stakeholders on their satisfaction level with respect to the banking platform conversion and T&O services. The preconversion survey amounted to a baseline and checkpoint on the conversion progress, whereas the postconversion survey provided validation with respect to lessons learned and service levels realized.

Overall, the executives voiced their high satisfaction with T&O in what was acknowledged to be a very challenging conversion year. Project management was cited as being a tremendous success and critical in delivering the bank integration and conversion and managing change effectively. Coordinating resources, managing interdependencies and milestones, mitigating risks, and tracking costs ensured the necessary discipline for project delivery. PMO portfolio management provided sound governance and organization to project management. The PMO was, in fact, referred to as a valued asset, essential to the success of NA Credit Union.

Read & Associates were engaged throughout the bank integration and banking platform conversion program, and subsequently engaged, for an additional 15 months, to assist in postintegration work. After bank integration, the extended assignment focused on the following IT value network management components: IT strategy, portfolio management, IT service management, and banking process management.

Strategic Plan and Portfolio Management: Recycle on the Second Degree of IT Value—IT Strategic Planning and Portfolio Management

After the successful bank integration and banking platform conversion, attention focused on delivering the five-year merger business plan, recycling on the second degree of IT value. The challenge was to:

- Facilitate and develop the technology and operations (T&O) strategic plan to deliver the merger five-year business plan and the promises to members and employees
- Reset the project portfolio, following banking integration, to align T&O investment to deliver the new IT strategy

Service and Information Management: Fifth Degree of IT Value—Technology and Operations Service Management

With a new T&O strategy and an aligned company-wide project portfolio, the fifth degree of IT value was deployed, building off previously enabled T&O capability and capacity (third degree) and an optimized PMO practice (fourth degree). T&O service management excellence required building and deploying:

- A service catalog and service level agreements
- A service-oriented architecture (SOA)
- A T&O service culture dedicated to creating outstanding stakeholder relationships

Value Chain and Process Management: First Degree of IT Value—Simplified Banking Operational Processes and Branch Processes

To deliver the five-year business plan, business process optimization was necessary for meeting volume growth without incremental cost. The first degree of IT value focuses on the value system and process excellence and thus on capturing higher T&O value opportunities. The approach consisted of:

- Identifying and cataloging bank operational and branch processes for streamlining and value capture
- Producing operational process playbooks to document best practices and to enable process improvements

Recycling IT Value Network Deployment—Enhancing Bank Integration for Higher Value

Following the banking platform conversion, attention focused on the enterprise strategy for delivering the five-year merger plan. Read & Associates were subsequently engaged to facilitate the T&O strategy, working with executives across the organization. Through the process of aligning the T&O strategy to the business objectives and stakeholder commitments and distilling the executive feedback from the satisfaction surveys, the following T&O strategic goals were ratified by the NA Credit Union Board:

1. **Exceed expectations—business focused.** Meet and exceed business and member needs and requirements, enabling outstanding relationship service; provide cost-effective and streamlined operational processes.
2. **Integrated platforms—standardization.** Build one banking platform, one IT infrastructure, and one IT operating environment through a buy, build, and integrate strategy.
3. **Managed infrastructure—stabilize.** Deliver cost-efficient, available, and reliable dial tone and data to business partners and clients.
4. **Banking applications and processes—optimize.** Deliver a cost-effective, integrated informational platform that automates operations and can scale nonlinearly with volumes. Include standard policies and procedures, facility environment, and back-office services.
5. **Secure the enterprise—protect assets.** Protect the members' and the credit union's money, assets, and information.
6. **Return on investment—maximize value.** Invest the firm's limited resources wisely for maximum returns through a project portfolio management methodology.

Exhibit 18.3 illustrates the T&O vision: to become a managed service provider for its stakeholders, delivering value-added services to its members and employees. T&O's strategic intent was to manage the delivery of services and provide innovative solutions to enable relationship-based financial services, as facilitated by its partners within the business. An integrated business and IT strategy was developed based on the alignment process illustrated in Exhibit 10.1 (Chapter 10). The technology architectural direction was based on a service-oriented architecture (SOA), separating the front-end service layer from the back-end applications, connecting through a Biztalk service bus. The NA Credit Union T&O service delivery architecture was similar to that portrayed in Exhibit 1.2 (Chapter 1).

The SOA approach is analogous to the cable TV delivery model in that new channels can be added transparently, providing new customer content without changing the underlying systems. Another advantage to this

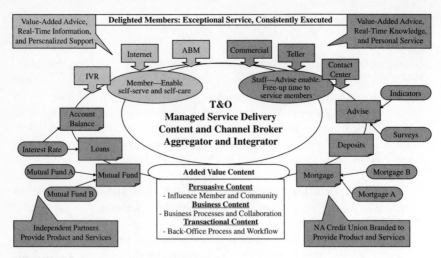

EXHIBIT 18.3 NA Credit Union T&O Vision

approach is that the services can be operated through software as a service (SaaS), enabling the ability to commission new content and services through third parties. Validation of the concept had already been successfully demonstrated at NA Credit Union with the implementation of an outsourced call center infrastructure and SaaS system, which provided a complete member service-desk capability remotely managed by a third party.

Maximizing returns from the T&O strategic direction required increased focus on investment portfolio management (IPM) and demand management, which proved successful during the bank integration. Exhibit 18.4 provides some insight as to the interdependent T&O processes and the approach applied for effective IPM and demand management, focused on value realization. The IPM scorecard becomes the dashboard for T&O networked value management. Projects, assets, and applications are measured through a weighted value index, consisting of cost/benefit, risk, flexibility, strategic, and technology. Utilizing the IPM approach, T&O was able to transfer 12 percent of the total IT investment spending, from operational systems (banking platform) and shared infrastructure to new strategic capability (i.e., Web-managed services) and enhanced stakeholder services in support of the business strategy. See Exhibit 18.5, IPM realizing value.

Operationalizing the T&O strategy required an immediate focus on service and process excellence. With the creation of an integrated banking platform and the early start in enabling an SOA, the critical focus was to define valued services and drive process efficiencies. A service catalog was built, similar to the approach shown in Exhibit 13.1 (Chapter 13), focused

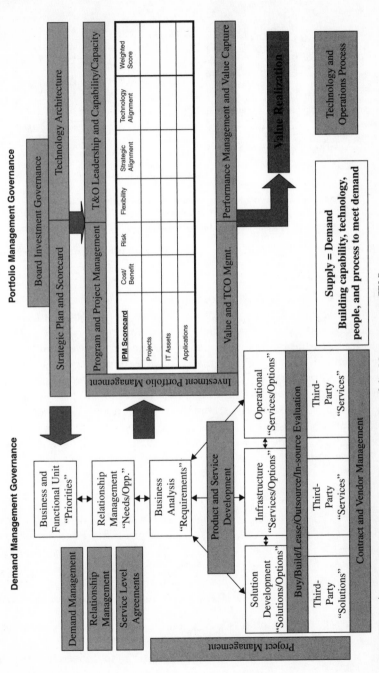

EXHIBIT 18.4 NA Credit Union T&O Investment Portfolio Management (IPM)

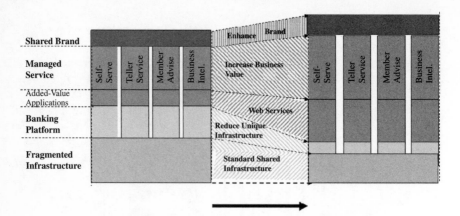

Realizing Value Through Investment Portfolio Management (IPM)
Transferring 12% of the total IT investment from shared infrastructure and
operational systems platform to higher-value services and strategic capability

EXHIBIT 18.5 NA Credit Union Realizing Value through Investment Portfolio Management (IPM)

on the measurement of service costs and benefits. Services were then clustered and categorized, rolling up into stakeholder or business-partner service level agreements (SLAs). In parallel, an extensive process study was completed for both the branch and operational functions. Over 150 processes were identified, which were depicted in an enterprise process map that showed relationships and data flows. Process playbooks were subsequently used to document current-state operational procedures. This exercise took six months, but it resulted in a comprehensive understanding of all bank operational processes. As discussed in Chapter 9, the process playbook is an excellent tool for documenting current-state processes and subsequently defining best practices, process improvements, and future-state optimized processes.

> NA Credit Union applied all six degrees of IT value, realizing stakeholder economic value at various levels, from a successful bank integration and banking platform conversion, to technology and operations (T&O) service excellence and process simplification, to a higher value IT investment portfolio.

Today, NA Credit Union is a competitive force within its communities, carving out a niche in the retail banking sector and providing value-added financial services to its members. NA Credit Union indeed represents a success story of the merger of two financial institutions, culminating in a reinvented community bank that offers outstanding member service. Stakeholder economic value realization was achieved at various levels, from a successful bank integration to service excellence and process simplification, through the effective deployment of the networked value management methodology and two cycles of IT value network management, deploying all six degrees of IT value.

PART V

Emerging Reality—Do IT, Value IT

Measuring and managing IT value has not changed with the times; it remains contained and constrained within traditional financial-based and conventional organization-based evaluation approaches. The current reality is that IT investments are invariably valued as an asset; treated no differently from property or machinery; and categorized as the cost of doing business. Financial views will remain important, but they are lag indicators of past and current capital valuations, whereas the IT value network assesses current and future potential value. Typically human resources are not treated as a booked asset; instead they are categorized as intellectual capital, contributing to intangible value, which is seen as the major contributor to shareholder value and market capitalization. Intangible value from IT investment should no longer be left on the table. The I in IT is the enabler to intellectual capital and therefore earns the right to be more effectively valued. The IT value network strives to meet the challenge, providing new multidimensional approaches to improve stakeholder economic value. Establishing confidence in future value provides the impetus to invest now, despite a recession. The emerging reality is that attitudes towards IT value are changing to accommodate the new paradigms that are driving intellectual capital.

Chapter 19 discusses how the IT value network addresses new paradigms specific to value networks, value systems, and value options, to maximize stakeholder economic value. See the following exhibit, the IT Value Network Extension. Social networking has been around for over 50 years, but has never been more prevalent than in today's world, where trillions of links have been created within value networks, connecting people, computers, and information. Value networks are complex relationships between social and technical resources or nodes, reaching across a business's points of presence and creating economic value. Value network clouds build, overlap, and layer and are consistently evolving, forming new shapes. Network portfolios are being created, requiring appropriate measurement and management. The value of the network can be determined through value network analysis, which maps information assets to the value system and connects stakeholder relationships and interdependencies. The value system extends the value chain, integrating processes and systems across suppliers, customers, partners, and alliances. Value options provide choices and build a flexible capability to address future opportunities for the business—not just the net present value of its parts. Maximizing stakeholder economic value for sustained competitive advantage or network advantage provides a more effective and measurable IT value proposition.

Chapter 20 provides an IT value network maturity model for companies to assess their IT value current practices. IT value client case examples are provided, illustrating different maturity levels. Advancing IT value network maturity needs to be carefully managed and involves evaluating a firm's readiness for organizational change. The chapter concludes with an IT value network checklist for execution along with some final thoughts on the art of collaboration for collective advantage—and ultimately for network advantage. The IT value network is a collaborative change effort between trusted partners for network advantage or sustained competitive advantage.

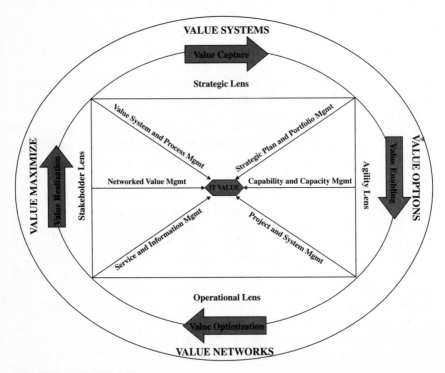

The IT Value Network Extension

CHAPTER **19**

Forward Thinking

Value Networks

With the advent of the Internet and the subsequent creation of trillions of connections, value networks will increasingly affect stakeholder economic value. New individual and business networks are extended and created daily. Value networks seek to determine the sociotechnical economic value of member relationships within a defined system. Loosely coupled with social networking, the focus of value networks is on the value created by the knowledge acquired through the application of technology, culminating in the eventual value exchanges of products and services. Enabling technologies driving knowledge acquisition include collaborative software, content management systems, expert systems, service desk tools, document management software, Web conferencing, wikis, blogs, and e-learning. In addition, mainstream ERP vendors are increasingly embedding knowledge management capability within their systems, including information workflows, process modeling, decision-support systems, real-time analytics, and business intelligence. Knowledge acquisition will create intellectual capital, which will be transformed into tangible returns over time.

> Integration of forward-thinking multidisciplinary evaluation (e.g., value network, value systems, and value options) enhances the IT value network framework and IT value proposition, transitioning from inconclusive shareholder value to maximum stakeholder economic value.

By extending the IT value network framework, as shown in the introductory exhibit in Part V, the goal is to maximize stakeholder economic value through quantifying member relationships, interdependencies, and

227

value exchanges, thereby extending the opportunity to capture, enable, optimize, and realize IT value. Value network analysis provides a methodology and modeling tool to visualize and optimize business networks. New IT investments should therefore consider the stakeholder value proposition of various intra- and interorganizational networks. Micro-functional or process networked goals should be mapped against macro-supplier, customer, and partner networked goals, for a balanced portfolio. Conflicting levels of network goals need to be better managed to maximize stakeholder economic value.

> Value networks seek to determine the sociotechnical economic value of member relationships within a defined system, through quantifying tangible and intangible value exchanges.

Social Networking

During the past century, social scientists have been concerned with social systems, attempting to understand members and the relationship between members at various levels, from interpersonal, to intra- and interorganizational. Traditional social scientists were more concerned with the individual member or actor attributes and their effect on norms and behaviors, and less on the structure or value of the relationship. This focus changed in the 1950s, when social networking became an accepted practice through the cited work of J.A. Barnes. Today, driven by the Internet, the concept of relationship value has become popular and mainstream. Connecting one-to-many and many-to-many has provided numerous permutations of networked relationships. The challenge is to understand the value equation for sustained membership. Whether driven by the intrigue of a school association (i.e., Facebook) or a potential opportunity through a business network (i.e., LinkedIn), it's not hard to understand the initial value proposition of becoming a member—assuming that the incremental effort or cost to join is less than the perceived upside. However, the effort to sustain or maintain membership may well outweigh any realized value over time, culminating in latent or abandoned membership.

The business of social networking is clearly driven by potential subscriptions and associated advertising revenues, as seen with Facebook, LinkedIn, MySpace, and Twitter. However, in applying social networking to value networks, the business value or relevance becomes much deeper and broader. Beyond the Internet excitement, social networks help us understand the value of organizational relationships. The strength of the relationship or interdependency determines the membership value or social capital. Interdependencies are quantified through shared or common values, ideas, or counsel, and through exchange of goods and services. The collective success in pursuit of individual or organizational goals determines the success of the social network. It's no surprise that large ERP vendors (e.g., IBM and SAP) are strong advocates of the underlying social networking themes, offering extended value network opportunities to firms. SAP offers an industry value network program for information sharing and building trusted long-term partnerships, through which network members leverage shared information, resources, and solutions.[1] Similarly, IBM advocates the importance of collaboration for innovation through social networking software tools (social software) and the linking of subject matter experts within the extended business network.[2]

The associations within the network determine behaviors and support systems in pursuit of shared goals and mold organizational functions and processes. Opportunities or new investments are shaped according to these shared goals. However, social networks operate at different levels. Conflicts of interests can occur in competing networks, whether at an individual, functional, organizational, or interorganizational level. The challenge is to quantify and compare relationship and exchange values over time, building a systematic approach to measuring stakeholder economic value for investment decisions. Customer relationships are often defined in dollar values or wallet share over the life cycle of the customer. Similar consideration should be applied to partners and suppliers. Further, employee relationships are frequently cited but rarely quantified, providing inadequate arguments for investment.

> Social networking is not new, but excitement over it has drawn renewed interest in value networks and stakeholder sociotechnical economic value, supporting the IT value network proposition.

Network Portfolio

Value network clouds build, overlap, and layer; they are consistently evolving and forming new shapes. Evaluating the value network takes time and involves identifying current and future valued members and value exchanges within defined system boundaries. Individuals seek associations that are tightly coupled based on known value and trust, but they also seek loose connections for new opportunities or potential value. Access to trusted information can create intellectual and social capital. Firms must understand the value they and others contribute to the network, either directly or through collaboration. In support, value networks should be classified according to stakeholder drivers, strategic assets, and core competencies.[3] Networks and their relationships require proactive management that assesses unique or differentiating firm value and associate value. Further, always remember that the network is valuable only if its valued links stay connected.

The network or system boundaries should be defined according to the level or intensity of interdependency between the members or roles. Internal company value networks are created by key activities, processes, and relationships, which cross the firm's conventional functional or organizational structure. Consider activities such as innovation, customer support processes, or common social interests, all of which can drive internal value networks. External value networks cross traditional interorganizational boundaries, driven by shared company or individual goals such as shared revenue or innovation agreements, market access, best practices, or open standards forums. The strength of the member relationship over time will be determined by the level of interdependency, moving from a casual to a symbiotic relationship. Casual relationships focus more on short-term value and are cost or effort conscious; whereas symbiotic relationships are the longer term and can be quantified in commitments or promises. Thus, value networks need to be well defined, with measurable interdependencies evaluated at various points in time.

Building a portfolio of value networks can be completed at the individual, functional, and organizational level. Executives should consider defining intra- and interorganizational value networks, assigning network owners or sponsors, similar to the current practice of assigning business process or IT system ownership. Customer relationships typically align to sales, supplier relationships to procurement, partner relationships to business development, and employee relationships to human resources. Therefore, it's not a stretch to then ask such executive owners to quantify and manage defined value networks. Perhaps an overarching value network chief or guru should be appointed, to provide best practice and value management, supported by the PMO in administration. The value network chief is the architect for knowledge acquisition and business development.

> Value network clouds build, overlap, and layer, consistently evolving and forming new shapes, requiring network portfolio management and a value network chief to govern knowledge acquisition across the business network.

Value Network Analysis

Social exchange theory considers the cost/benefit analysis of informal exchanges, but exchange value theory focuses on value conversion into hard financials or even price. Business relationships include contractual or formal agreements, along with informal exchanges of knowledge and intangible benefits. Contractual obligations or agreements are funded or budgeted and so are financially tangible, with a stated cost or price. Informal exchanges also need to be quantified through value network analysis, as they are often the key drivers of trust, innovation, and valuable intellectual capital. Value conversion algorithms can determine tangible and nontangible asset values. Ultimately, value network analysis can provide a current- and future-state view of the value of relationships, providing insights to incremental value. As a leading indicator, value network analysis is used by investors to assess a firm's business model and the firm's capability to create future value. It is also used in support of Securities and Exchange Commission (SEC) filings, providing a taxonomy for nonfinancial reporting.

Quantifying or measuring network value is the biggest challenge. Traditional financial-based and conventional organization-based valuation tools fail to identify sources of network value. Network analysis is focused on the structure and composition of the relationship, affecting norms and value propositions. Value network analysis provides a methodology and modeling tool to visualize and optimize business networks, depicting the members or roles (nodes) and their relationships (ties), which generate tangible and intangible value through complex dynamic exchanges. While tangible exchanges are easily quantified through a fair return for goods or services, intangible values are harder to measure but could account for up to 80 percent of a firm's market value. Mapping knowledge flows between members is a way to determine the intangible value of the current and the future potential value of knowledge creation or acquisition. Essentially, intangible values are transformed or converted into tangible values. Knowledge assets are mapped against the value chain or business processes, extending to include external stakeholders such as customers, suppliers, and partners. Information flows and knowledge asset transitions are captured through the value chain and value system, quantifying added value.

Categorizing the relationship contribution provides further insight into capturing the intangible value, aligning to impact areas like the business model, business processes, management reporting, innovation, collaboration opportunities, and service level agreements (SLAs).[4] Impact areas can be defined in term of mutually agreed-on intangible value outcomes, denoted by levels of privileges or knowledge access. SAP has successfully adopted a profitable value network through building a business network in support of its business model, transferring 80 percent of its R/3 software consulting business to partners. Driven by the collaboration with its partners, the global market demand has substantially grown through brand extension, increasing the pie of its retained 20 percent consulting practice.[5] Business models should depict how network relationships and knowledge exchange can create value.

> Business models should include value network analysis, thereby providing a methodology to optimize network member relationships and knowledge acquisition, which generate tangible and intangible value through complex dynamic exchanges.

IT Value Network Impact

Value networks are key to maximizing intellectual capital and stakeholder economic value and are therefore central to the IT value network framework. Chapter 1 referred to a number of IT investment trends, including open architecture and service-oriented architecture, virtualization, network clouds, integrated customer experience, real-time business intelligence, and social computing. The technology direction is without a doubt one that supports network computing. Consumers and businesses will move within and between branded or private clouds, depending on the required service or social network alliance. Thus capturing, enabling, optimizing, and realizing IT value must consider the broader value system across organizational boundaries. Tangible and intangible values within networks should be quantified and measured, providing leading indicators for strategic IT direction, system optimization, and service effectiveness. The portfolio of defined value networks needs to be proactively managed to maximize stakeholder economic value.

> Tangible and intangible values within networks should be quantified and measured, thereby providing leading indicators for strategic IT direction, system optimization, and service effectiveness.

Value Systems

Michael E. Porter's[6] value chain and value system was discussed in Chapter 9, referenced under the first degree in IT value network management. A key focus within the business should be on core competencies that will provide competitive advantage while shedding less-valued capabilities and building new strengths on key fundamentals. Based on the firm's strategic direction, the business model should be tuned to deliver the operational goals, ensuring that processes are optimized in delivering added value through the firm's chain of activities. The value system goes beyond the firm's value chain, including its network of customers, partners, suppliers, alliances, and potentially shareholders. The value chain is essentially extended to capture process optimization within the firm's stakeholder system or portfolio of networks.

Extending the IT value network framework, as shown in the exhibit in Part V, the goal is to maximize stakeholder economic value through optimizing the value system within the firm's business network. IT investment value can be captured by aligning to an optimized value chain and extended to include the value system. In support of a process culture, IT centers of excellence can be created to build process-centric system capability and core competencies for competitive advantage, thereby delivering added value within the value system.

> Value systems go beyond the firm's value chain, allowing processes and systems to converge across the firm's business network and so capture enhanced IT investment opportunities for competitive advantage.

Process and IT System Convergence

Capturing IT value requires mapping the firm's current- and future-state value chain and value system within the firm's business network, depicting interrelationships and IT dependencies or opportunities.[7] Overlaying investments in the IT shared infrastructure, systems, and services to the business processes provides visibility to the extended value chain dependencies on current IT investments. Projecting a future-state value chain or necessary process changes for competitive advantage subsequently provides insight into potential new IT investment opportunities. Consider Cisco's ecosystem, in which employees, suppliers, and customers are integrated into a single enterprise through a networked Web portal. IT investment dollars can be mapped to the current and future process map, providing insights to under- or overinvested processes and highlighting strategic or competitive advantage processes that require additional or reallocated IT investment.

Essentially, process redesign should be examined simultaneously with system capability. Completing major process redesign and then adapting or modifying systems to accommodate is time consuming and costly, especially when considering integration challenges. In addition to change management challenges, this caused many companies to fail in the implementation of large-scale business reengineering projects undertaken in the early to mid-1990s. Often ERP solutions advocate industry best practices, negating the need for process redesign, unless the effort is justifiably unique in providing competitive advantage. IT systems and business process redesign need to converge, chunking into more bite-sized change. The redesign should be evaluated through the IT value index, which captures the value from the strategic, operational, stakeholder, and agility value lenses. Convergence is particularly relevant for the business intelligence value chain, whereby system capability can liberate data (a form of raw material) from business processes, forming intellectual capital.[8] Consider an integrated IT infrastructure build in support of organizational knowledge creation, delivering business strategies through situational relevance of quality information.

New thinking suggests that IT capability can actually lead process change, providing completely new ways of conducting business for a firm and emphasizing agility. The most prevalent application is in the areas of CRM and product development. Consider Google's underlying shared infrastructure in support of the mainstream search business, which has been leveraged to provide a new value proposition for small- and medium-sized business hosting. Many of the processes are already automated creating a new operating model with relative ease. Business process reengineering drives radical new ways of conducting business, as opposed to process improvements. Perhaps business system reengineering will become a new paradigm, and IT may well become a driving change agent and not just an enabler or follower of processes.

> IT systems and business process redesign need to converge, considering business system reengineering and not be treated separately, enhancing core competencies within the value system.

Process Culture

Creating a process culture within an organization follows from a conscious decision by the leadership team, requiring significant effort down and across the firm's conventional organizational structure. Typically, key executive positions are created and then anointed as process champions or owners. In many cases, by default, the functional executive takes ownership of relevant processes, like the Sales VP owning sales processes. In other cases, there may not be an obvious choice, such as overseeing the supply chain or all procurement. Process owners ensure accountability of the firm's critical competencies, which create competitive advantage. Similarly, the IT organization should align to a process-centric organization, as in the Nortel case study presented in Chapter 16. Account managers, in this case, supported the business process owners and provided IT capability in support of process excellence.

IT organizations should enable process improvement. This would imply that the IT capability expands to include functional process knowledge. However, a clear distinction should be made between process knowledge and process design. The former considers process domain expertise, while the latter considers process engineering capability. Business analysts, typically reporting to the business function, may be best located within the IT organization, as seen at Indigo, providing process knowledge in proximity to system design. Converging process and IT system knowledge will optimize value through simplification, rationalization, and integration opportunities within the extended value chain. Process engineers are best served in support of the business process owners, in mapping current and future state processes. In the absence of an executive process champion, it is not uncommon for the CIO to become the process leader for the company.

> Converging process and IT system knowledge will optimize value through simplification, rationalization, and integration opportunities within the extended value chain.

IT Centers of Excellence

In addition to business process knowledge, the IT organizations should build centers of excellence in support of the firm's critical competencies or capability. Depicting the IT value chain is a good start; it is a way to identify infrastructure, systems, services, and supporting processes (i.e., ITIL, system development life cycle, project management), which add value to the business processes. Key performance indicators (KPIs) tie the IT value chain components to the business process. Business systems planning (BSP), popularized in the 1980s by IBM, provides a sound framework to identify sources of added value, aligned to processes, interfaces, and data sources and flows. Creating IT centers of excellence around core business competencies and capabilities increases the visibility of IT business priorities and focus. This, in turn, builds alignment and partnership between IT and the business.

In some cases a firm's core competencies could well include IT capability in itself. Consider an online business, where the competitive advantage or differentiating process is indeed a search capability. In fact, IT is now so embedded into the firm's value chain that in many ways it has become a critical differentiating or cost-leading competence. However, the investment in IT centers of excellence will depend on the firm's recognition of IT added value. Viewed as a cost center, IT is perceived to be a commodity or a utility, less concerned with added value and more concerned with service at the lowest cost. As a profit or investment center, IT is seen as a partner, identified as a key contributor to profits and competitive advantage options.[9] Aspiring CIOs should consider opportunities to build IT centers of excellence that provide enhanced business capability.

The value shop model, conceptualized by Thompson in 1967, provides an approach to building IT centers of excellence. The focus is on customer or client problem solving and solutions. While the value shop is not concerned about the end-to-end value chain, it can be aligned to business (client) process owners, providing system solutions. Required IT activities would include problem identification, problem solving, solution or system options, solution or system deployment, control management, and solution evaluation. These value shops or centers of excellence could be created within or external to the firm's IT organization. Through partnerships, outsourcing, or vendor agreements, the firm's IT value shop can be virtualized.

> Creating IT centers of excellence around core business competencies and capabilities increases the visibility of IT business priorities and focus, thereby aligning the IT value chain to business added-value processes.

IT Value Network Impact

Value systems are central to IT investment value, providing a firm with competitive advantage. This implies the IT organization must become more process-centric, aware of opportunities for process improvement within and beyond the firm's value chain. IT collaboration with the business is critical and is becoming increasingly important between IT and the firm's suppliers, partners, and customers. As the firm's business network evolves, so do the opportunities for reengineering or redesigning processes and systems. The IT value network framework advocates the integration or convergence of business process and system redesign as a way to capture higher levels of IT value. Enabling IT process capability and core competence around centers of excellence generates a more responsive and effective IT organization. System solutions and services are subsequently optimized across the value chain and value system.

> The IT value network framework advocates the integration or convergence of business process and system redesign, capturing higher levels of IT value; IT solutions and services are subsequently optimized across the value chain and value system.

Value Options

As discussed previously, living under uncertainty is becoming the norm, especially in a fast-paced globally connected world. The speed of events with respect to the recent global banking crisis and credit crunch took many by surprise and is a reflection of uncertain times. Equally, the speed of technology change and inter-networking shows no signs of easing. Trying to predict medium-term (two to three years) reality—let alone long-term (three to five years)—continues to be a challenge for most companies. Thus, the importance of the challenge for most companies. Thus, the importance of the agility value lens, as discussed in Chapter 7, for evaluating IT investments. Ensuring that IT investment decisions consider business flexibility is paramount for speed to market and profit, which, in turn, drive key enabling IT value capability. IT investment examples include open architecture, evergreen applications, and best practice ERP systems, as discussed in Chapter 1. Flexibility is equally served through the selection of strategic IT investments or IT value options. Under uncertainty, longer-term IT projects also require significant risk management to achieve desired outcomes.

Through extending the IT value network framework, as shown in the introductory exhibit in Part V, the goal is to maximize stakeholder economic value, through building, enabling, and executing IT value options at various points in time. In support of the business strategic direction, IT value options can be identified, which provides business flexibility. Such options can then be executed at the right time. Consider the IT value option to deploy "real-time" a series of CRM Web services as dictated by market changes or customer buying habits. Further, embedding options into the IT organization and IT infrastructure capability provides incremental added value, responding to future opportunities. An example would be the deployment of a service-oriented architecture or the migration to open systems.

> Value options provide competitive advantage during times of uncertainty, highlighting the importance of the agility value lens for IT investment evaluation and enabling a flexible and responsive IT capability for future business opportunities.

IT Agility with Scenario Uncertainty

Chapter 1 discussed the importance of considering agility or flexibility within IT investment decisions, building an IT capability to quickly respond to market and business changes, especially under uncertainty. Flexibility has the higher potential of enabling the upside while containing the downside. Future-state technology architecture should accommodate an open design, providing options or alternatives for changing business conditions or requirements. This may require additional system or infrastructure project investment, but the longer-term IT cost of ownership will likely be lower, through reduced integration, change management, and operating costs. Essentially, the objective here is to maximize long-term stakeholder economic value, thereby ensuring that total capital and all operating costs are accounted for within the value-creation business case.

IT agility is critical for strategic IT investments when there is outcome uncertainty. As discussed in Chapter 6, scenario planning is an excellent tool for devising flexible long-term plans and options. The focus is on critical strategic decisions, identifying parameters and uncontrollable variables. All possible outcomes are determined, identifying assumptions. Subsequently, "what if" analysis is applied, using decision trees, probability theory, and financial measures. The outcome with the highest return is then selected for execution. However, scenario planning requires significant time and expert knowledge. Thus, many companies conduct less formal scenario planning, resorting to executive knowledge and heuristics for outcome selection. The application of contingency planning is simpler and therefore more popular, where outcome decisions are made and "what if" analysis is applied to known individual risks or individual uncertainties rather than multiple combinations per scenario. Equally, sensitivity analysis would consider change in one variable at a time.

Applying scenario planning to IT strategy and investments requires a clear understanding of the business strategy, KPIs, and business drivers. Scenario planning advancement is taking place in the application of systems thinking, defining the value system, and subsequently mapping current and future state business processes with the supporting system applications. A value systems approach, discussed previously, hardens causal network relationships and supports plausible scenarios. Current-state and future-state technology architecture blueprints should be created that draw attention to technology migration opportunities for open systems and agility. Given such migration opportunities, the agility value lens can be quantified for new IT investment decisions, weighing agility with the other value lenses—strategic, operational, and stakeholder. Technology alternatives (i.e., proprietary or open) will have different IT value index outcomes, and the highest should be chosen based on the probable or likely scenario.

> Quantifying the agility value is critical for strategic IT investments that have outcome uncertainty, where systems thinking can advance scenario planning by discovering value options.

IT Risk Management Options

Due to the quick pace of technology, changing economic conditions, and volatility of market environments, IT investments and projects are inherently risk sensitive. The risks connected with an IT project are based on unique factors and thus are unsystematic or diversifiable. Chapter 1 discussed risk management treatment for controllable and uncontrollable risks, as applied to existing and new IT investments. Chapter 2 discussed risk and uncertainty, challenging conventional IT measurement norms according to which traditional capital investment and financial measures do not capture agility and flexibility. Chapter 5 outlined the IT risk management technique for evaluating an IT investment, consisting of an emerging decision support method for factoring or discounting various individual costs and benefit streams for a more rigorous NPV. This section expands on IT risk management options and mitigation strategies.

Within the IT investment portfolio, risk management is primarily concerned with the realization of overall investment returns, with a secondary focus on interdependency between programs and projects. Key risk considerations include strategic alignment risk (are we doing the right things?); architecture and integration risk (are we doing them the right way?); capability and delivery risk (are we getting them done well?); and benefit realization risk (are we getting the benefits?).[10] The objective is to achieve maximum stakeholder economic value within a balanced (i.e., short-term versus long-term) portfolio. In addition, interdependent variables across programs or projects need to be effectively managed; these include resource contention, sequencing within schedules, investment constraints, technology selection, and system availability. Program or project management applies risk management to achieve the stated business requirements with the expected quality, within approved budget and schedule. Whether at the portfolio, program, or project level, there are risk management options and mitigation strategies.

Risk management options or treatments include avoidance (elimination), transference (outsourcing or insuring), retention (acceptance and budgeting), and reduction (mitigating). Applied to IT investments, avoiding risk is idyllic. However, not proceeding with a cause of action to avoid risk may prevent a higher gain. For instance, not migrating applications to an open architecture would avoid risk of failure, but it would bypass the opportunity of system agility and simplification. Transferring risk is a viable option, typically seen in outsourcing deals, where a third party takes on the project and/or its operating risk. However, the IT organization still has to manage the business risk through governance and controls. Depending on the company's risk profile, retaining or accepting risk is an option, budgeting for the risk or probability of occurrence. Retaining risk on the books is typically seen in disaster recovery or information security situations, in which a company is not prepared to spend up-front on IT investment for 100 percent failsafe (if indeed that is possible) but would rather use reserves to fund the recovery from the unlikely event of failure. Finally, risk reduction or mitigation is probably the most commonly used option, the ultimate objective being to minimize the probability of failure or the severity of failure. IT projects can be created just to reduce operating risk, justified through risk and reward. In addition, contingency funds are often allocated within IT or project budgets to mitigate risk.

Risk management strategies should be governed through an enterprise risk management plan, which should identify known risks and acceptable treatments. IT risk management would be a subset, typically focused on information security, disaster recovery, audit concerns, and internal controls. There seems to be never enough money to cope with the all the information security needs, which include managing existing and new vulnerabilities as well as single points of failure. Disaster recovery deals with a number of trade-offs; the goal is to prevent the need to completely replicate costly production systems while retaining some residual risk. Audit issues need to be eventually remedied, allocating necessary resources and budget, with adequate internal controls having a clear priority.

Risk management and mitigation is invariably all about the risk-and-reward equation, prioritizing IT investment based on the potential highest gain or lowest loss. Applied to IT projects, risk mitigation is about ensuring that expected business outcomes are achieved on time and on budget. Applied to business cases, benefits should be discounted, factored for their risk of not occurring; also contingency funding should be allocated based on accuracy of planned cost estimates and possible risk occurrence in execution. Subsequently, for both IT investment and IT projects, although there are many different risk reduction strategies that should be managed, often IT risk mitigation defaults to incremental budget and resources.

> Risk management strategies should be governed through an enterprise risk management plan, which should identify known company risks and acceptable treatments, prioritizing IT investment based on the potential highest gain or lowest loss.

Real Option Techniques

A "real option" is the investment in physical and human assets that gives the ability to enable future opportunities, providing a higher future value to a firm. Firms need to hedge against adverse conditions in the future and retain an ability to capture the upside benefits. Real options were discussed in Chapter 5 as an emerging decision support technique for IT value measurement, supplementing traditional accounting and financial methods. The real option approach provides improved rigor to the value-based business case for capital budgeting, but it also provides an excellent addition to strategic decision making because this approach accounts for the value of future flexibility in times of environmental uncertainty. Real options can be used for IT value measures and methods in support of quantifying both the strategic and agility value lenses. In addition, the real options approach supports IT value management in the development and build of the IT strategy and IT capability, thereby capturing and enabling IT value.

Real option models originated from the John Henderson option model, which was successfully applied to financial transactions such as stock trades, currency arbitrage, and currency futures. The Cox-Rubinstein equation is central to the model and is used to assess the risks of a bet on the future price of a financial asset. Such option models are heuristic, but they adjust structure and coefficients based on volumes of transactions to determine future outcomes. The rigor of mathematical models to singular accounting measures and subjective IT investment decisions has excited early study. Real options can be simple in concept for identifying and evaluating IT strategic options or complex in capital budgeting and business case modeling.

The deployment challenge is in the transferability of adapted real option models to IT investment evaluation with respect to relevance and application simplification. There are many practical difficulties in applying real option techniques to capital budgeting and strategic decision making. Specifically, finding a model whose assumptions match the IT investment or project, capable of determining model inputs and having the ability to mathematically solve the option-pricing algorithm. Using standard options models (i.e., the Black-Scholes option valuation model) for strategic analysis could lead to poor strategic decisions. Customized models are required for each IT investment or project situation, thus perhaps explaining the current limited use of the real options approach in capital budgeting.[11] However, there have been some notable successes.

In building value-based business cases, many decision-support researchers question traditional capital investment measures; as such, metrics do not consider uncertainty, flexibility, and the opportunity of delay. Consider NPV as a measure that uses one risk-adjusted discounted rate for both the upside (positive outcome) as well as the downside (negative outcome) of risk. Further, NPV provides inadequate decision consideration in connection with investment irreversibility, uncertainty, and the opportunity of project delay. Therefore, the basic argument is to apply real options in the form of risk-adjusted rates according to probable outcomes of the different streams of benefits (tangible and intangible) and costs; subsequently, cash flows are discounted at a risk-free rate. Essentially, using a real option approach is applying an adjusted version of decision tree analysis.[12] Modeling takes time, but once completed it can be reused and tuned, providing a more realistic NPV for IT investment comparison and selection. Investing for growth options rather than cash streams is an important factor for justifying IT investment.[13]

Stochastic variability of uncertainty can be determined for IT projects; they need to achieve stakeholder economic value and business requirements, be on budget, be on time, and achieve quality or performance dimensions. The weighting and variability within these parameters can determine the real option value. Real option methodologies are proposed as a more effective approach to de-risking project investment. By applying real options for project flexibility, there is a higher potential of enabling the upside value, while limiting the downside or risk of no value.[14] Chatterjee and Ramesh propose a spiral-circle methodology for technology risk management in software development. Essentially, risk analysis is integrated at each stage of the project to provide for periodic evaluation and improved performance.[15]

Benaroch and Kauffman have successfully applied an adapted Black-Scholes model in a real-world case. Black's approximation was effectively used for the deployment timing of point-of-sale (POS) debit services at the Yankee 24 shared electronic banking network in New England. On the basis of this successful outcome the authors suggest that the application of the Black-Scholes model can be applied to different classes of IT project investment,[16] specifically:

1. **IT infrastructure investments,** which often do not provide immediate expected payback; therefore, there is a need to convert investment opportunities into the option's underlying asset (i.e., technology that support a revenue-generating sales process).
2. **Emerging technology investments,** in which technology is embedded in the underlying asset, posing a challenge to forecasting varied perceptions of future value payoffs; here the impact of stochastic cost (uncertain exercise price) is important (i.e., business analytic software is embedded into marketing software that supports a marketing research campaign).
3. **Application design prototyping investments,** in which the actual asset is less valuable than the potential value to react to business or

market change, providing necessary application functionality (i.e., Web applications).
4. **Technology-as-product investments,** where the project direction and decisions depend on the time remaining to exercise the option and value at a point in time (i.e., consideration of project time constraints and the value of a technology licensing agreements).

Real options can add value to individual IT investment or project evaluation; however, a possible greater value might come from deploying real option attributes in the management of the total IT investment portfolio. In considering a portfolio view of projects or IT investments, management can review a project's real option values, determining whether to explore, defer, abandon, expand, contract, or switch an IT investment within a project or apply it to the entire project investment. The key is to evolve the real options methodology to develop a repeatable and verifiable approach for the planning, allocation, and management of the portfolio of IT investments; this calls for consistently gathering and evaluating tangible and intangible costs and returns.[17] Such an approach will assist in resource allocation across IT investments and the business, with the goal of maximizing enterprise synergies and objectives.[18] There is a need to assess the overall value of IT and to consider portfolio decision scenarios, evaluating project trade-offs or option interactions and interdependencies.[19]

Grenadier and Weiss[20] studied two fundamental characteristics of investments in technological innovations: the impact of past decisions on future technological options and the uncertainty over future innovation opportunities. An optimal investment strategy for sequential technology innovations is proposed for a firm to pursue based on market and company-specific variables. Innovations are stochastically projected, based on their arrival times and their profitability. Four separate investment strategies are identified to determine firm policy based on the impact of past decisions on future technology options and the uncertainty over future innovation opportunities. These migration strategies include:

1. A compulsive strategy of purchasing every innovation
2. A leapfrog strategy of skipping an early innovation, but adopting the next generation of innovation
3. A buy-and-hold strategy of purchasing only an early innovation
4. A laggard strategy of waiting until a new generation of innovation arrives before purchasing the previous innovation

Kulatilaka and Venkatraman propose a strategic options navigator coordinated across three domains: business (CEO), IT (CIO), and finance (CFO).[21] Strategic options need to be assessed continually by the three domains, reevaluating the value and necessary actions to maintain, terminate, or develop the options. IT management often pays too much attention to cost management and not enough to IT capabilities that can grow future business opportunities. Deloitte Consulting has commercialized an idea that is similar to the strategic options navigator. A framework has been built for the application of strategic investment options, defined as a strategic flexibility framework, that determines four stages: anticipate, formulate, accumulate, and operate. Based on various business scenarios, necessary core program components are acquired and options placed on contingent parts. These options are either exercised or abandoned, depending on information at certain decision points; this is a way of meeting today's capability and developing capabilities for potential future opportunities.[22] Alternatively, an investment life cycle model can be used, as advocated by Benaroch, in which different options are relevant over time.[23]

Using a real options approach goes beyond the justification of a business case and project investments; it focuses the firm to assess opportunities, acquire options, nurture these options, and, when conditions are right, capture the value. Applied to IT value network management, the real options approach provides a theoretical platform for supporting strategies and building capabilities, through heuristics under uncertainty. IT executives have a more systematic approach in considering the uncertainty of several outcomes to a course of action and the available options. Depending on the decision-makers' view toward risk, the executive can subsequently apply risk and sensitivity analysis, determining probabilities of occurrence. Outcomes can be assessed based on the probability of success or highest added value. Embedding options through IT investment subsequently provides added-value capability for future opportunities. Executives should pay for flexibility after new information is received and before significant costs or revenues are incurred, assuming the probability of uncertainty is high.

A "real option" is the investment in physical and human assets that provides the ability to enable future opportunities, thus yielding a higher future value to a firm. Real options support strategic decision making and portfolio management and improve IT value-based business-case rigor for capital budgeting.

IT Value Network Impact

Value options provide agility and flexibility, especially under uncertainty, creating competitive advantage opportunities. The value options approach combines the theory of financial options with the fundamentals of strategic planning, risk management, organizational theory, decision analysis, and complex systems. Real options and risk management can be applied to project and portfolio management in addition to IT strategic planning and IT capability build. Applying a real options approach not only provides rigor to the IT value-based business case, enhancing traditional financial-based NPV measures, but it also can focus the firm to strategically assess opportunities, acquire options, nurture these options, terminate or keep options, and, when the time is right, capture the value. Real option and risk management methods can be used to quantify both the agility and strategic value lenses. Value options offer a valuable approach to building stakeholder economic value and competitive advantage because it combines a firm's innovation capabilities to address current and new markets, not just the net present value of its parts.[24] The IT value network framework advocates a value option approach to improve the capture, enablement, optimization, and realization of IT value.

> The IT value network framework advocates a value option approach to improve the capture, enablement, optimization, and realization of IT value, embedding options through IT investment maximizes stakeholder economic value.

Maximizing Stakeholder Economic Value

The traditional goal of a company is to maximize shareholder wealth through improving the stock price or paying dividends. Milton Friedman argued that the social responsibility of a business is to make profits. For shareholder value and stock price to increase, new corporate investment should provide a higher rate of return to the cost of capital investors would see in equally risky alternatives. However, attempts to isolate or determine the cause and effect of IT investment contribution to shareholder value have been inconclusive, as discussed in Chapter 2. Further, conditional prerequisites for IT investment are required, where complementary firm investments (i.e., change management) are essential for unlocking and realizing the full shareholder value. Studies have suggested that the success rate of IT on change initiatives is between 20 to 50 percent, emphasizing the importance of the inclusion of change management investment.[25] In addition, traditional financial measures, in pursuit of shareholder value, do not capture the range of perceived and realizable values from key stakeholders.

Maximizing stakeholder economic value from IT investments provides a more effective and measurable IT value proposition, especially when you consider the extended value network and value system, as shown in the introductory exhibit in Part V. The objective of the IT value network is to maximize stakeholder economic value (including social and moral responsibility). The stakeholder value lens provides a 360-degree perspective on defining stakeholder perceptions and expectations of value, which together with the other three value lenses (strategic, operational, and agility) cumulatively identifies stakeholder economic value. Determining stakeholder value is an art rather than a science; it requires extracting views and opinions through focus groups, surveys, reviews, and debriefings. Decisions are made based on intuition or best guess, not financials alone, requiring higher levels of information exchange and communication. Maximizing IT value requires effective stakeholder engagement, communication, and expectation management throughout the stages of value capture, value enablement, value optimization, and value realization.

Stakeholders will continually evaluate IT performance against SLAs, project deliverables, information management, and expected returns, in addition to functional or process capability, availability, flexibility, and if nothing else, perceived value at points in time. Therefore, the IT executive needs to continually assess the shared infrastructure, systems, services, and strategic investments, effectively measuring and communicating IT impact on the business network stakeholders. Network value management, the sixth degree of IT, as discussed in Chapter 14, is pivotal in driving stakeholder economic value. By applying value network analysis, as discussed previously, key stakeholders can be identified, depicting relationships and interdependencies across the value system. Network value management is a process to identify and deliver the stakeholder business drivers and expectations, as aligned to the strategic and operational objectives. The process builds on value network analysis to define member "loyalty" or satisfaction drivers. To understand expectations and perceived stakeholder value, it is wise to continually perform internal and external stakeholder satisfaction surveys and focus groups to identify areas of improvement and indeed areas of delight, in this way improving performance through a process of discovery and alignment.

Maximizing stakeholder economic value provides a more effective and measurable IT value proposition than questionable shareholder value; it builds a fan club of loyal and delighted stakeholders across the value network and value system.

IT Satisfaction and Value Loyalty

As discussed in Chapter 6, emerging organizational management techniques such as stakeholder surveys should be considered for measuring IT value. Stakeholder IT satisfaction and value loyalty are the main components of the stakeholder value lens. Building value loyalty across the network or value system drives realizable value. Network value management is essentially a loyalty business model for IT investment and the IT organization in itself. The loyalty business model assumes that when stakeholders are in pursuit of shared interests, there will be a convergence of minds, between seeking self-interest (IT—egotistical) and seeking the best interest of others (business—altruistic). Four critical factors drive IT loyalty: shared values or goals, relationship strength, potential alternatives, and critical events.

Identifying and nurturing company shared values in pursuit of common goals is often illustrated in the firm's mission and value statements, along with aligned objectives, through cascading balanced scorecards. The IT balanced scorecard, as discussed in Chapter 6, refers to the IT internal customer or client satisfaction, as a key measure of performance. Essentially, in an extended value network and system, this would incorporate all IT stakeholders, evaluating satisfaction and loyalty through the stakeholder value lens. The strength of the relationship between IT management and the business or extended stakeholders has a strong influence on IT loyalty and requires significant effort in building trust and managing expectations. In the Nortel business case, executive client managers were appointed to manage a business portfolio, with a remit to build trusted partnerships and strong relationships with the aligned business executives. Delighting stakeholders should be a key objective, especially when stakeholders have a choice whether to invest in IT or to outsource IT. Business dissatisfaction with IT can lead to a new CIO or complete IT outsourcing. Finally, critical events have key influence on loyalty; therefore, consider the impact of system crashes, project success or failures, service desk responsiveness, or network security breaches.

Value network analysis, as discussed previously, helps identify key stakeholder members and their relationships. Stakeholders should be categorized by common business drivers, considering external members (i.e., supplier, partner, customer segments, shareholders), internal functions (i.e., sales, marketing, finance), or by organization level (i.e., executives, management, employees). As discussed in Chapter 14, network value management (the sixth degree of IT value), the art of surveying, requires understanding the stakeholder landscape or context. Aligning to the firm's strategic goals and KPIs, the balanced scorecard cascades business objectives down the organization, defining key stakeholder critical success factors (CSFs). Satisfaction business drivers can be extrapolated and subsequently validated through focus groups and surveys, where IT investments are evaluated against these drivers, measuring perceptions of satisfaction and value. In addition, external stakeholders should be engaged in a similar "light" process, to establish satisfaction drivers within the business network. Extending the reach across the business network provides a line-of-sight to customer, supplier, partner, and shareholder perceived value. Stakeholders should be informed of consolidated feedback and performance outcomes, agreeing to targeted actions and improvements. Continuous review and stakeholder communication against targets should be conducted, deploying timely surveys and follow-up briefings as appropriate.

Although stakeholder satisfaction is essentially a state of mind, it has proved to be an effective tool for measuring perceptions and expectations of performance, correlating with value realization. The University of Michigan's American Customer Satisfaction Index (ACSI) is the scientific standard for customer satisfaction and a strong predictor of national gross domestic product growth. Applied to companies, the ACSI has proved to be an effective predictor of share or stock market performance. The Net Promoter score, trademarked by Frederick Reichheld, Bain and Company and Satmetrix, is another popular survey that is used to determine customer loyalty and the strength of customer relationships.[26] On a scale of 0 to 10, customers are asked, "How likely is it that you would recommend our company to a friend or colleague?" Although it uses customer-facing questions, the Net Promoter could be adapted and applied to IT. Promoters would be positive drivers of value realization, detractor stakeholders would be negative drivers, and passive stakeholders neutral drivers. The difference between the number of promoters and the number of detractors would determine the score; if greater than 75 percent, it would be considered high.

There are a number of different approaches to surveying stakeholders for satisfaction and value loyalty. IT customer or stakeholder satisfaction surveys can be compiled and administered online, in paper form, or by interview. Surveys can be designed to target IT services, shared infrastructure, systems, or all IT capability, capturing satisfaction and/or value. The audience can be targeted at various levels: executive, functional, general employee, supplier, partner, shareholder, or board executives, or can be based on events or projects. It is not uncommon to find IT organizations conducting an annual executive survey, a quarterly general employee survey, a project closure survey, and an IT service desk survey. Very few IT organizations survey or interview their suppliers, partners, or end customers; that is a more complex procedure, but failing to perform it does leave value opportunities on the table, unexplored. Consider the customer relationship build potential at Nortel, when Nortel's CALA (Caribbean and Latin America) regional CIO created the CIO forum for Nortel customers—or Indigo's annual IT supplier and partner conference for shared goals.

> Stakeholder IT satisfaction and value loyalty are the main components of the stakeholder value lens; building value loyalty across the value network and value system will realize economic value.

Perceptions and Trust

Shared or common values, as discussed previously, shape stakeholder behavior. However, organizational behavior and actions are also influenced by stakeholder perceptions of reality, not the reality itself. Therefore, it can be argued that the perception of reality is indeed reality in the eye of the beholder. Perceptions are produced and experienced in the mind.[27] Perception can be defined as the process stakeholders use to select, organize, interpret, and respond to information around them. Situations are perceived differently by stakeholders, who selectively interpret them and respond accordingly. Information is selectively screened to filter the most important issues. There are external and internal drivers affecting perception. External drivers include culture, size, intensity, contrast, motion, repetition, familiarity, and novelty. Internal drivers include personality, learning, and motivation.[28]

Perception of IT value is very subjective and stakeholder-specific. The challenge is to provide factual evidence of value, defendable by recognized expert opinion. Accepted value is more evident when there is a clear correlation between IT investment and performance improvement. Tangible value transferred to the bottom line is usually a convincing argument for broad acceptance of value, assuming that it is ratified by an impartial finance department. However, business executives could reject such direct correlation, due to other contributory factors (e.g., process change or staff competence). As discussed in Chapter 2, research has not validated the correlation between IT investment and profits. Isolating and determining the cause and effect between IT investment and tangible value is a challenging but not impossible task. The difficulty in building perceived intangible value across stakeholders is even more challenging, often becoming devalued to an unmeasurable "warm" or "cold" sense or feeling.

Stakeholder perceptions of IT value are likely to default to beliefs or heuristics, previous learning, or level of trust in IT. The art of managing perceptions is to provide information or knowledge that is consistent with stakeholders' preconceived ideas and experiences; if inconsistent, such information will be disregard or undervalued. Therefore, IT value will not be acknowledged unless stakeholders have satisfactory experiences. As discussed previously, IT satisfaction and loyalty provide the means to measure stakeholder experiences and perceptions. The value of managing customer experiences is well understood, but managing IT stakeholder experiences is typically overlooked. Building IT trust with stakeholder partners and delivering on the promise must take priority. Understanding the stakeholder audience is critical, as is empathy and being responsive to key concerns, issues, and priorities. Agreed IT commitments must be clearly documented. IT capability and solutions must be effectively delivered against the commitments. Communicating the value proposition consistently and with congruence through multimedia channels should be a continuous process. Only then will perceptions of IT value start to mature and deepen. Tangible value from IT investment are no longer challenged or questioned; warm feelings become more definable, and, ultimately, intangible value becomes measurable.

> Building IT trust with stakeholder partners and delivering on the promise must be a priority; however, managing IT stakeholder experiences is typically overlooked.

Managing Expectations

Managing expectations requires a clear understanding of and the separation of stakeholder fundamental needs or must haves from desired outcomes or wants. Differentiating between the two prepares the way for "contractual" expectations (must haves) and partnership expectations (wants). Without differentiation, stakeholders will have a higher expectation that goes beyond the committed IT capability to deliver. Contracts or formal agreements between IT and the business partners are popular, equating costs and capability and creating manageable expectations. For instance, SLAs provide clarity to the level of services or capability the service provider will support, at an agreed cost or budget. As discussed in Chapter 6, SLAs are actively used as an IT value approach for external and internal service providers. Additional formal contracts between IT and the business are also evident in project "success criteria" agreements and balanced scorecards. Interestingly, the informal agreements or understandings are becoming just as important in managing desired outcomes. Partnerships based on trust attempt to serve the wants and uncover hidden expectations, driving intangible value. However, stakeholder expectation should be positioned to accept that the wants are not an entitlement, but rather a pursuit.

Managing stakeholder expectations requires a fundamental understanding of the satisfaction level with the IT basic capability and service levels, before aspiring to higher levels of value. Viewed in the light of Maslow's hierarchy of needs, base survival needs must be in place before stakeholders show their willingness to pursue higher aspirations of actualization. IT must have a solid platform of operational excellence before higher-value propositions such as agility and competitive advantage can be promoted.[29] Equally, if the business expectations are that IT merely supports operations at the lowest cost, then this can become a barrier to higher-value propositions until the expectations can be reset. This applies to both internal and external service providers. Surveying stakeholder satisfaction is a prerequisite for setting a baseline and managing expectations. Further, linking business CSFs—and where possible the firm's KPIs—to service and solution provisioning will anchor IT delivery to the business drivers.

It is critical for any company to effectively market and promote itself to its customers, suppliers, partners, employees, and its shareholders. Marketing communication is a key element, one that focuses on sending the right message to the various stakeholders. The CIO must be able to orchestrate the key messages to the IT stakeholders, segmenting as appropriate and resonating with buying or touch points. Continual stakeholder communication is critical to manage expectations. Good communication occurs at various levels, from informal individual stakeholder check-ins, to formal company-wide "town halls" or newsletters. The IT value proposition and success stories should be known to both internal and external stakeholders (Chapter 16, see Nortel case). IT marketing is typically downplayed or overlooked, but with consistent and congruent messaging, the stakeholder network (including industry champions and market makers) will become believers, recognizing the firm's IT value and best practices. The right message at the right time in the right media packs a big punch, especially at annual budget reviews or quarterly reviews, to the point where the IT dollar value is perceived to have increased fourfold without an extra dollar having been spent.

> Managing stakeholder expectations requires a fundamental understanding of the satisfaction level with the IT basic capability and service levels, before aspiring to higher levels of IT value; comparable to the Maslow's hierarchy of needs, base survival needs must be in place before stakeholders are willing to pursue higher aspirations of actualization.

IT Value Network Impact

Maximizing stakeholder economic value drives the IT value network proposition, especially in view of the extended value network and value system.

Network value management, the sixth degree of IT as discussed in Chapter 14, is pivotal in realizing stakeholder economic value. Network value management is essentially a loyalty business model for IT investment and the IT organization in itself. Building trust and value loyalty across the value network and value system drives realizable economic value. The loyalty process builds on network value analysis, nurturing member relationships and satisfying stakeholder drivers. To manage expectations and define perceived stakeholder value, it is wise to continually perform internal and external stakeholder satisfaction surveys and focus groups, in order to identify areas of improvement and indeed areas of delight, thereby improving performance through a process of discovery and alignment. Stakeholder IT satisfaction and value loyalty are the main components of the stakeholder value lens. Stakeholder economic value should be broadly promoted across the business network. Through effective ongoing marketing communication, the IT value proposition and success stories should be known to both internal and external stakeholders; with the intent to build trust and the recognition of IT investment returns and ultimately the realization of economic value.

> Network value management is essentially a loyalty business model for IT investment and the IT organization in itself; the objective is to maximize stakeholder economic value—the IT value proposition.

This chapter has discussed some forward-thinking concepts to enhance and extend the IT value network framework. Renewed interest and the application of multidisciplinary approaches such as value network, value systems, and value options provide more depth for quantifying and managing IT value. Maximizing shareholder economic value should be the IT value proposition. Our attention now turns to the final chapter, in which the dots are connected. Here, along with a few final thoughts, we will consider the IT value network maturity model and complete a checklist for IT value network implementation.

CHAPTER 20

Connecting the Dots

Our journey through the IT value network has covered various multidisciplinary approaches to maximize the value of IT investments; this chapter consolidates these perspectives, with a pause for reflection, as we conclude the book. In the Oscar-winning film *A Beautiful Mind*, John Forbes Nash, Jr., played by Russell Crowe, was a renowned mathematician consumed with the pursuit of the "original idea." Nash struggles with many personal and interpersonal issues but is finally able to connect the dots, culminating in his winning of the Nobel Prize in Economics for his breakthrough work on game theory. In the shadows of brilliance and with a faint comparison, this book has attempted to connect the dots in the world of IT economics to discover the dynamics of stakeholder economic value.

Ultimately the journey is about returns to the IT dollar and transitioning IT investment to higher forms of stakeholder economic value for sustained competitive advantage or network advantage. Today, it is still common to find as much as 80 percent of IT investment spent on keeping the lights on and supporting baseline IT system operations and shared infrastructure. Optimizing the base provides opportunities to redirect IT investment to higher-value service and strategic capabilities, thus transforming IT investments to drive intellectual capital or intangible value, which typically accounts for 80 percent of a firm's market capitalization. This chapter provides an IT value network maturity model to assist companies in understanding their current state and so provides indicators for improvement and development. Subsequently, the chapter provides an IT value network checklist for implementation, with some final thoughts on the art of collaboration for collective advantage—and, ultimately, network advantage.

This book has attempted to connect the dots within the world of IT economics to discover the dynamics of stakeholder economic value; it presents a journey in the pursuit of returns to the IT dollar, transforming IT investment to higher forms of value for sustained competitive advantage or network advantage.

IT Value Network Maturity Model

The following recommended IT value network maturity assessment framework is advocated, as illustrated in Exhibit 20.1. The model consists of four maturity levels, with references to the U.S. General Accounting Office's IT Investment Management (ITIM) framework.[1] Each level is a build or development from the previous level. Companies should assess their IT value current practices across the IT value network maturity model and decide where to focus improvements, thereby advancing maturity.

Companies should assess their IT value current practices across the IT value network maturity model and decide where to focus improvements, thereby advancing maturity and enhancing stakeholder economic value.

State of Organizational Readiness

Prior to assessing a company's IT value network maturity model, the CIO should evaluate the firm's readiness for organizational change, which is a critical enabler for the deployment of the IT value network. An additional axis in the maturity model, beyond previously discussed attributes, has been added to accommodate organizational change readiness. As discussed in Chapter 19, if a firm's senior executives perceive that IT is purely a support organization, receptiveness to adopt a more strategic IT capability will be constrained. Similarly, if perceived IT value or satisfaction is low, baseline expectations could be limited to the fundamentals of improved shared infrastructure and IT operations.

Stakeholder economic value may need to be focused on cost reduction, treating IT as a commodity or utility, with little stakeholder notion of enhanced value opportunities. Organizational readiness for change could be equally low when there is little or no dissatisfaction with the base capability and a high perceived cost or risk of change. If a company does not see the

EXHIBIT 20.1 IT Value Network Maturity Model

IT Value Network	Level 1 Foundation	Level 2 Conventional	Level 3 Evolving	Level 4 Developed
IT stakeholder focus	**Operational value:** ■ Functional owners ■ General employee	**Strategic value:** ■ Cross-functional owners ■ Executives	**Value system:** ■ Executives ■ Extended process owners ■ External customers ■ Suppliers/vendors	**Value network:** ■ Executives ■ External customers ■ Board members ■ Partners/alliances ■ Market/industry analysts
Stakeholder economic value	Cost reduction	Investment returns	Competitive advantage	Network advantage
IT investment classification (four "S" category model)	Shared infrastructure systems	Shared infrastructure systems Strategic	Shared infrastructure systems Strategic Services	Future state scenarios
IT value portfolio management	Ad-hoc IT project management	IT program-project management	IT project management office (PMO)	Enterprise-wide business PMO
IT value index	Operational lens	Strategic lens Operational lens	Stakeholder lens Strategic lens Operational lens	Agility lens Stakeholder lens Strategic lens Operational lens

(Continued)

EXHIBIT 20.1 (Continued)

IT Value Network	Level 1 Foundation	Level 2 Conventional	Level 3 Evolving	Level 4 Developed
IT value network measurement	**Traditional accounting and financial:** ■ Budgeting ■ Business case cost/ benefit analysis ■ Investment review board ■ Audit	**Conventional strategic planning and financial:** ■ Level 1, plus ■ Strategic planning ■ Operational planning ■ Program-project management ■ ROI/DCF/NPV/IRR	**Emerging organizational mgmt and financial:** ■ Level 2, plus ■ Economic added value ■ Stock price trait ■ Value creation business case ■ Total cost of ownership (TCO) ■ IT governance ■ Critical success factors ■ IT balanced scorecard ■ Benchmarking ■ Internal service level agreements (SLA) ■ IT surveys	**Emerging informational economics and decision support:** ■ Level 3, plus ■ Decision trees ■ Real (value) options ■ IT risk management ■ Enterprise investment management ■ Enterprise portfolio management ■ Scenario planning
IT value network management	**4th-degree primary** **2nd-degree secondary**	**2nd-degree primary** **3rd–4th-degree secondary**	**1st-degree primary** **2nd–5th-degree secondary**	**6th-degree primary** **1st–5th-degree secondary**

256

Organizational change readiness	Low readiness for change	Moderate readiness for change	High readiness for change	Systematic readiness for change
– **Value capture**	■ Project and system management	■ Strategic plan	■ Value system and process management ■ Strategic plan	■ Networked value management ■ Value system and process/system integration management ■ Strategic plan and portfolio management
– **Value enabling**	■ Capability and capacity management	■ Capability and capacity management	■ Capability and capacity management ■ Project and system management	■ Strategic plan and portfolio management ■ Capability and capacity management ■ Project and system management
– **Value optimization**	■ Project and system management	■ Project and system management	■ Project and system management ■ Service and information management	■ Capability and capacity management ■ Project and system management ■ Service and information management
– **Value realization**	■ Project and system management	■ Project and system management	■ Project and system management ■ Service and information management	■ Project and system management ■ Service and information management ■ Networked value management

value of mobilizing executive energy to improve the effectiveness of measuring or managing IT value, which comes with a cost, attempts to introduce change will be resisted. In today's world, this may seem unlikely, but often the idea is supported in principle and not in execution. Placing increased rigor and discipline in the management of IT investments can be frustrating to business executives who want investment control and the deployment of fast solutions. But applying improved investment governance is particularly popular these days, when increased scrutiny of the board's accountability to shareholders continues to be prevalent.

Although change management has been extensively discussed with respect to IT investment deployment or project management, changing the firm's approach to IT investment governance is an undertaking of another order of magnitude. Driving awareness for the need for change must be the first step. As change champion and educator, the CIO should earn the respect of business partners, reaching out across the value network to socialize best practices and to solicit priorities, issues, and sensitivities. Building desire or motivation for change is the next step. Cultivating the IT value proposition (vision) for change is an art, connecting the dots for an insightful picture of current and future reality. CIOs need to gauge political support for change, engaging the business partners for a mutually agreeable and compelling IT value proposition. Building execution plans and IT value network deployment capability would follow. Business partners must become the advocates and ambassadors of change, participating in the design and acknowledging the desired value. Subsequently, new processes, roles, techniques, and tools can be built and deployed in support of the customized IT value network model. Finally, business partner reinforcement is essential to sustain the desired state, from recognizing early wins to supporting longer-term benefits. At maturity level four, organizational readiness for change has become institutionalized or systematic, always on, receptive to the search for continual improvement and ways to maximize stakeholder economic value.

> CIOs need to assess the firm's readiness for change and gauge political support for IT value network transformation by engaging the business partners to arrive at a mutually agreeable and compelling IT value proposition.

Assessing Maturity

Firms should assess the current state of their IT value network, if only to answer the basic question:

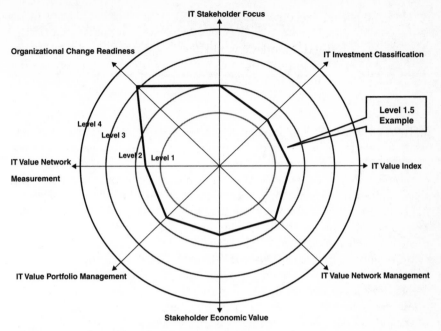

EXHIBIT 20.2 IT Value Network Maturity Assessment

How do we know the value of our IT investment?

Without a reassuring answer, confidence in IT wanes and more questions are asked, specifically:

Is there value in our IT?

If these questions remain unanswered, a firm may start engaging in IT outsourcing discussions or worse, it may start to think of replacing the IT management. IT executives should be well prepared to address challenges to IT value. Assessing current practices across the IT value network framework is the first step. Exhibit 20.2 provides an IT value network maturity grid for firms to use in making an assessment. Eight axes are identified, corresponding to the maturity model, mapped alongside concentric circles of maturity. Based on research and cited cases, it is not uncommon to find many firms' baseline falling between level one and level two, as illustrated in the example. Providing there is a moderate to high level of readiness for organizational change, most companies will aspire to a higher level of IT value network maturity.

Providing there is a moderate to high level of readiness for organizational change, most companies will aspire to a higher level of IT value network maturity.

MATURITY LEVEL ONE: FOUNDATION   On level one, IT stakeholders' primary focus is on the firm's functional owners and support of employee productivity. IT investment decision making is IT dependent, and stakeholder economic value is focused on cost. IT investments are classified as basic shared infrastructure and application systems. There is no IT value portfolio management, defaulting to ad hoc and inconsistent project management. The company's annual operating plan drives a budget process for IT investment availability and selection. An IT value index does not exist, defaulting to an operational focus on costs and benefits. Traditional accounting and financial techniques are typically used in assessing and measuring IT investments. Business cases justify IT investments by applying inconsistent and questionable financial measures. Sponsoring business executives apply judgment and strength of conviction to gain investment approval. Audit may provide direction for investment selection.

IT project management and systems management (fourth degree) are the essential means to capture, optimize, and realize value, with some capability management (second degree) for value enablement. Investment performance measurement and value realization are loosely tracked. IT investment management is minimal and governing processes inconsistent, resulting in variable project and investment outcomes.

MATURITY LEVEL TWO: CONVENTIONAL   On level two, IT stakeholders' primary focus is upgraded to the senior executive level, with attention to cross-functional owners and initiatives. IT investment decision making tends to be business unit (BU) dependent and focused on interim or shorter-term investment returns. IT investments classification broadens to include strategic investments. IT value portfolio management is absent, but disciplined program and project management methodology is deployed. The BU strategic and operating planning process drives a negotiated budget (between IT and BU) for the allocation of IT investments. The IT value index starts to mature, balancing operational and strategic benefits. Conventional strategic planning and financial techniques are typically used in assessing investments. Business cases justify IT investments by applying consistent financial measures (e.g., IRR, ROI), based on tangible values. The BU leadership team approves investments.

The BU strategic and operating plan (second degree) drives value capture, enabled by capacity and capability management (third degree). IT project management and systems management (fourth degree) remain as the IT value network management focus for optimizing and realizing value. Investment performance measurement is tracked to project completion, but postproject value realization is not captured. IT system investment management is basic. However, governance of project-level and system management processes are consistent and repeatable, producing manageable project and investment outcomes.

MATURITY LEVEL THREE: EVOLVING On level three, IT stakeholders' primary focus now includes extended process owners across the value system, touching external customers and suppliers. IT investment decision making is at the enterprise level, focused on future profits and competitive advantage. Classification of IT investments broadens to include service investments in support of the extended stakeholder network. IT value portfolio management has evolved, with the establishment of an IT project management office (PMO). Investments are selected based on the IT strategic plan, which is aligned to the business strategic and process objectives, using techniques such as the balanced scorecard. Audit and IT surveys also provide direction for investment decisions. IT investment benchmarks provide competitive and market positioning. The IT value index now includes the stakeholder value lens to complement the operational and strategic value lens. In addition to conventional strategic planning and financial techniques, emerging organizational management methods would typically be used in assessing investments. Business cases justify IT investments by applying consistent value creation or economic added-value measures, based on tangible and intangible values. Investments are aligned to long-term stock price measures (traits). An IT investment committee governs and approves investments.

Integrated process and system improvements (first degree), together with the enterprise strategic and operating plan (second degree), drives value capture. Value enablement is managed through capacity and capability management (third degree), plus project and system management (fourth degree). The latter also drives value optimization and realization, with service and information management (fifth degree). Investment performance measurement is tracked to project completion. Postproject reviews are conducted. System investments are linked to process improvements across the value chain and system. Stakeholder service levels are tracked and information assets managed. IT investment management has significantly evolved, with emphasis on stakeholder economic value, producing measurable IT value outcomes.

MATURITY LEVEL FOUR: DEVELOPED On level four, IT stakeholders' primary focus extends to include board members, the firm's alliances and partners, also touching and influencing market and industry analysts. IT investment decision making is now an integral part of the overall enterprise-wide investment assessment and is focused on network advantage or sustaining competitive advantage. IT investments classification matures to future-state scenarios in support of the evolving value network. IT value portfolio management is now centralized within an enterprise-wide business PMO. IT investments are selected based on networked value management considerations and identified through integrated process and system objectives and through an integrated business and IT strategic plan.

Scenario analysis, value options, and risk management provide additional direction for investment decisions. The IT value index now includes the agility value lens to complete optimal IT investment evaluation. In addition to traditional financial measures, conventional strategic planning, and organizational management, emerging informational economics and decision-support techniques would typically be used in assessing IT investments. Value-creation business cases justify IT investments, based on tangible and intangible values and applying value options. Scenario planning assists in the evaluation of strategic projects over longer life cycles, considering market changes under uncertainty. The business PMO will oversee an integrated IT and business project management team, governed by the corporate investment review board.

Networked value management (sixth degree), together with value systems (first degree), and strategic planning and portfolio management (second degree), drives value capture. Value enablement is managed through the second degree, in addition to capacity and capability management (third degree), and project and system management (fourth degree). Together with the third and fourth degrees, service and information management (fifth degree) drives value optimization. Finally, value realization will materialize from the fourth and fifth degrees, in addition to networked value management (sixth degree), thereby instigating a new circle of higher value. Investment performance measurement is tracked throughout the life of the project and for several years after project completion, capturing the total investment value. System investments realize process improvements across the value chain and system. Stakeholder service levels are exceeded, and intellectual capital is quantified. Networked value management produces stakeholder loyalty, converted into stakeholder economic value. Enterprise IT investment management and IT portfolio management are advanced, with emphasis on maximizing stakeholder economic value and producing optimal IT value outcomes.

Advancing Maturity

Referencing client assessments, most firms initially baseline between maturity levels one and two, where the IT organization is relatively conventional in the management and measurement of IT investments. Depending on the "state of the burning deck" or impetus for change, the CIO should target an advancement in IT value network maturity over a stated period of time. To aspire to level four just might not be practical and necessary. The amount of transitional change, risk, or costs could be prohibitive. Alternatively, IT stakeholders may perceive little value in pursuing level four. Changing the fundamentals of IT investment measurement and management can challenge traditional practice, particularly financial justification, and so needs to be carefully managed. As discussed previously, evaluating the state of readiness for organizational change is paramount.

Once having gained the support of the new IT value proposition or vision from the business partners or broader stakeholders, including the company board, the CIO should be ready to address "how" to execute. Assessing current practices against the IT value network maturity model determines the current state, depicting key processes or attributes for improvement as mapped along the axis. Subsequently, applying evolution and not revolution, specific IT value network processes and metrics can be targeted for reengineering or improvement. Stretched but achievable objectives should be set, focused on quick wins to provide a platform for sustained sponsorship and further change. Step by step, a customized IT value network framework will evolve, providing increasingly higher stakeholder economic value.

> Depending on the "state of the burning deck" or impetus for change, the CIO should target an advancement in IT value network maturity over a stated period of time, but it may not be necessary or practical to aspire to level four.

IT Value Client Cases

The IT value network maturity model was applied to the four IT value clients discussed in Chapters 15 to 18. In each case, the maturity level was evaluated before and after implementation of the IT value network approach. Each client case transitioned to a higher maturity level and a higher level of IT value realization.

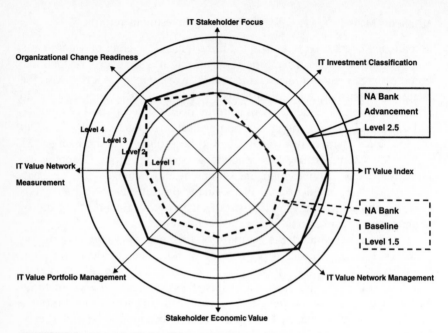

EXHIBIT 20.3 NA Bank IT Value Network Maturity Assessment

NA BANK: TRANSITIONING FROM LEVEL 1.5 TO 2.5 MATURITY NA Bank's
initial baseline IT value network maturity assessment was conducted in
the beginning of 2002. Subsequently, IT value network measurement
and management methods were deployed—specifically, elements of networked value management (sixth degree) and strategic planning and
portfolio management (second degree). Maturity assessment was reevaluated, approximately one and half years later, toward mid-2003. NA Bank
had transitioned from level 1.5 to 2.5. Exhibit 20.3 depicts the NA Bank IT
value network maturity assessment. Referencing Chapter 15, NA Bank case,
the following advancements can be summarized:

- **Organizational change readiness was moderate to high.** Key stakeholders were starting to question the IT value. NA Bank's CIO was also
  concerned that the IT spending or investment was not effectively aligned
  to the bank's strategic direction.
- **IT stakeholder focus moved from level 2.0 to 2.5.** In addition to
  cross-functional owners and executives, process owners and suppliers
  were considered.
- **Stakeholder economic value moved from level 1.5 to 2.25.** IT
  investment moved from primarily operational cost reduction to more

rigorous IRR and ROI for shorter-term investment returns, with some movement toward targeting longer-term competitive advantage.

- **IT investment classification moved from level 1.0 to 2.5.** IT classification moved from traditional shared infrastructure and systems to include strategic investments, with some movement toward service investments. This significant swing supported advancements to IT value portfolio management.
- **IT value portfolio management moved from 1.5 to 2.5.** Project management moved from an ad hoc practice to a best practice with stronger IT investment transparency and governance. An IT investment portfolio was created, redirecting investment to higher-value informational and strategic investments.
- **IT value index moved from level 1.5 to 3.0.** The IT investment evaluation scorecard transitioned significantly from primarily operational (lens) measures of value to include the strategic lens and the stakeholder lens thus targeting short-term and long-term returns, in addition to stakeholder satisfaction.
- **IT value network measurement moved from level 1.5 to 2.5.** Improved IT investment measurement techniques were deployed. A new IT strategic plan was aligned to the business with balanced scorecards. IT investment governance was formalized, with improved performance management. Improved project management metrics were developed. Increased rigor was applied to business-case financial measures, with IRR and ROI thresholds. IT surveys was used for the first time to measure value.
- **IT value network management moved from level 1.75 to 3.0.** Improved management practices were deployed for IT investment value capture; transitioning from primarily project and system management (fourth degree) to a new aligned IT strategic plan (second degree) and process optimization improvements (first degree). Value optimization and value realization improved with the inclusion of rigorous project management practice (fourth degree), service levels agreements (fifth degree), and IT satisfaction surveys (sixth degree).

INDIGO CHAPTERS: TRANSITIONING FROM LEVEL 1.5 TO 3.0 MATURITY Indigo Chapters' initial baseline IT value network maturity assessment was conducted in mid-2006. Subsequently, IT value network measurement and management methods were deployed—specifically, elements of project and system management (fourth degree) and strategic planning and portfolio management (second degree). Maturity assessment was reevaluated over two and half years later, toward the end of 2008. Indigo had transitioned from level 1.5 to 3.0. Exhibit 20.4 depicts Indigo's IT value network maturity

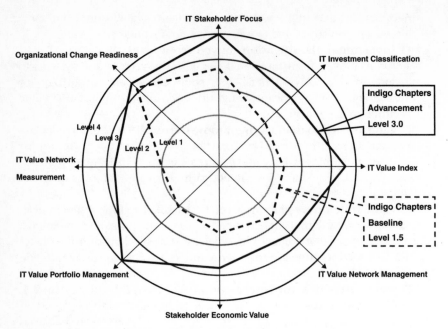

EXHIBIT 20.4 Indigo Chapters IT Value Network Maturity Assessment

assessment. Referencing Chapter 17, the Indigo Chapters case, the following advancements can be summarized:

- **Organizational change readiness was high.** Project management had become a significant challenge to Indigo, culminating in some large strategic projects exceeding budget and schedule. Indigo's leadership team acknowledged that improved project management was indeed a priority when delays in these projects started to impact the business through increased operational risk and quality concerns.
- **IT stakeholder focus moved from level 2.75 to 4.0.** Indigo started with a high level of extended IT stakeholder focus, which improved further in support of all IT stakeholders, including employees, executives, process owners, suppliers, partners, alliances, external customers, board members, and market/industry analysts. Indigo is an excellent example of an IT organization that has a complete stakeholder focus across its business network.
- **Stakeholder economic value moved from level 1.5 to 2.75.** IT investment moved from primarily operational support with some focus on short-term returns to a balanced perspective with long-term invest-

ment returns, including competitive advantage. Significant change was due to adoption of a more strategic approach and a portfolio view of IT investments.

- **IT investment classification moved from level 1.5 to 2.75.** IT classification moved from traditional shared infrastructure and systems to include strategic investments, thus enabling portfolio investment management.
- **IT value portfolio management moved from 1.0 to 4.0.** Major impact to IT value was realized through the maturity of IT project management, from ad hoc project management to a fully developed enterprise-wide business PMO. IT investment governance was managed by the senior leadership team, aligned to the strategy, with complete PMO accountability for investment management and project delivery. The PMO practice included a comprehensive "life cycle" toolkit of processes, policies, procedures, and deliverables.
- **IT value index moved from level 1.5 to 3.5.** The IT investment evaluation scorecard significantly transitioned from primarily operational (lens) measures of value to include the strategic lens, the stakeholder lens, and, to some extent, the agility lens. IT investment decisions were based on short-term (opportunistic) and long-term (strategic) IRR, plus stakeholder key performance indicators for shared infrastructure and informational investments.
- **IT value network measurement moved from level 1.0 to 2.75.** Improved IT investment measurement techniques were deployed. The IT strategic plan was integrated into the business strategy with cascading objectives and measures. Enterprise investment governance was formalized, with agreed-on portfolio investment levels and a rigorous process for investment justification, prioritization, and selection. An enterprise-wide business PMO was established, promoting best practices and strong performance management. IT strategic and opportunistic investments were required to produce an IRR above 18 percent, showing hard, tangible benefits. Key performance indicators and intangible values were quantified, in the absence of hard benefits, as a means of investment justification and selection within finite shared infrastructure and informational investment envelopes.
- **IT value network management moved from level 1.5 to 2.5.** Improved management practices were deployed for IT investment value capture; transitioning from primarily project and system management (fourth degree) to an enterprise strategic plan and investment portfolio management (second degree) and, to some extent, through system alignment to processes (first degree). Value enablement improved with the advancements in the second and fourth degrees, along with some

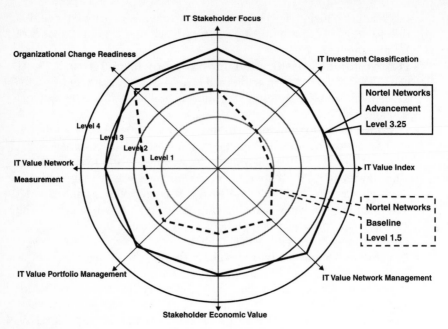

EXHIBIT 20.5 Nortel Networks IT Value Network Maturity Assessment

developments in capability and capacity management (third degree). Value optimization and value realization improved with the deployment of the enterprise PMO (fourth degree), along with service levels agreements and some improved information management (fifth degree).

NORTEL NETWORKS: TRANSITIONING FROM LEVEL 1.5 TO 3.25 MATURITY Nortel Networks' initial baseline IT value network maturity assessment was conducted in mid-1997. Subsequently, IT value network measurement and management methods were deployed—specifically, elements of capability and capacity management (third degree) and strategic planning and portfolio management (second degree). Maturity assessment was reevaluated more than two years later, toward the end of 1999. Nortel had transitioned from level 1.5 to 3.25. Exhibit 20.5 depicts Nortel Networks' IT value network maturity assessment. Referencing Chapter 16, the Nortel Networks case, the following advancements can be summarized:

- **Organizational change readiness was high.** The CIO announced the intention to reorganize Nortel's IT organization and realign the IT strategy in order to enable a new capability in support of Nortel's change in direction, the "right-angle turn." The challenge was to transition from a fragmented support organization to a strategic and service based added-value capability, aligned to support process excellence and customer engagement.

- **IT stakeholder focus moved from level 2.0 to 3.5.** A complete IT reorganization and refocus was undertaken, moving from traditional attention to functional owners and employee support to satisfying: employees, executives, process owners, suppliers, partners, alliances, and external customers. In this way Nortel's IT organization became Nortel's best service provider and customer.
- **Stakeholder economic value moved from level 1.5 to 3.0.** IT investment moved from primarily operational support and cost reduction to a focus on both short-term and long-term investment returns, including competitive advantage from IT deployment of Nortel's own leading technology.
- **IT investment classification moved from level 1.0 to 3.0.** IT classification moved from traditional shared infrastructure and systems to include strategic and service investments in support of a business service-centric model.
- **IT value portfolio management moved from 2.0 to 3.0.** IT project management was sound, but it moved from being fragmented across the IT organization to a federated PMO practice, with stronger IT investment transparency and governance. IT executive client managers were assigned to business units and process owners to manage IT investment, governed by an IT investment council. A comprehensive charge-back system was deployed to ensure business unit IT accountability.
- **IT value index moved from level 1.0 to 3.5.** The IT investment evaluation scorecard transitioned significantly from primarily operational (lens) measures of value to include the strategic lens, the stakeholder lens, and, to some extent, the agility lens. IT investment decisions were based on a weighted IT value index in which agility was known as R&D, with the deployment of Nortel's own new technology.
- **IT value network measurement moved from level 1.5 to 3.0.** Improved IT investment measurement techniques were deployed. A new IT strategic plan was aligned to the business with balanced scorecards. IT investment governance was formalized through IT executive client management and an investment council. A federated PMO was established, promoting best practices and strong performance management. IT surveys were used for the first time to measure value. Total cost of ownership models were created. IT costs were charged back to the business for IT accountability, corresponding to internal service level agreements. IT strategic investments were required to produce a positive net present value (NPV), with a return on assets (ROA) of between 16–19 percent.

- **IT value network management moved from level 1.75 to 3.5.**
  Improved management practices were deployed for IT investment value
  capture, transitioning from primarily project and system management
  (fourth degree), to an aligned IT strategic plan and portfolio management (second degree) and through system alignment to centralized
  process owners (first degree). Value enablement increased significantly
  with enhanced capability and capacity management from the IT reorganization (third degree), together with the second and fourth degree
  improvements. Value optimization and value realization improved with
  the inclusion of the federated PMO (fourth degree) and service levels agreements with IT charge-back (fifth degree), along with client
  management and IT satisfaction surveys (sixth degree)—Network value
  management was evolving to include external customers, suppliers,
  partners, and alliances.

NA CREDIT UNION: TRANSITIONING FROM LEVEL 1.5 TO 3.5 MATURITY   NA Credit
Union's initial baseline IT value network maturity assessment was conducted
in the mid-2000s. Subsequently, IT value network measurement and elements of all six degrees of the IT value network management were deployed.
Maturity assessment was reevaluated over two years later. NA Credit Union
had transitioned from level 1.5 to 3.5. Exhibit 20.6 depicts NA Credit Union's

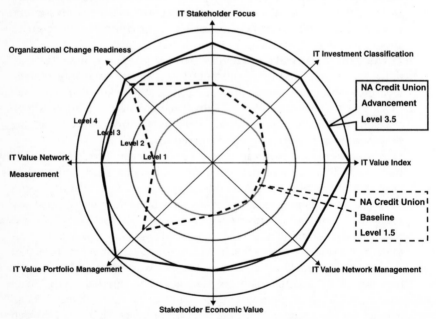

EXHIBIT 20.6 NA Credit Union IT Value Network Maturity Assessment

IT value network maturity assessment. Referencing Chapter 18, the NA Credit Union case, the following advancements can be summarized:

- **Organizational change readiness was high.** NA Credit Union was created through the merger of two credit unions, both with a long history of serving their local communities. The challenge was to integrate the banking operations, processes, and systems under one organization within 15 months. After bank integration, there was high business expectation for improved IT capability, operational excellence, and process simplification, cumulatively the expectation was for improved IT value.
- **IT stakeholder focus moved from level 2.0 to 3.5.** A complete IT reorganization and capability build was required for banking integration, moving from traditional attention to functional owners and employee support, to satisfying employees, executives, process owners, suppliers, partners, alliances, board members, and external customers (members). IT had to focus on its network stakeholders to ensure seamless bank integration throughout the value system, especially because there was a number of banking platform interdependencies with suppliers, partners, and alliances.
- **Stakeholder economic value moved from level 1.0 to 3.0.** IT investment moved from primarily operational support and cost reduction to an initial focus on short-term capability, then postintegration to a matured focus on short-term and long-term investment returns, meeting the board and member commitments, and merger promises.
- **IT investment classification moved from level 1.5 to 3.5.** IT classification moved from traditional shared infrastructure and systems to include strategic and service investments in support of a managed service model. Postintegration, future-state scenarios were projected based on a service-oriented architecture (SOA).
- **IT value portfolio management moved from 2.5 to 4.0.** IT project management was sound, but it matured into a mission-critical enterprise business PMO for bank integration execution, with stronger IT investment governance and performance management. Post integration, the IT investment portfolio aligned to strategic and operational priorities, migrating 12 percent IT investment to higher-value business capabilities and stakeholder services.
- **IT value index moved from level 1.0 to 4.0.** IT investment evaluation significantly transitioned from primarily operational (lens) measures of value to include a mature IT value index. Project, asset, and system capital were assessed through a weighted value index, consisting of quantifiable measures—specifically, the cost/benefit, risk, flexibility, strategic, and technology value lenses.

- **IT value network measurement moved from level 1.0 to 3.0.** Improved IT investment measurement techniques were deployed. The IT strategic plan became an integral element to the business strategy with measurable key performance indicators. IT investment governance and metrics was formalized through an IT investment council managed by the business enterprise PMO. IT surveys were used for the first time to measure value. Total cost of ownership models were created. IT costs were aligned to internal service level agreements.
- **IT value network management moved from level 1.0 to 3.5.** Improved management practices were deployed for IT investment value capture, transitioning from project and system management (fourth degree) to an integrated business-IT strategic plan and portfolio management (second degree) and through system and process simplification (first degree). Value enablement increased significantly with enhanced capability and capacity management (third degree), from IT reorganization, managed service model, and SOA, together with the second and fourth degree improvements. Value optimization and value realization improved with the developed third and fourth degrees, along with service cataloging and service level agreements (fifth degree) and IT satisfaction surveys and business focus sessions (sixth degree). Network value management was evolving at various levels to include the board, external customers (members), suppliers, partners, and alliances in pursuit of outstanding stakeholder relationships.

IT Value Network Checklist

If the firm's mission is to maximize stakeholder economic value, the following six questions need to be addressed:

What are the IT stakeholder's perceptions and expectations?

Where do we spend our IT investment?

How do we know the value of our IT investment?

What is the value of our IT investment or spending?

Do we have appropriate IT value network management?

Should we expect more value from our IT?

Depending on your confidence in the answers to these questions, your company might consider conducting a baseline assessment of its IT value network maturity to determine its current state. This initial maturity view will provide a foundation for executive discussions, drive awareness, facilitate consensus, and provide directional improvements for advanced maturity. The IT value network checklist, along with consolidated IT executive opinions, makes a good starting point to determine the company's current-state IT value network maturity level. Review your company's current IT practices against the following IT value network key activities or checklist, and then assess your company's initial maturity level. The six steps within the IT value network checklist are as follows.

> The IT value network checklist, along with consolidated IT executive opinions, makes a good starting point to determine the company's current-state IT value network maturity level.

1. Define the IT Value Network: Networked Value Management

What are the IT stakeholder's perceptions and expectations?

1. **IT value network portfolio.** Identify your stakeholders (internal and external) categorizing them into primary, secondary, and tertiary members (nodes)—build a portfolio of network clouds.
2. **IT value network map.** Depict the relationships and interdependencies between stakeholders or members (links).
3. **IT value network analysis.** Build a high-level view of expected stakeholder value (value statements).
4. **Networked value management baseline perceptions.** Conduct a survey to create a baseline of IT stakeholder satisfaction and value (survey).
5. **Networked value management expectations.** Follow up with stakeholder focus groups to understand perceptions and determine expectations (focus).

2. Categorize IT Investment: Four "S" Category Model

Where do we spend our IT investment?

1. **The four "S" category model.** Categorize IT investment/spending into shared infrastructure, systems, services, and strategic buckets.
2. **Current, projected, historical trend, operating budget.** Determine associated operational or ongoing costs.
3. **Current, projected, historical trend, capital budget.** Determine associated capital and one-time project costs.
4. **Cost of ownership and residual value.** Conduct a high-level cost assessment of IT assets.
5. **IT investment predictors.** Identify main causes, drivers, or influences on IT investment.

3. Triangulate IT Value: IT Value Network Measurement

How do we know the value of our IT investment?

1. **Key performance indicators (KPIs) and value-creation business cases.** Determine business objectives and corporate goals and validate the rigor within investment business cases.
2. **Stakeholder critical success criteria (CSC).** Align KPIs to stakeholder expectations and IT investment categories.
3. **IT value index and value lens.** Determine the enterprise measures within the value lens—strategic, operational, stakeholder, and agility—and create the enterprise value index.
4. **IT value network measures.** Quantify and baseline IT investment value, using financial and organizational techniques.
5. **Stakeholder economic value.** Consolidate tangible and intangible value by IT investment category, across the IT portfolio.

4. Build the IT Value Portfolio: Stars and Black Holes

What is the value of our IT investment or spending?

1. **Current-state IT value portfolio.** Depict the current-state IT stakeholder value against timeline expectation.
2. **Future-state IT value portfolio.** Project initial future-state IT stakeholder value against timeline expectation, based on strategic and operational objectives.
3. **Stars and black holes.** Assess IT portfolio strengths and weaknesses, opportunities and threats (SWOT).
4. **Star gazing.** Consider some scenario views applying scenario planning and value options.
5. **Transitional plan and value proposition.** Produce an initial investment transition or migration plan and value proposition.

5. Manage the IT Value Network: IT Value Network Management—Six Degrees of IT Value

Do we have appropriate IT value network management?

1. **IT value network management.** Audit and review value management processes to capture, enable, optimize, and realize value.
2. **Six degrees of IT value.** Evaluate the six degrees of IT value effectiveness.

3. **Reclaim lost stakeholder value.** Identify process, people, and technology improvements.
4. **IT performance measurement and balanced scorecards.** Review alignment and IT reward and recognition objectives.
5. **Investment management and BPMO.** Review your IT investment and portfolio governance.

6. Maximize Stakeholder Economic Value: Connect the Dots

Should we expect more value from our IT?

1. **Organizational readiness for change.** Understand the "state of the union" and "IT health and wealth."
2. **IT alignment and collaboration.** Ensure key stakeholder (i.e., executives, board) ongoing alignment and collaboration.
3. **IT value proposition.** Continually report and communicate IT value and key initiatives to all stakeholders.
4. **Networked value management.** Monitor stakeholder satisfaction, compare to industry best practices, target advancements or improvements, and manage stakeholder expectations.
5. **IT value loyalty and trusted partnerships.** Recycle the IT value network; build and extend the value network, value system, and value options.

> Aspiring for higher IT value network maturity in pursuit of maximum stakeholder economic value requires an iterative cycle through the six degrees of IT value, building IT value loyalty.

Collaboration for Network Advantage

To maximize stakeholder economic value is to deliver sustained competitive advantage or network advantage. The desire for change or advancement of IT value network maturity needs to be carefully managed. The senior IT leadership team has to keep its eyes on the big picture and aim for the big wins for enterprise advancement; excellent collaborative skills are needed. Setting the bar too high will draw stakeholder resistance or establish an unrealistic stakeholder expectation. It is wise to seek sustained support and permission to proceed, rather than seeking the ideal situation, utopia, or the perfect desired state. The senior IT leadership should ensure business partner consensus across the targeted stakeholder network. Building trusted partnerships enables mutually agreed-on outcomes and a collective advantage.

Collaboration is required to achieve the desired IT value network state to accommodate stakeholder interests and manage trade-offs between stakeholders. Compromises will need to be made to gain agreement on mutually acceptable terms, balanced across the various stakeholder groups. While compromise suggests a watered-down solution, it is nonetheless a solution at a point in time, which provides the starting point of change. Subsequently, through quick wins and further collaboration, higher states or maturity levels can be pursued. The IT value network is a collaborative process, not an event.

> While compromise suggests a watered-down solution, it is nonetheless a solution at a point in time, which provides the starting point for change. Subsequently, through quick wins and collaboration, higher states or maturity levels can be pursued for network advantage.

Firm in Mind, Agile in Execution

As commander and chief of IT investment, the CIO should continually survey the environment or landscape and not lose sight of the big picture. The IT value proposition for change provides the vision and mission statement. Blueprinting the current and future IT value network state provides the context or situational assessment. The migration or transitional plan provides strategic direction. Execution tactics require marshalling the necessary capability and resources as well as strong communication lines. But things can go wrong in the battlefield. The landscape changes or execution tactics fail; consider operational issues, new business imperatives, financial constraints, or just poor change management. Diminished stakeholder confidence or new priorities are always a threat. The CIO needs to choose the battles and battle tactics wisely in pursuit of IT value network maturity. Understanding IT value mission-critical events and the path of least resistance should be priorities. *When in the trenches, the vision is contained, but the radar should always be on.* Trying to achieve success on all frontiers is highly risky. *Back on the hill, the vision is expansive, but with no reality check.* Keep the eyes on the big picture, but ensure that there are regular checkpoints throughout the journey and be ever prepared to adapt to a given situation. IT value network leadership is about being firm in mind and agile in execution.

> As commander and chief of IT investment, the CIO should be firm in mind and agile in execution, cognizant of IT value mission-critical events and wise in choosing battles and battle tactics.

Trade-Offs and Compromises

A trade-off is a stated situation that involves giving up one quality or value in return for gaining another quality or value. To appease stakeholders, choices must be made where the upside and downside of stakeholder values must be quantifiable. Stakeholder opportunity cost quantifies the most preferred alternative given up. The art of advancing IT value network maturity lies in gaining stakeholder collective advantage, where the collective value in support of change is higher than the collective opportunity cost. This, however, requires negotiating compromises with stakeholder interest groups, where deals are struck based on perceptions of value. The art then is to give away low values, which are perceived by others as high value. Thus, compromises should be agreed on when critical requirements for moving change forward are being secured, with allowance made for flexibility to accommodate stakeholders' perceived high-value interests. Give away your low value to others, who perceive it as a higher value and defend your high perceived value. Optimal outcomes are found through discovery of stakeholder interests in pursuit of a common cause. The IT value network proposition should reflect the collective advantage in support of change.

> The art to advancing IT value network maturity lies in gaining stakeholder collective advantage, where, through trade-offs, the collective value in support of change is higher than the collective opportunity cost.

Collective Advantage to Network Advantage

Gaining agreement or permission to proceed with IT value network change will require excellent relationship building and negotiation skills across the IT leadership team. In pursuit of IT value network maturity, a collective advantage should be sought across the stakeholder interest groups. Focusing on underlying stakeholder interests and requirements, as opposed to stated "negotiation" positions, is a means to uncover collective or mutual gains. Principled negotiation strives for win-win propositions, as supported in economic game theory. However, the connotation of gaming can make the playing field very competitive, which does not provide for collective gain through creative outcomes. Thus, IT leadership should create open stakeholder forum(s) for dialog on change, stimulating creative outcomes for collective advantage and mutual ownership.

Negotiation may then default to a focus on IT value network deployment tuning and timing exercise, not whether or not it should be pursued. Relationships between IT and the stakeholder interest groups are perhaps the most important element for deriving collective advantage. Building trusted partnerships enables effective negotiation and mutually agreeable outcomes. The IT value network is a collaborative change effort between trusted partners, building collective advantage, which ultimately converts to network advantage or sustained competitive advantage.

> Building trusted partnerships enables effective negotiation and mutually agreeable outcomes for collective advantage, where IT value network becomes a collaborative change effort between trusted partners evolving to network advantage or sustained competitive advantage.

Value IT

Taking the first step is always the hardest, but you will be surprised how many "dots" of IT value already exist in your company's value system or value network; it's a question of how best to connect then for a more compelling IT value proposition. IT value network measurement and management points of presence may be vague or dim in your company, but it does not take a lot of effort to brighten and increase visibility for stargazing. Subsequently, building your own IT value network, through connecting relationships and leveraging nodes of value, becomes a collaborative journey of discovery aimed at realizing maximum stakeholder economic value. Managing the IT value network life cycle for network value or sustained competitive advantage is an iterative process not an event, rejuvenating for higher levels of IT value—Value IT.

Glossary

Black Hole IT investments that fall short of most or all of the baseline IT value network index thresholds, providing unsatisfactory value. IT investments that fall into black holes should not be pursued.

Chief Value Network Officer (CVO) Company chief or guru providing value network and value management best practice, supported by the program management office (PMO) in administration. The value network chief is the architect for corporate value networks or network clouds, stakeholder relationships, and valued exchanges; the CVO's domain encompasses knowledge acquisition, intellectual capital, portfolio value management, and business development.

Conventional Planning Techniques These include strategic planning, operational planning, and program and project management. Such techniques are popular approaches used in IT investment management.

Customer Network Management (CNM) An approach used to build social and economic value from customer relationships and exchanges by leveraging the extended value network (network clouds). CNM goes beyond customer relationship management (CRM), which strives for increased profits from cross-selling, up-selling, or wallet and account share opportunities. CNM includes customer economic and social value derived from knowledge transfer, business intelligence, and collaboration; it is used for building a firm's intellectual capital.

Emerging Decision-Support Techniques These include risk management, decision trees, management information systems (MIS), management science, and real options or strategic options. Decision-support systems provide mathematical models or structured approaches to IT investment evaluation. Decision-support techniques can assist in unstructured or complex processes (i.e., IT investment management) for which there is no singular solution; where in the absence of structure would usually default to human intuition for decision making.

Emerging Financial Techniques These include economic value added (EVA), stock price traits, and total cost of ownership (TCO). Such techniques provide more rigorous shareholder value measurements for IT evaluation.

Emerging Information Economic Techniques   These include IT investment management, IT portfolio management, and scenario planning. Such techniques apply a comparable weighting and point system to various projects or investments, based on respective benefit (tangible and intangible), cost, and risk outcomes. Probabilities of success are attached to the weight and estimates, where the project or investment selected is based on the highest score. Such techniques are ideal for project and investment comparison.

Emerging Organizational Management Techniques   These include critical success factors (CSFs), balanced scorecards (BSC), benchmarking, surveys, service level agreements (SLAs), and IT governance. Such techniques are becoming increasingly popular for IT investment evaluation, providing ideal tools for measurement and management in less structured or uncertain conditions.

Fifth Degree of IT Value Management   This includes service management and information management. It is concerned with the transition from IT value optimization to IT value realization, where stakeholder economic value materializes through service level agreements (SLAs), and through liberated information for intellectual capital across the business network.

Financial-Based Measurement Techniques   Traditional and emerging accounting and financial IT investment value measurement approaches. Such techniques are more structured and are based on strict formulas and assumptions, as compared with organization-based approaches.

First Degree of IT Value Management   This includes value systems and process management or improvement. It is concerned with IT value capture, whereby IT investments are identified based on enhanced competitive advantage or operational effectiveness from changes to the firm's processes across the business network or system.

Four "S" Category Model   Classification of specific types of IT investment and spending, which are categorized based on differentiated or unique characteristics or attributes. IT investment categories include shared—infrastructure, systems—operational, services—stakeholder, and strategic—informational.

Fourth Degree of IT Value Management   This includes project management and system management. It is concerned with IT value optimization, where cost-effective solutions and quality outcomes are expected for stakeholder economic value.

Intellectual Capital   Appreciated intangible assets that increase the firm's market value through quantifiable returns or yielding intellectual rights or property; a principal driver for stakeholder economic value. Intellectual capital can also be considered as the premium over the cost of knowledge that the stakeholders are willing to pay. The business network intellectual capital is the accumulative stakeholder intellectual capital derived within the enterprise sphere of influence. Venture capitalists continue to demonstrate the importance of intellectual capital, valuing firms at multiples much higher than the underlying tangible asset base would support. However, with the exception of research and development and acquisition accounting, intellectual capital rarely appears on the firm's books. It is particularly relevant in the information age, outgrowing traditional productivity measures, which relate more to an industrial age.

IT Centers of Excellence Core IT competencies and capabilities in support of the company value system or IT value chain. IT centers of excellence increase the visibility of IT business priorities and focus, building alignment and partnership between IT and the business. IT centers of excellence or value shops can be created within or external to the firm's IT organization. Through partnerships, outsourcing, or vendor agreements, the firm's IT value shop can be virtualized.

IT Intangible Assets or Benefits IT investments that provide embedded or unseen value in support of knowledge-based strategies or capabilities. Typically intangible assets or benefits are hard to accurately measure and possess outcome uncertainty. However, they produce intellectual capital, accounting for 85 percent to 90 percent of shareholder value, thus explaining excess company returns and higher market valuation.

IT Investment Broad inclusion of both IT capital and IT operational spending, differentiated between existing and new investments. Costs associated with technology hardware and software capital (e.g., support and services) should be included within IT investment management. Although ongoing operational support and services are not normally seen as an investment, human (intellectual) capital is more important than physical assets and thus operational expense should accordingly be treated as an IT investment.

IT Stakeholder Experience The management of IT stakeholder relationships and exchanges, which is typically underinvested. It is an approach similar to customer experience or relationship management but focused on IT stakeholders. The IT organization should be aligned to its business partners, managing associated IT investments and building IT trust, thereby delivering on the promise.

IT Value Network An approach used to maximize stakeholder economic value from IT investment. The IT value network consists of various techniques, methods, models, and processes for IT value measurement and management. It requires a collaborative change effort between IT and its trusted partners, with the objective to sustain the firm's competitive advantage or network advantage.

IT Value Network Checklist   A series of six steps to evaluate the current state and maturity level of an organization's IT value network. It includes (1) defining the IT value network—networked value management; (2) categorizing IT investments—the four "S" category model; (3) triangulating IT value—IT value network measurement; (4) building the IT value portfolio—stars and black holes; (5) managing the IT value network—six degrees of IT value; and (6) maximizing stakeholder economic value—connecting the dots.

IT Value Network Index   An IT investment valuation scorecard, consisting of four value lenses: (1) strategic, (2) operational, (3) stakeholder, and (4) agility. The IT value network index captures and triangulates the total stakeholder economic value of an IT investment. Companies should standardize on appropriate financial- and organization-based measures or techniques for each lens, ensuring design simplicity for IT investment valuation.

IT Value Network Management   A set of techniques and methods for IT investment management—capturing, enabling, optimizing, and realizing IT stakeholder economic value, as depicted in the six degrees of IT value.

IT Value Network Maturity Model   Determines the organizational level of the IT value network advancement. Eight axes are identified, with four maturity levels—foundational, conventional, evolving, and developed. The maturity model provides insights into areas of IT value measurement and management improvement for enhanced stakeholder economic value. The IT value network checklist, together with consolidated IT executive opinions, makes a good starting point for determining the company's current-state IT value network maturity level.

IT Value Network Measurement   A set of financial- and organization-based measures or techniques for IT investment measurement and evaluation, consisting of six steps: (1) identify, (2) justify, (3) prioritize, (4) select, (5) perform, and (6) realize.

IT Value Portfolio   An enterprise or business unit framework to evaluate the collective portfolio of IT programs and projects, assets, and spending. It provides a snapshot of total IT investments relative to stakeholder economic value over time. The IT value portfolio approach considers risk and return relative to IT investment type or the four "S" category model. Once the current IT investments have been consistently defined, categorized, benchmarked, and mapped against stakeholder economic value, a future-state IT value portfolio can be projected. The future-state IT value portfolio defines the mix of programs and assets that require investment over the next three years, based on the business and IT strategic and operational objectives. The IT portfolio enables stargazing, providing a helpful—if not interesting—visual of IT investments and their relative stakeholder economic value over time.

IT Value Proposition An IT internal or external marketing communication to the business network of the value of IT. Maximizing stakeholder economic value from IT investment is the value proposition of the IT value network approach. Stakeholder economic value should be broadly promoted across the business network. Through effective ongoing marketing communication, the IT value proposition and success stories should be made known to both internal and external stakeholders. Informed stakeholders build IT trust, enabling the recognition of IT value and the realization of IT value.

Network Advantage Equates to sustained competitive advantage through a systematic process to maximize stakeholder economic value across the business or value network. Network advantage is the collective stakeholder advantage or economic value gained from a firm's investments.

Network Cloud An association of virtual members (nodes) based on interests, relationships, exchanges, or dependencies (links). Network clouds are extended value networks, consisting of connected stakeholders with common interests or value pursuits.

Network Portfolio A concept used to manage a firm's value networks or network clouds. Value networks or clouds build, overlap, and layer, consistently evolving and forming new shapes, requiring network portfolio management and a value network chief to govern. Building a portfolio of value networks can be completed at the individual, functional, and organizational levels.

Networked Value Management The sixth degree of IT value management, which is essentially a loyalty business model for IT investment and the IT organization in itself. Networked value management is a critical process for identifying and realizing stakeholder economic value through managing business-critical success factors, and stakeholder satisfaction and expectations. It goes beyond internal IT satisfaction surveys; it involves building IT value loyalty and trust over the business or value network, continually delivering stakeholder value while material benefit is being transformed and realized on the books.

Organization-Based Measurement Techniques Conventional planning, organizational management, and information economics IT investment value measurement approaches. Such techniques are more process driven and less definitive or structured compared with financial-based approaches.

Real Option The investment in physical and human assets that provides the capability to enable future opportunities, thus providing a higher future value to a firm; it assists in strategic decision making, portfolio management, and improves IT value-based business case rigor for capital budgeting. It also enhances the evaluation rigor of IT investment projects under uncertainty. A cost/benefit analysis example of using real option techniques would encompass the decision tree analysis and the NPV model. In deriving an embedded option value within a cost/benefit analysis, the cash flow subjective probabilities need to be replaced with certainty probabilities for the option, and then the value of the option needs to be discounted by the risk-free (not risk-adjusted) rate. The option value will change over time and can be accelerated, terminated, or postponed at various points in time.

Second Degree of IT Value Management   Includes strategic planning and portfolio management and governance. It is concerned with IT value capture; whereby IT investments are identified, prioritized, and selected for stakeholder economic value.

Services—Stakeholder   One of the four "S" IT investment categories. IT services accommodate stakeholder needs and expectations, and are managed through service level agreements. Service-based IT investments are emerging, as IT organizations evolve to become service oriented. Examples include process inputs/outputs, transactions, information exchange, service desk, alerts, or reporting. Such services provide the visible value of underlying systems or infrastructure. They also extend the value of underlying IT investments by providing enterprise insights through digital dashboards, or by protecting assets through information security.

Shared Infrastructure   One of the four "S" IT investment categories. Typically, the IT infrastructure is shared across a firm's business units, functions, or processes. Examples include computers, servers, data centers, and operating systems, along with data, video, and voice network facilities. Network and computing infrastructure remains a large portion of the overall IT spending across industries, typically accounting for 50 percent to 60 percent of the total.

Shareholder Value   The firm's cumulative net present value of future cash flows, plus residual value, less debt. Shareholder value can also be defined as the total estimated economic value of investments, which is the sum of cash flows discounted by the cost of capital plus the residual value of the investments. Shareholder wealth is derived by improving the stock price or paying dividends.

Six Degrees of IT Value   A series of interrelated IT value network management steps that will increase the value of existing and new IT investments. If the chain of events is broken, the targeted value becomes suboptimal—hence, the notion of degrees of IT value. Ideally the starting point is the first degree, but depending on the firm's IT value network maturity, the initial focus may be on any one of the degrees, progressing to other degrees as necessary. Six degrees of IT value is cyclical moving from the sixth degree to the first degree, in pursuit of higher stakeholder economic value.

Sixth Degree of IT Value Management   Includes networked value management. It is concerned with IT value realization, whereby stakeholder economic value is gained through delivering the business's critical success factors, and stakeholder satisfaction and loyalty, meeting stakeholder expectations. In parallel, IT investments are being transformed and returns materializing on the firm's books.

Six Degrees of Separation   The transition from IT investment to stakeholder economic value is a process that suggests that there are six connections or steps to maximize IT value. Psychologist Stanley Milgram introduced the famous phrase "six degrees of separation" in 1967. Based on a small-scale experiment, it took six steps to pass a message along a chain of acquaintances to subsequently reach a targeted person. Similarly, for IT investment there are six steps within the business network to reach the targeted IT value.

Stakeholder Economic Value   The measurable tangible and intangible value from IT investment, determined through the IT value network index and value lenses: strategic, operational, stakeholder, and agility. Financial-based and organization-based measures are applied within the value lens to determine the total stakeholder economic value for an IT investment. Maximizing stakeholder economic value across all IT investments drives sustained competitive advantage or network advantage.

Star   IT investments that meet or exceed most or all of the baseline IT value network index thresholds. Stars shine brightly when measured IT investments exceed all index thresholds. Star shapes can be depicted for an IT investment category index or for a subgroup index—for example, telecommunications, a subgroup of shared infrastructure.

Stargazing   Graphically mapping IT investments within an IT value portfolio, showing their positions relative to each other; comparing size of investment and value over time. Stars and black holes become visual, showing their relative positioning, as depicted by various indexed star shapes on the IT value portfolio grid.

Strategic—Informational   One of the four "S" IT investment categories. Strategic or informational IT investments typically align to new customer, new market, new channel, new product, or business intelligence and knowledge-based opportunities. The business strategy defines strategic IT investments, which may well develop from current infrastructure, systems, or services. There are also strategic IT initiatives unto themselves that formulate long-term IT direction—for example, architectural road maps, investment management, and integrated middleware. These IT investments must contribute to a company's future earnings and thus to future shareholder value.

Systems—Operational   One of the four "S" IT investment categories. IT system or application investments that are operation based or transactional in nature, supporting the business's operational processes. IT systems include software applications, quality assurance, system integration, and support.

Tangible—Assets or Benefits   IT investments that provide hard benefits (i.e., cost savings or revenue increase), determined through financial-based measurement rigor and validated by finance. Such assets or benefits materialize on the firm's books and provide realized returns but do not account for intangible value.

Third Degree of IT Value Management   Includes enterprise capability and capacity management for IT systems and infrastructure as well as for IT organization and its people. It considers whether the company has the right technology and IT resources to meet current and future business needs. Further, it is concerned with IT value enabling, with a focus on where IT investments are required to enable agility or options for current and future business solutions.

Traditional Financial and Accounting Techniques   These include return on investment (ROI), payback, net present value (NPV), internal rate of return (IRR) cost/benefit analysis, budgeting, investment review board, and audits. These techniques attempt to provide more rigorous shareholder value measurements for IT evaluation, but generally they measure the past and not the future residual value, which is a significant contribution to a firm's market value. In addition, they do not capture agility and flexibility within IT investments that have outcome uncertainty and potential options.

Triangulating IT Value   An approach used to determine the complete value from an IT investment, synthesizing data from multiple sources. Triangulating is typically known for finding the coordinates and distance to an entity, such as a ship from the shoreline, using the law of sines, through the calculation of a triangle from two reference points. Triangulating IT value applies multidisciplinary techniques through the IT value network index, using more than one measure of valuation. Data from different sources, whether qualitative or quantitative, corroborate value, overcoming specific flaws in any one measurement or approach. It requires designing a standard corporate IT value network index, aligning the IT investment four "S" category model with specific measures within the four value lenses.

Value Capture   The first consideration for IT value network management. It includes identifying, justifying, prioritizing, and selecting IT investments. This encompasses evaluation of the business processes within the value chain and value system, IT alignment to the business strategy, IT governance, and portfolio management. Capturing IT value requires the first degree of IT value management, mapping the firm's current and future potential IT investments to key processes within the firm's value chain and value system and showing embedded IT value and dependencies for process improvement. Subsequently, the second degree of IT value management is required for capturing value by identifying IT investments through integrating the IT strategy with the business strategy and prioritizing and selecting IT investments through portfolio management. Networked value management, the sixth degree or IT value management, will also identify and capture IT value.

Value-Creation Business Case A rigorous IT investment business-case approach; accounting for all of a project's capital, project's one-time costs, and operational ongoing costs, in addition to tangible and risk-free intangible benefits. It applies various risk-adjusted and discounted rates to calculate the net present value (NPV), internal rate of return (IRR), or economic value added (EVA).

Value Enabling The second consideration for IT value network management. It builds off value-capture decisions and considers the underlying enterprise capability and dependency enablers along with the capacity and resource constraints. It includes the third degree of IT value network management, whereby value options should be considered to provide capability and capacity flexibility or agility, through IT technology and organizational capability and capacity planning.

Value Lenses Used to build IT value network indexes, measuring IT investments from four views: (1) strategic, (2) operational, (3) stakeholder, and (4) agility. One or more primary or secondary financial- and organization-based measures and techniques are defined and applied to each value lens, corresponding to IT investment types (the four "S" category model).

Value Loyalty Ongoing and unquestionable stakeholder commitment and support for IT investment and for the IT organization. Stakeholder IT satisfaction and value loyalty are the main components of the stakeholder value lens. Building value loyalty across the business network or value system drives realizable value. Network value management is essentially a loyalty business model for IT investment as well as for the IT organization in itself. The loyalty business model assumes that when stakeholders are in pursuit of shared interests, there is a convergence of minds between seeking self-interest (IT—egotistical) and seeking the best interest of others (business—altruistic). Four critical factors drive value loyalty: (1) shared values or goals, (2) relationship strength, (3) choices of potential alternatives, and (4) critical events.

Value Network   Consists of complex relationships and transactions (links and ties) between social and technical resources (nodes) across a firm's value system or points of presence, creating stakeholder economic value.

Value Network Analysis   A methodology and modeling technique to visualize and optimize business networks, depicting the members or roles (nodes) and their relationships (links and ties). Information assets are mapped to the firm's value chain and value system, connecting stakeholder relationships and interdependencies. Value network analysis seeks to determine the sociotechnical economic value of member relationships within a defined system through quantifying tangible and intangible value exchanges.

Value Optimization   The third consideration for IT value network management. It builds off value-enabling decisions and focuses on IT execution or deployment. Value optimization materializes primarily at the fourth degree of IT value network management—project management and system management. The management effectiveness of IT operations and existing IT investments and assets impacts the effectiveness of new IT investment execution. In other words, IT project deployment depends on the effectiveness of the IT organization's existing processes, people, and technology, building off value enablement. The fifth degree of IT value network management—service management and information management—also drives value optimization.

Value Option   A complementary or supplementary IT investment that enables choices or provides a flexible capability to address future business opportunities. Embedding options into the IT organization and technology provides incremental added value, enabling network advantage, especially during times of uncertainty. Value options are a critical component of the agility value lens for IT investment evaluation, enabling a flexible and responsive IT capability for future business opportunities. At the IT value portfolio level, the value option approach focuses the firm on assessing opportunities, acquiring options, nurturing these options, terminating or keeping the options, and, when the time is right, capturing their value.

Value Realization   The fourth consideration for IT value network management. It builds off value-optimization decisions and focuses on IT returns and benefits. Value realization is most evident when returns are booked on the company's ledgers or budgets are reset to accommodate benefits. Audited value becomes the final proof point, providing independent validation of realized booked IT value. However, IT stakeholders continually evaluate IT performance and value, especially as IT value takes time to transform onto the books. Thus, value realization should materialize throughout the six degrees of IT value network management, but it is most evident at the sixth degree, networked value management. Business value realization starts to materialize when service level agreements (SLAs) are met, projects deliver on the business case, business solutions are delivered to business requirements, and information is liberated for improved decision making. Ultimately, at the sixth degree, the IT stakeholders' expectations are met, satisfaction is high, IT loyalty is strong, and booked value materializes.

Value System   The value chain was popularized by Michael Porter in 1985, on the release of his best seller *Competitive Advantage: Creating and Sustaining Superior Performance*. Porter is a university professor at Harvard Business School and is considered as a thought leader in business strategy and competitive advantage. Porter's notion of the value system encompasses the firm's internal value chain and extends to include the firm's customers and suppliers. Extending further, the firm's value system could include partners and alliances across the business network. The value system consists of a series of activities that add customer value to a firm's products or services, whether through differentiation or lower cost to competition. The objective is to offer the customer, buyer, or client a level of value that exceeds the cost of these activities, thus providing the firm a profit margin or competitive advantage. Opportunities for process improvement or reengineering should be identified within the extended value chain or value system, targeting higher stakeholder economic value and showing IT system dependencies. Systems and business process redesign should converge, enhancing core competencies within the value system.

Notes

Chapter 1

1. *The Financial Express* (2008, June). "Gartner sees 2.5% global IT spend growth." *The Financial Express, Infotech.* Retrieved June 26, 2008, from http://www.financialexpress.com/old/print_latest.php?content_id=103929
2. Retrieved June 26, 2008, from http://www.ideasmerchant.com/go/useful/facts-quotes. Also from *The Quotations Page.* http://www.quotationspage.com and from *Wisdom Quotes* http://www.wisdomquotes.com/cat_computers.html
3. Microsoft (2008, June). "Sixty years of world's first modern computer." MSN Technology. Retrieved June 29, 2008, from http://computing.in.msn.com/articles/article.aspx?cp-documentid-1501063
4. See note 2.
5. Jonathan Fildes (2008, June). "One tonne 'baby' marks its birth." BBC news. Retrieved June 29, 2008, from http://newsvote.bbc.co.uk/mpapps/pagetools/print/news.bbc.co.uk/1/hi/technology/746511
6. See note 2.
7. See note 2.
8. Jaques, R. (2007, October). "Global IT spend to top $3tn in 2007." *Vnunet.* Retrieved June 26, 2008, from http://www.vnunet.com/vnunet/news/2200735/2007-global-spend-set-top-3tn
9. Kaplan, R., and Norton, D. (2001). *The Strategy-Focused Organization.* Boston: Harvard Business School Press.
10. Brynjolfsson, E., and Yang, S. (1998). "The intangible benefits and costs of investments: Evidence from financial markets." Massachusetts Institute of Technology, Sloan School of Management, 147–166.
11. Marchand, D., Davenport, T., and Dickson, T. (2000). *Mastering Information Management.* Upper Saddle River, NJ: Prentice Hall.
12. Ross, J., and Beath, C. (2002, Winter). "Beyond the business case: New approaches to IT investments." *MIT Sloan Management Review,* 51–59.
13. Phillips, C., and Rathman, R. (2002, December). "Morgan Stanley CIO survey series: Release 3.8." Morgan Stanley Retrieved January 21, 2003, from Morgan Stanley Inc. Web Site: http://www.morganstanley.com/mrchuck
14. Porter, M. (1990). *The Competitive Advantage of Nations.* New York: The Free Press.
15. Homann, U., Rill, M., and Wimmer, A. (2004). "New architectures for financial services: Flexible value structures in banking." *Communications of the ACM, 47,* 34–36.

16. *The Banker* (2004, August). "FSIs to up external spend." Retrieved June 26, 2008, from www.thebanker.com

17. Ferguson S., and Preimesberger, C. (2008, April 21). "Virtualizing the client." *Eweek*, 14.

18. Burrows, P. (2008, April 21). "Amazon takes on IBM, Oracle, and HP." *Eweek*, 9.

19. Pallatto, J., and Boulton C (2008, April 21). "An on-demand partnership." *Eweek*, 22.

20. Pohlmann, T. (2003, February). "Benchmarking North America." *Forrester Research Inc., Technographics Research*.

21. Cap Gemini. (2001, October). Global financial services: Paths to differentiation. *2001 Special Report on the Financial Services Industry* (10th ed.). Toronto: Cap Gemini Ernst & Young, Canada.

22. Dandapani, K. (2004). "New architectures for financial services: Success and failure in web-based financial services." *Communications of the ACM, 47*(5), 31–33.

23. Cawthon, R. (2001, July). "Creating IT harmony for Bank One: The bank's new CTO composes a score for bringing an ensemble of systems into accord." *Bank Technology News, 14,* 8–13.

24. May, D. (2003, March). "Getting the most from technology: Keys to better decision-making." *American Banker, 168,* 7–8.

25. Pan A., and Vina, A. (2004). "New architectures for financial services: An alternative architecture for financial data integration." *Communications of the ACM, 47,* 37–40.

26. Donston, D. (2008, June 2). "5 ways the desktop will be different." *Eweek*, 2008, 32–37.

27. Mallat, N., Rossi, M., and Tuunainen, V. (2004). "New architectures for financial services: Mobile banking services." *Communications of the ACM, 47,* 42–46.

28. Slewe, T., and Hoogenboom, M. (2004). "New architectures for financial services: Who will rob you on the digital highway?" *Communications of the ACM, 47,* 56–60.

29. Weill, P., and Broadbent, M. (1998). *Leveraging the Infrastructure*. Boston: Harvard Business School Press.

30. See note 17.

31. See note 21.

32. Batiz-Lazo, B., and Wood, D. (2003). "Strategy, competition, and diversification in European and Mexican banking." *International Journal of Bank Marketing, 21,* 202–216.

33. McKinsey and Company. (1998, September). *The Changing Landscape for Canadian Financial Services: Research Paper Prepared for the Task Force on the Future of the Canadian Financial Services Sector.* (Publication No. BT22-61/3-1998E-1). Ottawa, ON: Canadian Department of Finance.

34. See note 21.

35. See note 28.

36. Slater, D. (2002, June). "Strategic planning don'ts and do's." *CIO Magazine*. Retrieved June 23, 2003, from http://www.cio.com/archive/060102/donts .html

37. Hackney, R., Burn, J., and Dhillon, G. (2000, April). "Challenging assumptions for strategic information system planning: Theoretical perspectives." *Communications of the Association for Information Systems (AIS), 3*(9), 1–23.

38. Ernst & Young. (1998, September). *Canadian Financial Institutions and Their Adoption of New Technologies: Research Paper Prepared for the Task Force on the Future of the Canadian Financial Services Sector* (Publication No. BT22-61/3-1998E-5). Ottawa, ON: Canadian Department of Finance.

39. Hoffman, K. (March, 2020). "E.banking online banking aligns practices." *Bank Technology News, 15*, 3.

40. Bills, S. (2002, April). "Online banking: B of A makes its case." *American Banker, 167*, 69.

41. See note 29.

42. See note 38.

43. Benko, C., and McFarlan, W. (2003). *Connecting the Dots: Aligning Projects and Objectives in Unpredictable Times*. Boston: Harvard Business School Press.

Chapter 2

1. *Software Mag*.com (2004, January). "Standish: Project success rates improve over 10 years." *Software Mag*.com. Retrieved July 25, 2008, from http://WWW.softwaremag.com/L.cfm?doc=newsletter/2004-01-15/Standish

2. Brynjolfsson, E. (1993, December). "The productivity paradox of information technology." *Communications of the ACM, 36*, 67–76.

3. CIO. (2003, December). "Maximizing value from IT vendors, part 11." CIO Research Report. *CIO Magazine*. Retrieved January 16, 2004, from http://www.cio.com/research/surveyreport.cfm?id=66

4. Seddon, P., Graeser, V., and Willcocks, L. (2002). "Measuring organizational IS effectiveness: An overview and update of senior management perspectives." *The DATA BASE for Advances in Information Systems, 33*, 11–28.

5. Carr, P. (January, 2003). "Third annual Canadian IT issues study." Athabasca University, Canada. Retrieved January 21, 2003, from Athabasca University Web site: http://www.mba.athabascau.ca

6. Rappaport, A. (1998). *Creating Shareholder Value*. New York: The Free Press.

7. Strassmann, P. (1997). *The Squandered Computer*. New Canaan, CT: Information Economics Press. 24.

8. See note 7.

9. Lewis, W., Palmade, V., Regout B., and Webb, A. (2002). "What's right with the U.S. economy." *The McKinsey Quarterly, 1*, 31–40.

10. Thorp, J., and DMR's Center for Strategic Leadership. (1998). *The Information Paradox*. Toronto, ON, Canada: McGraw-Hill Ryerson Ltd. (Gartner citation).

11. Costanzo, C. (2003, January). "Web getting short shrift again in back-to-basics budget." *American Banker*. Retrieved January 24, 2003, from http://167.26.24.16/IndustryWatch/factiva/web%20Getting%20Short%20Shift.htm

12. Schwartz, S., and Zozaya-Gorostiza, C. (2003, January). "Investment under uncertainty in information technology: Acquisition and development projects." *Management Science, 49*, 57–70.

13. Olazabal, N. (2002). "Banking: The IT paradox." *The McKinsey Quarterly, 2*, 47–51.

14. Brynjolfsson, E., and Yang, S. (1996). Information technology and productivity: A review of the literature. *Advances in Computers*, Academic Press, 43, 179–214.

15. Brynjolfsson, E., and Hitt, L. (1998, August). "Beyond the productivity paradox." *Communications of the ACM, 41*, 49–55.

16. Brynjolfsson, E., and Hitt, L. (1996, April). Paradox lost? Firm-level evidence on the returns to information systems spending. *Management Science, 42*, 541–558.

17. See note 7.

18. See note 15.

19. Dedrick, J., Gurbaxani, V., and Kraemer, K. (2003, March). "Information technology and economic performance: A critical review of the empirical evidence." *ACM Computing Surveys, 35*, 1–28.

20. Anderson, M., Banker R., and Ravindran, S. (2003, March). "The new productivity paradox." *Communications of the ACM, 46*, 91–94.

21. See note 19.

22. Brynjolfsson, E., and Yang, S. (1998). "The intangible benefits and costs of investments: Evidence from financial markets." Massachusetts Institute of Technology, Sloan School of Management, 147–166.

23. See note 2.

24. See note 7.

25. See note 4.

26. See note 4.

27. Sai On Ko, A., and Lee, S. (2000). "Implementing the strategic formulation framework for the banking industry of Hong Kong." *Managerial Auditing Journal, 15*, 469–477.

28. Mintzberg, H. (1994). *The Rise and Fall of Strategic Planning*. New York, NY: The Free Press.

29. Hackney, R., Burn, J., and Dhillon, G. (2000, April). "Challenging assumptions for strategic information system planning: Theoretical perspectives." *Communications of the Association for Information Systems (AIS), 3*(9), 1–23.

30. See note 28.

31. Ahituv, N., Zviran, M., and Glezer, C. (1999, April). "Top management toolbox: For managing corporate IT." *Communications of the ACM, 42*, 93–99.

32. Sassone, P. (1988). "Cost benefit analysis of information systems: A survey of methodologies." *Communications of the ACM*, 126–133.

33. Weill, P., and Broadbent, M. (1998). *Leveraging the Infrastructure*. Boston: Harvard Business School Press.

34. See note 31.

35. Meta Group. (2002). "2003 worldwide IT benchmarking report." META Group Inc.

36. See note 20.

37. See note 7.

38. See note 6.

39. See note 33.

40. Clemons, E. (1991, January). "Evaluation of strategic investments in information technology." *Communications of the ACM 34*(1), 22–36.

41. Colkin, E. (2002, October). "Getting Tough on ROI." *InformationWeek.com*. Retrieved September 10, 2003, from http://www.informationweek.com/shared/printableArticle.jhtml?articleID=6503764

42. See note 20.

43. Kaplan, R., and Norton, D. (2001). *The Strategy-Focused Organization*. Boston: Harvard Business School Press.

44. Nokes, S. (2000). *Taking Control of IT Costs*. Upper Saddle River, NJ: Prentice Hall.

45. See note 7.

46. See note 2.

47. Alter, A. (2003, January). *Research: How bad is the bite in your budget?* CIO Insight.

48. See note 7.

49. See note 43.

50. See note 28.

51. Chatterjee, D., and Ramesh, V. (1999). Real options for risk management in information technology projects. *IEEE, Proceedings of the 32nd Hawaii International Conference on System Science, 6*, 1–7.

52. Bowman, E. (2001, November). "Real options analysis and strategic decision making." *Organization Science, 12*, 772–777.

53. Huchzermeier A., and Loch, C. (2001, January). "Project management under risk: Using the real options approach to evaluate flexibility in R & D." *Management Science, 47*, 85–101.

54. Schwartz, S., and Zozaya-Gorostiza, C. (2003, January). "Investment under uncertainty in information technology: Acquisition and development projects." *Management Science, 49*, 57–70.

55. See note 52.

56. See note 32.

57. Sommer, B. (2002, January). "A new kind of business case." *Optimize Magazine*. Retrieved January 13, 2003, from http://www.optimizemag.com/issue/003/roi.htm

58. See note 10.

59. Remenyi, D., and Sherwood-Smith, M. (1997). *Achieving Maximum Value from Information Systems*. New York: John Wiley & Sons.

60. See note 43.

61. See note 22.

62. OWASP. (2007, January). Business justification for application security. *OWASP*. Retrieved July 25, 2008, from http://www.owasp.org.

63. *SecurityPark*. (2008, April). "Justification and return on investment of automated penetration testing." *SecurityPark*. Retrieved July 25, 2008, from http://www.securitypark.co.uk

64. Nichols, S. (2008, July). "McAfee: Small firms naïve about security." *SC Magazine*. Retrieved July 25, 2008, from http://www.scmagazineus.com

65. 12manage. (2008). "Total Cost of Ownership." *12manage– E-learning community on management*. Retrieved July 25, 2008, from http://www.12manage.com/methods_tco.html

66. Ross, J., and Beath, C. (2002, Winter). "Beyond the business case: New approaches to IT investments." *MIT Sloan Management Review*, 51–59.

67. See note 4.
68. See note 20.
69. See note 40.
70. See note 57.
71. See note 66.
72. Visitacion, M. (2001, February). Selecting metrics and using then effectively (Issue Brief No. RPA-022001-00006). *Planning Assumption Update, Giga Information Group.*
73. See note 41.
74. See note 4.
75. See note 72.
76. See note 44.
77. See note 41.
78. See note 20.
79. Hackney, R., Burn, J., and Dhillon, G. (2000, April). "Challenging assumptions for strategic information system planning: Theoretical perspectives." *Communications of the Association for Information Systems (AIS), 3(9)*, 1–23.

Chapter 3

1. Costanzo, C. (2003, January). "Web getting short shrift again in back-to-basics budget." *American Banker.* Retrieved January 24, 2003, from http://167.26.24.16/IndustryWatch/factiva/web%20Getting%20Short%20Shift.htm
2. Cap Gemini. (2001, October). "Global financial services: Paths to differentiation." *2001 Special Report on the Financial Services Industry* (10th ed.). Toronto: Cap Gemini Ernst and Young, Canada.
3. Schwartz, S., and Zozaya-Gorostiza, C. (2003, January). "Investment under uncertainty in information technology: Acquisition and development projects." *Management Science, 49,* 57–70.
4. Pohlmann, T. (2003, February). "Benchmarking North America." *Forrester Research Inc., Technographics Research.*
5. Jegher, J. (2007, December). "IT spending in financial services: A global perspective." *Celent.* Retrieved July 24, 2008, from http://www.celent.com
6. Forrester. (2007). "US IT spend hits $761bn next year; global IT spending to surpass $2 trillion mark." *Metrics2.0.* Retrieved July 24, 2008, from http://www.metrics2.com
7. Lund, V., Watson, I., Raposo, J., and Maver, C. (2002, September). "Optimizing distribution channels: The next generation of value creation." *Directions: Executive Briefings, 11,* 1–7.
8. McKinsey and Company. (1998, September). *The Changing Landscape for Canadian Financial Services: Research Paper Prepared for the Task Force on the Future of the Canadian Financial Services Sector* (Publication No. BT22-61/3-1998E-1). Ottawa, ON: Canadian Department of Finance.
9. Kroeger, B. (2004). "Banking continuing prosperity." *Ernst and Young Cross Currents Special Report, 8–11.*
10. Coy, P. (2008, July 16). "The Future of Fannie and Freddie." *Business Week.*
11. See note 5.

12. Lum, B., and Hildebrand, R. (2002, April). "Canadian banking in the 21st century, strategic differentiation." *Dominion Bond Rating Services Ltd. (DBRS), Annual Review of the Canadian Banking Sector.*
13. See note 8.
14. See note 2.
15. See note 12.
16. See note 12.
17. Holland, C., and Westwood, J. (2001). "Product-market and technology: Strategies in banking." *Communications of the ACM, 44,* 53–57.
18. See note 7.
19. See note 8.
20. *Potomac* (2004, January). "Bank One/JPMorgan Chase, Bank of America/Fleet mergers raise questions." *Potomac, 15,* 1.
21. See note 8.
22. See note 12.
23. See note 7.
24. See note 8.
25. See note 8.
26. See note 8.
27. See note 8.
28. Graeber, C. (2003, January). "Want to get more online bill payers?" *TechStrategy Research*. Forrester Research Inc.
29. See note 7.
30. Hoffman, K. (2002, March). "E.banking online banking aligns practices." *Bank Technology News, 15,* 3.
31. See note 8.
32. See note 7.
33. See note 7.
34. Dandapani, K. (2004). "New architectures for financial services: Success and failure in web-based financial services." *Communications of the ACM, 47*(5), 31–33.
35. See note 9.
36. See note 7.
37. Olazabal, N. (2002). "Banking: The IT paradox." *The McKinsey Quarterly, 2,* 47–51.
38. Dedrick, J., Gurbaxani, V., and Kraemer, K. (2003, March). "Information technology and economic performance: A critical review of the empirical evidence." *ACM Computing Surveys, 35,* 1–28.
39. Strassmann, P. (1997). *The Squandered Computer*. New Canaan, CT: The Information Economics Press.
40. Meta Group. (2002). 2003 worldwide IT benchmarking report. META Group Inc.
41. See note 40.
42. See note 40.
43. See note 4.
44. See note 39.
45. Zhu, F., Wymer, W., and Chen, I. (2002). "IT-based services and service quality in consumer banking." *International Journal of Service Industry Management, 13,* 69–90.

46. Batiz-Lazo, B., and Wood, D. (2003). "Strategy, competition, and diversification in European and Mexican banking." *The International Journal of Bank Marketing, 21*, 202–216.

47. See note 7.

48. See note 9.

49. See note 7.

50. Bills, S. (2002, April). "Online banking: B of A makes its case." *American Banker, 167*, 69.

51. See note 8.

52. Hussan, M., and Hoque, Z. (2002). "Understanding non-financial performance measurement practices in Japanese banks." *Accounting, Auditing and Accountability Journal, 15*, 162–183.

53. See note 40.

54. See note 8.

Chapter 5

1. Rappaport, A. (1998). *Creating Shareholder Value*. New York: The Free Press.

2. Anderson, M., Banker R., and Ravindran, S. (2003, March). "The new productivity paradox." Communications of the ACM, 46, 91–94.

3. Strassmann, P. (1997). *The Squandered Computer*. New Canaan, CT: Information Economics Press.

4. Turban, E., and Aronson, J. (2001). *Decision Support Systems and Intelligent Systems* (6th ed.). Upper Saddle River, NJ: Prentice Hall.

5. Colkin, E. (2002, October). "Getting Tough on ROI." *InformationWeek.com*. Retrieved September 10, 2003, from http://www.informationweek.com/shared/printableArticle.jhtml?articleID=6503764

6. Huchzermeier A., and Loch, C. (2001, January). "Project management under risk: Using the real options approach to evaluate flexibility in R and D." *Management Science, 47*, 85–101.

7. Weill, P., and Broadbent, M. (1998). *Leveraging the Infrastructure*. Boston: Harvard Business School Press.

8. Clemons, E. (1991, January). "Evaluation of strategic investments in information technology." *Communications of the ACM 34(1)*, 22–36.

9. Schwartz, S., and Zozaya-Gorostiza, C. (2003, January). "Investment under uncertainty in information technology: Acquisition and development projects." *Management Science, 49*, 57–70.

10. Benaroch, M., and Kauffman, R. (2000, June). "Justifying electronic banking network expansion using real options analysis." *MIS Quarterly, 24(2)*, 197–230.

11. See note 4.

12. Sommer, B. (2002, January). "A new kind of business case." *Optimize Magazine*. Retrieved January 13, 2003, from http://www.optimizemag.com/issue/003/roi.htm

13. Ross, J., and Beath, C. (2002, Winter). "Beyond the business case: New approaches to IT investments." *MIT Sloan Management Review*, 51–59.

Chapter 6

1. Kaplan, R., and Norton, D. (2001). *The Strategy-Focused Organization*. Boston: Harvard Business School Press.
2. Visitacion, M. (2001, February). "Selecting metrics and using then effectively" (Issue Brief No. RPA-022001-00006). *Planning Assumption Update, Giga Information Group.*
3. Hussan, M., and Hoque, Z. (2002). "Understanding non-financial performance measurement practices in Japanese banks." *Accounting, Auditing and Accountability Journal, 15,* 162–183.
4. Sai On Ko, A., and Lee, S. (2000). "Implementing the strategic formulation framework for the banking industry of Hong Kong." *Managerial Auditing Journal, 15,* 469–477.
5. Peffers, K., and Gengler, C. (2003, January). "How to identify new high-payoff information systems for the organization." *Communications of the ACM, 46(1),* 83–88.
6. Schiemann, W., and Lingle, J. (1999). *Bullseye!* New York: The Free Press.
7. See note 1.
8. Van Grembergen, W., and Saull, R. (2001). "Aligning business information technology through the balanced scorecard at a major Canadian financial group: Its status measured with an IT BSC maturity model." *IEEE, Proceedings of the 34th Hawaii International Conference on System Science, 8,* 8061–8071.
9. Seddon, P., Graeser, V., and Willcocks, L. (2002). "Measuring organizational IS effectiveness: An overview and update of senior management perspectives." *The DATA BASE for Advances in Information Systems, 33,* 11–28.
10. Weill, P., and Broadbent, M. (1998). *Leveraging the Infrastructure*. Boston: Harvard Business School Press.
11. Strassmann, P. (1997). *The Squandered Computer*. New Canaan, CT: Information Economics Press.
12. U.S. General Accounting Office. (2000, May). *Information Technology Investment Management (ITIM): A Framework for Assessing and Improving Process Maturity* (GAO/AIMD-10.1.23).
13. Benko, C., and McFarlan, W. (2003). *Connecting the Dots: Aligning Projects and Objectives in Unpredictable Times*. Boston: Harvard Business School Press.
14. Turban, E., and Aronson, J. (2001). *Decision Support Systems and Intelligent Systems* (6th ed.). Upper Saddle River, NJ: Prentice Hall.
15. Marchand, D., Davenport, T., and Dickson, T. (2000). *Mastering Information Management*. Upper Saddle River, NJ: Prentice Hall.

Chapter 7

1. Weill, P., and Broadbent, M. (1998). *Leveraging the Infrastructure*. Boston: Harvard Business School Press.
2. Ross, J., and Beath, C. (2002, Winter). "Beyond the business case: New approaches to IT investments." *MIT Sloan Management Review*, 51–59.

Chapter 9

1. Harmon, P. (2006, January 31). "Value Chains vs. Silos." *Business Process Trends, 4, 2*. Retrieved from http://www.businessprocesstrends.com/publicationfiles/bptadvisor2006Jan31.pdf

Chapter 10

1. Slater, D. (2002, June). "Strategic planning don'ts and do's." *CIO Magazine*. Retrieved June 23, 2003, from http://www.cio.com/archive/060102/donts.html
2. Ernst and Young. (1998, September). *Canadian Financial Institutions and Their Adoption of New Technologies: Research Paper Prepared for the Task Force on the Future of the Canadian Financial Services Sector* (Publication No. BT22-61/3-1998E-5). Ottawa, ON: Canadian Department of Finance.
3. Hackney, R., Burn, J., and Dhillon, G. (2000, April). "Challenging assumptions for strategic information system planning: Theoretical perspectives." *Communications of the Association for Information Systems (AIS), 3*(9), 1–23.
4. Kaplan, R., and Norton, D. (2001). *The Strategy-Focused Organization*. Boston: Harvard Business School Press.
5. Mintzberg, H. (1994). *The Rise and Fall of Strategic Planning*. New York, NY: The Free Press.
6. Henson, S., and Wilson, J. (2002). "Case study strategic challenges in the financial services industry." *Journal of Business and Industrial Marketing, 17*, 407–418.
7. Cawthon, R. (2001, July). "Creating IT harmony for Bank One: The bank's new CTO composes a score for bringing an ensemble of systems into accord." *Bank Technology News, 14*, 8–13.
8. See note 3.
9. Marchand, D., Davenport, T., and Dickson, T. (2000). *Mastering Information Management*. Upper Saddle River, NJ: Prentice Hall.
10. See note 1.
11. Kaplan, R., and Norton, D. (1996). *The Balanced Scorecard*. Boston: Harvard Business School Press.
12. Benko, C., and McFarlan, W. (2003). *Connecting the Dots: Aligning Projects and Objectives in Unpredictable Times*. Boston: Harvard Business School Press.
13. Thorp, J., and DMR's Center for Strategic Leadership. (1998). *The Information Paradox*. Toronto, ON, Canada: McGraw-Hill Ryerson Ltd.
14. U.S. General Accounting Office. (2000, May). *Information Technology Investment Management (ITIM): A Framework for Assessing and Improving Process Maturity* (GAO/AIMD-10.1.23).

Chapter 11

1. Bentley, W. (2007). *Systems Analysis and Design Methods*. New York: McGraw-Hill Irwin.

Chapter 12

1. Childs, P., and Triantis, A. (1999, October). "Dynamic R and D investment policies." *Management Science, 45,* 1359–1377.

Chapter 13

1. U.K. Office of Government Commerce (2007, June,). "Information technology infrastructure library, ITIL v3.0." Retrieved September 25, 2008, from http://www. itil.org.uk/

Chapter 14

1. Reichheld, F. (1996). *The Loyalty Effect.* Boston: Harvard Business School Press.

Chapter 16

1. IT Value Network: Nortel Networks Case. (2009, January). Nortel Networks Corporation. *Printed with permission.*

Chapter 17

1. IT Value Network: Indigo Books & Music Case. (2009, February). Indigo Books & Music Inc. *Printed with permission.*

Chapter 19

1. SAP (2008). "Leverage industry Value Network to drive growth: Collaboration that fosters innovation and creates value." SAP Solution Brief, SAP AG.
2. IBM. (2007). "Achieving tangible business benefits with social computing." IBM, Armonk, N.Y.
3. Benko, C., and McFarlan, W. (2003). *Connecting the Dots: Aligning Projects and Objectives in Unpredictable Times.* Boston: Harvard Business School Press.
4. Peppard, J., and Rylander, A. (2006). "From value chain to value network: Insights for mobile operators." *European Management Journal, 24, 2.*
5. Daum, J. (2001, November). "Value drivers intangible assets: Do we need a new approach to financial and management accounting?" Available at: http://www. juergendaum.com.
6. Porter, M. (1985). *Competitive advantage.* New York: Free Press.

7. See note 5.
8. Brackett, M. (1999, March). "Business intelligence value chain." *DM Review Magazine*. Retrieved September 13, 2008, from http://www.dmreview.com/issues
9. IBM. (2005). "IT optimization: Driving infrastructure value." IBM Global Services, Somers, N.Y.
10. McCracken-Hewson, J. (2004). "Where is the value in IT?" Fujitsu, Australia. Retrieved May 15, 2008, from http://fujitsu.com/au
11. Bowman, E. (2001, November). "Real options analysis and strategic decision making." *Organization Science, 12,* 772–777.
12. Benaroch, M. (2002). "Managing information technology investment risk: A real options perspective." *Journal of Management Information Systems, 19,* 43–84.
13. Zhu, K. (1999, December). "Evaluating information technology investments: Cash flows or growth options?" *Presented at the Workshop on Information Systems Economics (WISE'99),* Charlotte, N.C.
14. Huchzermeier A., and Loch, C. (2001, January). "Project management under risk: Using the real options approach to evaluate flexibility in R and D." *Management Science, 47,* 85–101.
15. Chatterjee, D., and Ramesh, V. (1999). "Real options for risk management in information technology projects." *IEEE, Proceedings of the 32nd Hawaii International Conference on System Science, 6,* 1–7.
16. Benaroch, M., and Kauffman, R. (1999). "A case for using real options pricing analysis to evaluate information technology project investments." *Information Systems Research, 10* (1).
17. Strassmann, P. (1997). *The Squandered Computer.* New Canaan, CT: Information Economics Press.
18. See note 12.
19. Kumar, R. (1999). "Understanding DSS value: An options perspective." *Omega: The International Journal of Management Science, 27,* 295–304.
20. Grenadier, S., and Weiss, A. (1997). "Investment in technological innovations: An option pricing approach." *Journal of Financial Economics, 44,* 397–416.
21. Kulatilaka N., and Venkatraman, N. (2001). "Strategic options in the digital era." *Business Strategy Review, 12* (4).
22. Raynor, M. (2001). "Strategic flexibility in the financial services industry: Creating competitive advantage out of competitive turbulence." *Deliotte Consulting and Deloitte and Touche: Deloitte Research.*
23. See note 12.
24. Kogut, B., and Kulatilaka, N. (2001, November). "Capabilities as real options." *Organization Science, 12,* 744–758.
25. Hackney, R., Burn, J., and Dhillon, G. (2000, April). "Challenging assumptions for strategic information system planning: Theoretical perspectives." *Communications of the Association for Information Systems (AIS), 3*(9), 1–23.
26. Reichheld, F. (1996). *The Loyalty Effect.* Boston: Harvard Business School Press.
27. Goddard, I. (2003, September). "What do we perceive and how do we perceive it?" *Montgomery College Student Journal of Science and Mathematics, 2.*
28. Hellriegel, D., Slocum, J. (2009). *Organizational Behavior.* Mason, OH: Southwest Cengage Learning.

29. IBM. (2004). The IT value model: Winning the business "battle" with the right IT "nails". IBM Global Services, Somers, N.Y.

Chapter 20

1. U.S. General Accounting Office. (2000, May). *Information Technology Investment Management (ITIM): A Framework for Assessing and Improving Process Maturity* (GAO/AIMD-10.1.23).

About the Author

Tony J. Read, Ph.D. has more than 20 years of international IT experience in the high-tech, computing, telecommunications, financial, banking, and retail industries. Tony has led global IT teams and successfully implemented key corporate initiatives, contributing millions of dollars to the top and bottom line. He established Read & Associates in 2002, an international IT value-based management and project delivery consultancy practice (www.readassociates.net). The aim of the company is to provide IT value network solutions, delivering stakeholder economic value and network advantage. Prior to establishing Read & Associates, he served as CIO and IT senior vice president within several international corporations.

Dr. Read is also a visiting professor at various universities, with several published papers on the subject of IT investment portfolio value, IT strategy, and IT governance. He graduated with a bachelor's degree in management science and subsequently earned an M.B.A. and an M.Ed. in organizational change management. In 2005, Tony earned his Ph.D. in information systems and was elected into the Honor Society of Computing Sciences, being awarded the Upsilon Pi Epsilon. Tony is a dual U.K.–U.S.A citizen presently, residing in Canada. He regularly travels for speaking engagements at various conferences and corporate events.

The Vision =IT VALUE and the Mission =VALUE IT.

Index